Young

JUDY

Frances at age twelve imitating Helen Morgan on cross-country tour in 1934.
Courtesy of The Garlandia Collection of Wayne Martin

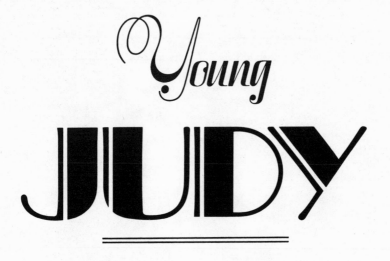

Young JUDY

DAVID DAHL and BARRY KEHOE

MASON / CHARTER

NEW YORK 1975

First Printing, August 1975
Second Printing, August 1975

Printed in the United States of America

Library of Congress Cataloging in Publication Data

Dahl, David, 1940-
  Young Judy.

  Bibliography: p.
  1. Garland, Judy. I. Kehoe, Barry, 1941-   joint
author. II. Title.
ML420.G253D25   784'.092'4 [B]   75-11500
ISBN 0-88405-106-4

For our parents,
Marion and Gladys,
Jeremiah and Margaret

When I was very young
the world was younger than I
as merry as a carousel

The circus tent was strung
with every star in the sky
above the ring I loved so well

Now the young world has grown old
gone are the tinsel and gold

CONTENTS

ix

PREFACE

What more is there to say about the girl "sentenced to martyrdom and sainthood in a show-biz world that cries too easily but shies from the true cause of the tears that Judy has been crying from Andy Hardy onward"?[1] Her life has been described in detail in hundreds of articles and numerous books. We know the fixed image of the troubled singer, the pathos of her private life, her theatrical accomplishments and failures, her legendary status and the myths thereof. The truth shall make you free, the old adage goes; yet in the several biographies already written, Judy remains imprisoned in her legend, no more comprehensible than before, as elusive as ever—the "little girl lost" who escapes us. After almost 40 years of public notoriety, Judy seems doomed to be a martyr and a secular saint.

A good biography should answer some fundamental and perennial questions about its subject, and we hope this one does this for Judy Garland. Schulberg's intuition was right: people have shied away from the truth about Judy, not only from her early MGM days on, but from the deeper recesses of her history, the years before she became famous. This book is about the source of her crushing anguish which increased as her life went on, the cause of the tears that she cried.

Her accomplishments and tribulations have been well documented. In Mel Torme's *The Other Side of the Rainbow,* which deals with less than a year in Judy Garland's later life, she emerges as disturbing and fascinating, as much from her own sheer indomitability as from Torme's portrayal of her from his love-hate viewpoint. Mickey Dean's and Ann Pinchot's *Weep No More My Lady* explains Judy's life from the perspective of her last few years. Her fifth husband sympathetically tries to make a whole meaning of her life through this association, and he succeeds as far as such a factual chronology can.

Anne Edwards' approach is self-explanatory in its title, *Judy Garland: A Mortgaged Life,* in which she maintains that Judy's "childhood was a nightmare from which she never recovered" and that "perhaps no woman in theatrical history has been as exploited" as she was. Yet another one, *Little Girl Lost* by Al DiOrio, affectionately relates what Judy meant to her innumerable fans, written from a fan's point of view, supplying more data about her career, especially performances and reviews of her concert career. But neither this book nor the others offers insight into her behavior, nor do they solve the basic enigma of Judy Garland and why so many were drawn to her.

When we began work on this book in January 1971 we did not expect to solve an enigma. As we reviewed the public facts of her life, we deviated, gravitating toward the less familiar period, the years before she became famous, instead of the highly publicized later years. In focusing on this obscure period, we learned more than we had expected to. We found a motive for Judy's life turning out as it did. Until her death in 1969 she persistently tried to find the same thing. Just a year before she died, she asked the one family friend who had known her and her parents longer than anyone, what really happened between her mother and father in those last years before the MGM contract was signed in 1935. In her later life she complained that everyone always kept the truth from her, trying to shield her from reality. The family friend didn't tell her the truth either, later saying of Judy's query about her mother and father: "I didn't see what sense it would make to tell her."

He may have been right; she had suffered so much pain already. But today Judy's question deserves an answer; her memory requires the truth as far as it can be determined. In exposing and reconstructing a part of her life that has never been treated before, we encountered the very phenomenon Norman Mailer denied was possible in his biography, *Marilyn*—transcendence. Mailer admitted that he was not willing to write a psychohistory of his subject that would "consume years." He questioned, but didn't refute, the traditional process of hard work, meditation, and diligence—all the qualities necessary in "the logic of transcendence" in such biographies which attempt to "force an impossible solution out of the soup. . . ." Notwithstanding Mailer's advice, we have—we think—forced just such an impossible solution, and from an authentic perspective.

The search for the real Judy is important if for no other reason than that it answers her own desperate musings about her life. *This book is her story,* as close to an objective memoir of her family and early life as we could get. In it we have tried to retrieve Judy, as well as her mother and father, from the purgatory they have lived in as a result of the tragedy that engulfed them and the subsequent cruel picture drawn of them. In addition, the search for Judy is important because there is a lesson in the way we perceive celebrity and success—ritualistically, often with no regard for the person within the celebrity.

Young Judy is a nostalgic evocation, through the life of one of the most remarkable entertainers of all time, of a period in America. Depicted is the origin of those marathon, uninhibited, equilibrium-upsetting stage performances that became her hallmark. We show what impelled Ethel Gumm to promote her daughter's singing career, hence not only how but why a star was born. Judy's life as a child is reenacted, showing the psychological and social influences on the woman she became. The life of a commonplace yet talented child is contrasted with the persona of the celebrity who became a part of the public domain. These formative "buried years" revealed, childhood comes to an end for Judy with a loss that makes all of her later success and tragedy seem inevitable.

Real success in life was doomed because of the life Judy left behind. Ultimately success was empty for her. A year before her death she wrote: "Do you know how difficult it is to be Judy Garland? . . . I certainly didn't ask to be a legend . . . I was totally unprepared for it. . . ." Success failed, but Judy triumphed and prevailed. She transcended. With pure feeling, talent, and determination she overcame everything in her lifetime. She didn't need answers to her despairing questions about her life because she was bigger than life. For as Mailer says, transcendence is more a "miracle" than a rational process in which a person can be comprehended by the facts of his or her life.

ACKNOWLEDGMENTS

These people and sources made the writing of this biography possible: in the South, John M. Webb, Dean of Men at the University of the South, and Edward J. Tribble, former university archivist, also at the University in Sewanee, Tennessee; in Tullahoma, Tennessee, Floyd Mitchell, and in Murfreesboro, Tennessee, Briley Adcock, of the Linebaugh Public Library; in Nashville, Tennessee, the *Nashville Banner* and the *Nashville Tennessean*. The help of the University of the South Archives was invaluable.

We are very grateful to Mrs. Barbara Knotts of the Superior Public Library, Superior, Wisconsin, without whom we could not have filled in the Superior part of our story. We also wish to thank the Douglas County Historical Museum and the *Evening Telegram* for allowing us to see its old issues.

We appreciate the assistance of and interviews with Mrs. Elsie Kirkes at the Itasca Memorial Hospital; Wallace Aiken; Father Paul Berg, rector at Christ Memorial Church; Mrs. George O'Brien; Mr. Stan Helmer; Mrs. Ralph Comstock of the Historical Room of the Courthouse; Ken Hickman, editor of the *Herald Review;* Mr. Bob Bentz; Mr. Rossman, publisher of the *Herald Review;* Mrs. Mabel Beckman; Mr. and Mrs. Allen Doran; Mr. and Mrs. L. L. Huntley; and Mrs. Louis

Laurent. All of these people were in Grand Rapids, Minnesota. Special thanks go to Margaret O'Brien and her staff at the Grand Rapids Public Library for their tireless work on our behalf and to Mr. and Mrs. Allen Doran for their cooperation. The old issues of the *Grand Rapids Herald-Review* and the *Grand Rapids Independent* were quite valuable. We thank Lilian Esala of the Virginia Public Library, Virginia, Minnesota, for her help.

We would like to thank those persons who live in Lancaster, California, or who lived there in the 1920s and 30s, Adelaide Kinnamon Ladd and Arne and Lois (Wakefield) Wirta for their thoughtful help, Mrs. Vernon (Wakefield) Ward, Sam Ming, W. D. Carter, Mr. and Mrs. Glenn Settle at the Tropico Gold Mine in Rosamond, Bob Herbert, Shirley Eyler, George Badgely, Walt Austin, Bill McAdam, Irma Story, Ralph Rosas, Ed White, Gayland Reed, and Ethel Oman. We are indebted to Bill MacKenzie at the *Daily Ledger Gazette* and particularly to the old issues of the *Antelope Valley Ledger Gazette*. We are also grateful to the Lancaster Regional Library and the *South Antelope Valley Press*. Special thanks to the close friends of Judy and her family, John and Billie Perkins, who saved the letter from Frank Gumm, and to Ina Mary Miller, Judy's childhood friend, and her husband, Earl Miller, for their recollections.

In Lomita, California, Corena Green of the *Peninsula News,* and the Lomita Chamber of Commerce. Also the old issues of the *Lomita News* and the *Lomita Progress*.

In Los Angeles many thanks to Maurice L. Kusell, Dr. Marcus Rabwin, Harry Rabwin, Sherrill C. Corwin, and to Terry Helgesen for his information about vaudeville and the old movie theaters. We acknowledge assistance from Metro-Goldwyn-Mayer Inc. for the details of Judy's contract, and KFI Broadcasting and Wayne Martin for the "Shell Chateau" transcripts. The libraries in the Los Angeles area that we used were the Los Angeles Public Library (Main Branch), the Alhambra Public Library, the South Pasadena Public Library, the Pasadena Public Library, the Academy of Motion Picture Arts and Science's Library, and the Pacific Telephone Library of Old Listings. Thanks also to the Hollywood Professional School for information obtained.

These newspapers, past and present, assisted us in reconstructing Judy's vaudeville career: the *Detroit Free Press; Chicago Daily Tribune; Post Advocate,* Alhambra, California; *Los Angeles Examiner; Los Angeles Mirror; Los Angeles Evening Herald and Express; Los Angeles Evening Express; Los Angeles Times; Los Angeles Herald-Examiner; Lewiston Morning Tribune,* Lewiston, Idaho; the *San Diego Union; Chalfant Press (INJO Register),* Bishop, California; *Long Beach Press Telegram,* Long Beach, California; *San Francisco Chronicle;* the *Wenatchee World,* Wenatchee, Washington; the *Spokesman-Review,* Spokane, Washington; the *Shelby Promoter,* Shelby, Montana; the *Herald-Republic,* Yakima, Washington; *Santa Barbara News-Press,* Santa Barbara, California.

These movie magazines were perused: *Movieland, Photoplay, Quick Magazine, Screen Guide,* and *Modern Screen.*

Of the dozens of persons we interviewed, we reiterate our gratitude to them, especially the Dorans, Perkinses, Ina Mary Miller, Mr. Kusell, Mr. Harry Rabwin, and Dr. Marcus Rabwin, all of whom were close friends of the Gumms and had fond memories of Judy and her family.

We wish to thank our friends who helped us: Bob O'Farrell, for his special assignment in Grand Rapids; the late Freda Olson for her recollection of young Judy in San Francisco; John Ferjo III, Clara and Irving Rosenbluth, Anne and Jerry Kehoe, and Marcus Haines, for their special assistance; Louis Ortega for musical consultation; Nancy and Dean Hill and Glenn Siebert for their critiques of the first drafts of this book, and their insightful editorial suggestions; and Lola Rubio and Florence Bolden for their particular efforts in manuscript preparation and typing the book.

We wish to thank the publisher, Orlando Petrocelli, the managing editor, Jane Rogers Tonero, and the staff of Mason/Charter.

PROLOGUE

As one commentator has pointed out, when she died there didn't seem to be any American over the age of five who did not know something about Judy Garland. Most had been touched by her in *The Wizard of Oz,* an MGM movie made in 1939, which has been shown many times on television. Some lost track of her after that, while many followed her astounding career. Many last heard of her triumphs at the Palace Theater in the fifties, Carnegie Hall in the sixties, or gave up on her while watching her nervous gestures and diminishing talent on television in 1963.

In those later years, everyone heard that things had gone bad for Judy, that she was a casualty and even something of an "indecency," as one critic put it. They either felt sorry for her or lost patience, getting snatches of stories about pills and booze, marriages and divorces, breakdowns and illnesses, debts and professional failure. It was downhill and dead end; she knew that it was over, that nothing more was expected of her. After four decades, few had great hopes for her.

The loss of her talent was a psychic crisis. Without it, she could no longer tell who she really was; the source of power and hope was gone. Less than two years before her death a critic and friend wrote that "the voice—as of last night's performance, anyway—is now a memory. . . ."

Another wrote of the same show, asking how long she would be able "to continue in this manner without reaching a point of absolutely no return."

No one was more aware of or sensitive to her waning talent than Judy herself. She knew she was losing the gift that had been the focal point of her life as long as she could remember and which had brought her fame and joy. But she continued to tour the world, doing the only thing she knew how to do: sing in public.

In early 1969 she went to London to appear at the Talk of the Town nightclub for a lengthy engagement. It was thousands of miles and 45 years from her stage debut with her two sisters—a lifetime ago in Minnesota. In London she still considered herself to be "in vaudeville." But the gaiety and vigor of youth were gone. As she sang a song, painfully aware of her cracking, rasping voice, she would apologize to the audience and herself: "My dear, I sound like a train." At other times she would say, "I've been singing for 45 years," as if that would explain what was happening to her. The run in London was marred by pathos resulting from illness and a disintegrating voice.

She arrived an hour late one night. The restless audience had begun to chant, "Why are we waiting?" When she emerged on stage, the chanting continued. She sang "I Belong To London." Customers threw bread rolls, cigarette packages, and other assorted rubbish at her. Interrupting her already disjointed song, she asked: "What's the matter with you out there?" Then she began her second song, "Get Happy." As the heckling continued, she tried the last resort—"Over the Rainbow." Amid boos and catcalls she yelled: "That's it. I have had enough."

Was this floundering 46-year-old minstrel the same one who had been hailed as the greatest entertainer of her time, the single most creative talent ever to pass through the theater and motion pictures, the last of the legendary stars? She, too, asked this question, as well as how long she could continue. The answer came within five months of that grim and prophetic show. She died on June 22, 1969. Yet her death itself seemed to bring an achievement, a phenomenon:

The more than 20,000 who, in 36 hours, viewed Judy Garland's body in a glasstopped casket . . . attest anew to the charisma that distinguished this

unique thrush . . . songstress was an extraordinary personality . . . the appeal
lasted right to the end . . . the thousands, from all walks, who paraded under
a hot June sun into Campbell's [Funeral Parlor] were decorous as they attested to deep-felt public affection.[1]

The obituaries of her dwelled on the morbid aspects of her life. In
talking or writing about her, people responded to an image that had become fixed in their minds. Huntley/Brinkley suggested that her life had
been wasted singing about "bluebirds" and "rainbows." Budd Schulberg
said that she "was a victim of a system she couldn't beat,"[2] while Vincent
Canby spoke of her as an object of America's propensity for conspicuous
consumption, like "glass containers, automobiles, uranium" and as a symbol of "loneliness and loss."[3] The *New Yorker* saw her as the "food of
millions," but she herself as "fearfully hungry." Van Horn called her a
"pathetic ornament of our times."

The diffused (or fixed) impression of Judy Garland continues to this
day. Beyond the confusion lies a mystery about her. Part of the difficulty
is that she was a "legend," and legends are often impenetrable. They
dispel an adequate comprehension of the person. Judy Garland knew
this all too well, saying late in her life: "If I'm such a legend, then why
am I so lonely?" She accepted this status: "All right, so I'm Judy Garland. But I've been Judy Garland forever. . . ."

Judy's daughters, Liza Minnelli and Lorna Luft, speak of her frequently, trying to counter the tragic image of her with memories of the
gay and funny Judy, the talented and impish woman who was their
mother.

Liza recalls "the joy she had for life . . . she wanted the pinnacle of
excitement . . . she had lived eighty lives in one." They recall the witty
and mischievous side of their mother. She could joke about the Internal
Revenue Service which was about to repossess her luxurious Hollywood
home in 1967, saying: "I never liked it. It looks like a Gloria Swanson
reject." Or referring to her many marriages and divorces: "I'm not in the
munitions business! Why should I always be rejected?" This indestructible
humor is cited by Liza in an instance when Liza was about 14, and a
strange lady came up to her mother in a restroom. She said: " 'Oh, Judy,

never forget the rainbow,' and Mama said, exiting grandly, 'Madam, how could I forget the rainbow, I've got rainbows up my ass.' "

Lorna says of her mother's performing achievement: "It doesn't bother me to be compared to Mama, but neither Liza nor I can be truly compared because nobody can be compared to Mama. Nobody will ever beat her. Streisand? Don't make me laugh . . . even when Mama was bad, she was better than everybody else put together." At least, she may have been more competitive than everybody else put together, for the overriding fact about Judy is that she was a vocal athlete whose track record extended over 45 of her 47 years. Somewhere in those years viable alternatives for her ceased to exist. On stage and before the cameras, she was always the picture of innocence and wistfulness, serenity and melancholy, joy and yearning. Picasso should have painted her among his acrobats and clowns and harlequins—the eternal troubadour.

What of her art, her voice itself? Controversy was extended here, as well. The dissenting view revolves around "a vibrato out of control" versus the "voice of the century." Many couldn't see beyond the low-brow nature of her repertoire and medium, the histrionic performances and the fanaticism of the audiences. Because of her "show business" orientation and because many made a distinction between being a "belter" and a "singer," she was not given the critical recognition of that of her contemporaries. Critics who did not involve themselves in her music and who perhaps did not find a sociological link between her experience and what she sang, would not speak of her in the same breath as a Piaf or a Holliday. Not only did she seem to defy aesthetic classification, but her life did not appear tragic enough. Her suffering appeared to be more "hysterical." Few knew to what extent her existence had been predetermined. Other critics did attest to her being a true artist, the very best, an original. Although denied the consensual acclaim granted to many others by the literary-musical establishment, she was content, more than compensated by personal recognition, audience loyalty, and mass adulation.

Beyond the legend, the pathos, humor, and talent of Judy Garland, there is a fascination, a pull that persists today. Three of her husbands have announced that they would memorialize her in either a book or a movie. "There's not one day that my father doesn't talk about her," says

Lorna. In the research for this book, we encountered a man who had known Judy throughout her life. In 30 years no one had approached him about her; then in the course of one month he had four requests for interviews. Amazed at the extraordinary interest in her, he remarked that she was becoming "the new Bernhardt." One of the writers who interviewed him, a famous mystery-crime writer, speaks of the "unfathomable Judy" and of trying to find out what it was Judy Garland was searching for.

No twentieth-century personality has been more obscured by myths. When Liza Minnelli received the Oscar in 1973 an older actress remarked: "That girl deserved it, but she got it because this town destroyed her mother, and now they're doing penance." This sentiment parallels the typical story about Garland, found in memoirs of Hollywood, such as this one in *The MGM Stock Company* by James Parish and Ronald Bowers: "No longer is there a member of the film cognoscenti who does not know about Louis B. Mayer's haste in the transformation of Judy Garland into a star. . . . Using his auditor's brain, he found a beautiful vein of gold in a little vaudevillian girl and turned her into what street people term a 'junkie' and social workers tag an addict."[4]

Did Hollywood destroy Judy Garland? Was she a "property" of the Metro-Goldwyn-Mayer Studio, which introduced her to an assortment of drugs as an adolescent in order to meet a demanding schedule, which was allied with her mother to make sure personal matters did not interfere with her career, and which even thwarted the efforts of a federal narcotics agent to help her, all because of her value to the studio? Was MGM justified in turning her out of the studio for which she had made $100 million or more, set adrift at the age of 28, broken and spiritless? Was the young Judy as sweet and good-natured as she appeared to be in the *Wizard of Oz* and other Metro films? Was her mother a monstrous stage mother and her father an ineffectual, muzzled figure, as the story goes? Was she a child who never grew up, or worse, a woman without a childhood, who grew up on vaudeville stages and whose early years were abnormal and terrible?

These are some of the myths that had to be surmounted in order to see this idolized and mythologized show business person in a new—and fresh—light. We began by following the few clues Judy gave about the early years of her life. We found that her recollections were either uncannily lucid or grossly distorted. In the latter instance, she either repressed the truth, lied, or found her early life too painful to recapture honestly—she buried the memory of the life she left behind her. Breaking through the barrier of Judy's remembrances, we found a part of her life no one knew about, not even Judy herself, although it was a story she tried to tell.

We started tracing her footsteps, based on her vivid recollections, reconstructing the places and times she had known when she was Frances Gumm, the youngest daughter of Frank and Ethel Gumm. Our picture of this period became clearer as we headed out to Lancaster, California, for the first time—in search of Judy Garland's youth.

We entered the town fully aware that this was the place Judy had many unhappy memories of, which she had expressed on numerous occasions in the 1960s in some popular magazines. She had come down hard on the town, saying that here she was lonely and persecuted because her family were show people. She made remarks which, understandably, were not calculated to endear herself to the desert town, such as: "The people in the town were like the countryside around them—barren and harsh."

We thought of these remarks as we spotted a building with an old marquee in front. It must have been Frank Gumm's old theater. This was confirmed as we talked to the proprietor of the barbershop in the building which was no longer a theater. Another man entered, a barber from down the street. It turned out that he used to give Frank Gumm a shave every day during the 1930s; he even had a letter Gumm had written to him years ago. He said he'd look for the letter if we were interested in it.

With this beginning we walked over to the old Lancaster School, Judy's resolute opinion of her former home echoing in our minds. We asked a lady in the school whether she had been familiar with the family and if it was common knowledge that Judy had grown up in the town. She replied with little interest, saying she recalled them but adding, "I don't think Lancaster is going to erect a monument to Judy Garland."

We asked if she knew of others who had known them. Softening, she picked up the phone and dialed. "Hello, Lois, Hi! Say, did you know the Gumm girls real well? . . . The two older ones! . . . Did you know Judy, too? . . . Would you like to talk to two young men who are writing a book about her? . . . Okay, they'll be right over."

What follows is based on the fact that no one ever attempted to establish the reality of the person who became Judy Garland or to ask what was gained and lost in the process. We will show how the youngest Gumm daughter was transformed from a typical American child into the ultimate theatrical phenomenon—artist and commodity, legend and enigma, troubled woman, and lifelong object of both pity and adulation. What caused Judy's mother to seek a show business career for her three young daughters, thus insuring her youngest child's disenchantment? What happened during these years to create the later, disturbed woman and great theatrical personality?

The answer lies in Judy Garland's childhood because no one paid attention to Judy's fragmented reveries nor examined them in light of what she left behind and what she became. No one went to Lancaster, California; Grand Rapids, Minnesota; or Murfreesboro, Tennessee. No one asked about a particular family of the 1920s and 30s, about those places in an era of small towns, hard work, ambition, success, innocence, and corruption. This is the story of Frances Ethel Gumm who, a half century ago, became a singer.

Young
JUDY

1

MARIPOSA—LOOKING BACK

I was just an ordinary girl of twelve
with a healthy voice.

In 1935 the family lived together for the last time at 842 North Mariposa Avenue in the heart of Los Angeles, a few blocks from where the Hollywood Freeway would later pass.

There was a down-to-earth quality about the Gumms in spite of the fact that the past decade or more of their lives had been unusual by most standards. The three daughters of Frank and Ethel Gumm had served an apprenticeship in the family business—show business.

Known as the Gumm Sisters, the trio had plugged along for years, getting good and bad reviews, lots of applause and practically no applause. They had been booed. One of the girls recalled being hit with a piece of cheese. Of the three, Frances, the youngest, had gotten most of the attention and praise and had been the star of the act. Her older sisters, Mary Jane and Virginia, were now merely providing background for the diminutive prodigy of the family.

In April 1935 the family engagements were nearing an end. These were the last days of the trio, which, under the auspices of Frank and Ethel Gumm, had appeared hundreds of times on stages all over the United States. The year before, the girls had changed their last name and were now appearing as the "Garland Sisters." It took this vaudeville family 10 years to concede that there were more theatrical-sounding names than Gumm. But even with a new name, the act seemed to have reached a plateau; good bookings, good reviews, and "breaks" for the trio and Frances led nowhere.

This didn't matter to them, though, especially Mary Jane and Virginia who were pursuing the typical life of teenage girls in Los Angeles, including, of course, boys. Young Frances, whom everyone called "Babe" or "Baby," was left out of this activity; but her father, surveying his girls, quipped that even Babe was "beginning to give the boys the once over." None of the girls really knew what a big break would mean to them. Even Ethel Gumm, the most determined of them, couldn't imagine how success would affect them. Known to everyone as a woman of endless enterprise and productivity, her relentless promotion of the singing and dancing Gumm Sisters had not yielded fame or fortune.

Their father, a vaudevillian, but a man with a Southerner's sense of tradition, wanted security for them. He relished the thought of stability for his family, especially his beloved Frances, his youngest, then 12 years old. Disheartened at having had to leave their last home, and now living in the city, Frank was running another movie theater, this time in Lomita, an outlying area of Los Angeles.

Mariposa Avenue was more eastern-looking, with its large, wood-frame and brick houses instead of the common California-Spanish stucco homes. The Gumms lived in a white, two-story house with a colonial facade. Frances went to school in the mornings, freeing her for practice and performances in the afternoon, but she could frequently be seen running and cycling down the street. As neighbors watched this energetic child playing on the block, it was inconceivable that events would soon overwhelm her, that time was running out for Frances Gumm.

She was aware that both her mother and father had theatrical hopes for her. Also, she was becoming a singer who could really sing.

Frances idolized her father, and Frank worshipped the ground she walked on. And no wonder; she was an irresistible child, quite ordinary looking but with an appealing quality that drew one's eyes to her. She was small and slender, with gangly legs and the slightest hint of chubbiness. Her personality fluctuated from moods of serious introspection to effervescent good-naturedness. She had a forlorn, sensitive face with large brown eyes which became animated and excited when people paid attention to her and which were an accurate index of her thoughts and feelings. She was impish, and there was a definite sparkle to her.

She had inherited her father's outgoing and genial nature, but there was also a sad and melancholy side to him. By 1935 he had lost his dapper good looks; aside from his clear, striking eyes, he now looked old. He tended to look back, full of nostalgia and sentiment. Intermittent periods of depression found him reflecting on his past life and the dreams of his youth.

The past few months had become almost unbearable as the last hope of relieving the torment he and Ethel had shared for the past two decades was finally sealed off. Here in their last home, a few months before the ambitious family enterprise would disintegrate and set adrift its youngest member, Frank wrote to a college chum, perhaps out of self-pity but more likely with a vaudevillian's sense of irony about the course of his life:

Tomorrow is my birthday . . . and I can think of no better way of celebrating it than by sending you herewith my check, in order that I may become, in a humble way, a "paying" member of Sewanee's great alumni. Boy, I will never forget the six years I spent at Sewanee; they were six of the happiest, the most beautiful years of my life.

As Frank Gumm, the founder of a yet-unknown theatrical dynasty, pondered his Southern boyhood and college days, which now looked so idyllic to him, the Gumms pursued their lives like countless families on the bright, palm-treed streets of Los Angeles. Although Frances had a special place in the hearts of her sisters and parents (they were slightly in awe of her exuberant personality and musical talents), no one in April 1935 was aware that Frances Gumm was on her way to becoming "a little Mozart of song and dance."[1]

2

SOUTHERN ROOTS

*I guess if I had any talent . . .
it was inherited.*

"I adored him. And he had a special kind of love for me, the youngest of his three daughters. We sang together."[1] Judy Garland always spoke of her father with such warmth. In a lifetime of blunted, deceitful, and contradictory remarks about her family, he was the one person who never diminished in her mind. All of her remembrances of him have this mutually adoring tenor. When she raged against her mother for the way her life turned out, not a single negative word was uttered about her father. She recalled him as being "so friendly," the man who laughed good and loud like she did, with a funny Irish sense of humor, who praised and protected her. He had a beautiful voice which she inherited, and they sang together. He sang spirituals to her as a baby while she cuddled up to him in her flannel pajamas. He gave her everything she wanted.

But he left her. She would be possessed by him for the rest of her life. He became her standard in everything. When she went to Hollywood, she wrote on the MGM questionnaire that she was born in Murfreesboro, Tennessee because her father was born there. When she had a television series, she sang as her weekly closing theme a song she said he wrote. She would tell her friends how her father had run away with a

5

traveling show as a boy, that that was part of her tradition. He was handsome and a gentleman. Later, in love, she looked for men who were very much like him.

Judy Garland inherited her father's looks, his talent, the sweet timbre of his Southern voice, his romantic bent (a whimsical and dream-like attitude), as well as his dark, melancholy side. Frank Avent Gumm became his daughter's lifetime ideal—a life force whose inspiration was one of the strongest and most perplexing in the history of the theater, one which gave her a dream and left her bereft, made her great but insured her doom.

That her ideal may have become a fallen idol if she had viewed him maturely does not matter, since we are speaking of a young girl's impression of a charming and glamorous father whose aura would persist as a unifying emotion in her psyche. Her impression was not an inaccurate one, as can be seen as their story unfolds. Fittingly, she never learned the full dimensions of his nature any more than he could ever see the fate of his beloved daughter as an anguished, idolized, caricatured human commodity. Their love for one another survived the true story of the intricate friendship between them which had its roots and beginnings almost a century ago in the Old South.

George Darrow sat at his desk at Oak Manor, having completed his task. He had a sense of accomplishment. He truly believed in the boy and was impressed with his special qualities. He was the godfather to the boy and an old friend of the family. But it was more than loyalty to his neighbors and Episcopal brethren that impelled his action. The lyric quality of the boy's voice had caught his attention; he was pleased with his trusting and gentle nature, as well as his apparent intelligence. Young Frank was also fanciful and a bit of a dreamer, but his benefactor had no way of knowing this.

Mr. Darrow was an influential churchman, the treasurer of the diocese and a patron of Sewanee. He sent a letter to the school. With it began the odyssey of a young Southern boy, choir singer and minstrel, carrying a dream of love and music, eventually all over the land and even near the gates of fame. It was June 7, 1899, the beginning of a hot summer in Murfreesboro, Tennessee. In a few days Benjamin L. Wiggins, vice-chancellor of the Sewanee Grammar School, would receive the letter:

My Dear Mr. Wiggins:
Your kind letter regarding my young friend Frank Gumm, has given me great pleasure. I will bring the boy up Tuesday morning. I am sure neither you, or any of those interested will ever have cause to regret helping this bright boy along—He knows that he is taken for his services in the Choir, and that he must be ever anxious to render service to his benefactors. With warmest regards.

Sincerely yours
G. M. Darrow   June 7–99

It seemed fitting that as the Gilded Age, or Age of Innocence, came to an end, Francis Avent Gumm, age 13, of Murfreesboro, should be starting his adventure in the world. He was a stocky, healthy-looking boy of Irish descent, friendly and agreeable and very impressionable. Through his personal charm and good singing voice, he had already learned that he could draw attention to himself, in addition to the possibility that these attributes might earn him a dispensation from the ordinary life. Already his personal assets were allowing him to leave home to go to a preparatory school for the university. A college career was conceivable, which was not the lot of the average boy in a small American town in 1899. The plan for Frank was timely, since he had already experienced the usual restlessness of a rural youngster. Later in life he told of running away with a minstrel show when he was 10. Whether he did or not, there is no doubt that he would have wanted to do so.

Not that there were such unfavorable circumstances that they would drive him from home; on the contrary, he came from one of Murfrees-boro's most genteel families. They might have been considered part of the "impoverished gentry" of the South, but they were at least com-fortable, now living in a society more closely identified with the national spirit of the Gay Nineties than with the depressing postbellum years. In the Gumm home there was a happy union of the old order with the new, which was imparted to the children.

Frank Gumm's boyhood home in Murfreesboro, Tennessee. *Courtesy of the University of the South*

William T. Gumm had married Clementine Baugh, and they raised three boys. Frank, who was the youngest, was born on a Saturday evening, March 20, 1886, in the family home on East Main Street near the town square.

William Gumm was active in the commercial life of the small town, which had once been the state capital but was now known for its livestock and cotton. The city was located near the Stones River, less than 50 miles southeast of Nashville. The Gumms lived in an elegant, two-story, white-brick, Georgian residence, an antebellum home which Will's father had built. From the beginning the youngest of the three boys was called "Baby Gumm," a nickname that would persist in the Gumm lineage.

So if Frank had other dreams, they didn't grow out of revolt but were nourished in an atmosphere of comfort, affection, and love. Theirs was a proud and gentle life, a world of Tiffany lamps and horse-drawn carriages, home entertainments and town hall recitals, and other delights of a period drawing to a close.

By the time Frank entered grade school, his interests tended toward music. His pleasant boy-soprano voice was in sharp contrast to his older brothers who had little aptitude for music. Will and Clementine indulged this tendency, and Frank sang at home and at school. Mr. Darrow, a visitor to the home, saw to it that the boy joined the church choir. The family attended St. Paul's Church quite faithfully and now with even more pride as they listened to young Frank in the choir loft.

There was no conflict between this and Frank's equal attraction to more worldly music—the minstrel shows, circuses, and tent vaudeville shows that passed through Murfreesboro. It was a time when the world impinged more and more on the lives of rural people in America, and Frank was no exception to being lured toward the glitter of travel, the big city, and the glamor of theatrical life. Further influences were the now popular weekly magazines, advertisements, and billboards showing trapeze artists, Gibson girls, blackface minstrels, and the stars of the New York stage. Also in New York in the mid 1890s, Edison's vitascope, photographs projected on a screen with movement of the images, was being demonstrated in vaudeville houses.

The Gumms traveled some, and it is quite possible that they took

Frank Gumm (right, second from bottom) at age thirteen in St. Paul's Church choir, Murfreesboro, Tennessee, 1899. *Courtesy of the University of the South*

the boys to the Chicago Exposition of 1893, which would have further whetted Frank's appetite. But locally he saw enough of the touring shows —the potpourri of singing and dancing, comedy, melodrama, and acrobatic and juggling acts—to know that this was for him. He sang the songs of the nineties, "The Band Played On," "When You Were Sweet Sixteen," "After the Ball," and others. He knew of the leading actors and actresses of the time—John Drew, William Farnum, William Gillette, Lillian Russell, Anna Held, and Sarah Bernhardt. Another was Minnie Maddern Fiske, who started her career as a child entertainer on a showboat and had emerged as the "first lady of the theater." And in 1899 the Four Cohans, including young George M. with his sister and parents, were performing on Broadway. All of this was part of Frank's dream. Two songs of the year 1899 expressed the universal conflict of life that was experienced by many—"The Curse of the Dreamer" and "Stay in Your Own Back Yard."

The Gumms knew that their son had a romantic bent and an artistic temperament which, they hoped, with a good education, could be channeled appropriately. Other than being a rather impulsive and rambunctious boy, Frank had not given his parents any reason for disapproval. He did well in school and remained faithful to his choir duties. The latter he executed with much fervor and style, and his voice was remembered in Murfreesboro for its warmth and beauty. He sang hymns with unabashed ardor, which was somewhat unusual in a church choir. He was also recalled throughout his youth and young manhood as "handsome and very, very charming." A classmate of Frank's in Murfreesboro recalled that he could "see him now as he came down the street with his straw hat on and his coat over his shoulder. He was invariably whistling or singing."

For the time being he would accept the decisions of others and repress any vagabond dreams, but within him the artistic temperament would always be at war with his more provincial self. In later life he would try to reconcile his Southern tradition of roots with the less respectable life of a vaudeville trouper.

But this struggle was all in the future as the family bid farewell to their youngest at the city depot on June 13, 1899. With Mr. Darrow next to him, he waved good-bye as the cars pulled out of Murfreesboro, along the Nashville, Chattanooga and St. Louis line, toward the Cumberland Plateau and Sewanee.

He would be starting at Sewanee in midterm since the academic year ran from March to December, a provincial adjustment to allow the students, most of whom came from the low country, to attend school in the mountains during the summer to avoid the outbreaks of malaria at home. Vacations were during the winter months, starting at Christmas time.

The train arrived at Sewanee about midday. Frank was introduced to Mr. Wiggins, and it was decided that he would begin classes the next Wednesday, so as to have time to settle into his new home. He was taken to the dormitory at Quintard Hall and there said farewell to Mr. Darrow. He was given a tour of the campus, or at least part of it, since it was nearly 10,000 acres, 8,000 of which were in forest. He was shown the classrooms, playing field, Forensic Hall, and the chapel before being introduced to the house mother, one of the many house mothers at this time who were usually widows of bishops or Confederate generals. Sewanee, totally ravaged during the Civil War, was a "repository for the hopes and dreams of the Old South." Frank took an immediate liking to it. He would spend the next five years or more there.

He was the equivalent of a high school freshman. The Grammar School, as it was called, was actually a prep school with a rigid program. He made friends quickly, spent arduous hours learning Latin, Greek, history, and mathematics, and studied voice privately. He took little interest in athletics, quickly gravitating toward the musical and theatrical events of the school year, in addition to his choir duties. By this time his voice had matured to what some remembered as a rich, high baritone, although some recall him as a tenor.

By his second year (and after his first vacation home) he was entrenched in life at Sewanee. At the beginning of his second year Frank participated in an impressive service at St. Augustine's Chapel on Easter Sunday, 1900. He drew favorable attention, garnering a note in the campus newspaper, the Sewanee *Purple* of April 17: "To speak the truth briefly, the music was by odds the best that has ever rung through that

Frank Gumm's residence at the Sewanee campus, where he attended prep school and college. *Courtesy of the University of the South*

chapel, so far as we know. . . . Master Frank Gumm, of Murfreesboro, sang with accuracy and purity of tone the solo part of Stainer's 'They Have Taken Away My Lord.' "

It was a far cry from vaudeville. Frank was proud of his first notice and strived to improve. The choir repeated their performance, and again the paper noted it, distinguishing Frank's efforts: "In spite of the everlasting 'croakers,' it was well and sympathetically sung. Master Gumm gained confidence with experience, and sustained his solo part creditably."

The good word was passed on to his parents and to Mr. Darrow. The term went on, with studies, play, church and choir, and an occasional "German," or cotillion. Frank brought distinction to himself this year by winning the medal for excellence in declamation. His oratorical skills having been rewarded, the 14-year-old would-be thespian now made the transition to the theater. The *Purple* of October 9, 1900 praised the cast of "The Seven Little Dwarfs":

The summer girls and college beaux of ten years hence charmed and delighted a house full of grown-ups with their singing, dancing, and play-acting. . . . The play, "The Seven Little Dwarfs," was the *piece de resistance*. . . . The prince was duly and instantaneously amorous, as he should have been, in the person of Master Frank Gumm.

Back home during vacations, Frank was a "light-hearted lad." According to one Murfreesboro lady,

he had dark hair, dark eyes, was of medium height, medium build, and was well read, a good conversationalist. I couldn't say enough nice things about him. He was always happy, laughing. When he would come in a crowd, everybody would gather around the piano and sing. In those days young people didn't date the way they do now, but on Sunday afternoon the whole crowd would get together, usually at one of the girl's houses. When Frank dropped around, the music began.

During the next three years at the Grammar School, Frank was involved in musical and theatrical productions. He lived up to all the expectations of his "benefactors" and was well known on campus for his abilities and ebullient, courteous manner. He had become a Sewanee gentleman.

He graduated from the Grammar School in June 1903 and was a ready candidate for the college as one of its 300 students. He entered the college—later known as the University of the South, but known then, as well as today, as Sewanee—in June 1903. The college was to leave an indelible impression on him.

Sewanee afforded its students what has become a cliché in liberal arts college catalogues—an idyllic setting, a classical education, a spiritual foundation—in general, preparation for the "good life." A fellow student, William Alexander Percy, later described the Sewanee experience:

There's no way to tell of youth or Sewanee, which is youth, directly [he speaks of the qualities of the students]. . . . Personable youth greets you with not irreverent informality, puts your house guest at ease, flirts with your daughter, says grace before the evening meal with unsmiling piety, consumes every variety of food and drink set before him with unabashed gusto, leaves a wake of laughter, pays delightful attention, affable under the general disapproval, sits at last on the doorstep in the moonlight, utterly content. . . .[2]

Ironically, Frank, who would leave Sewanee after his sophomore year, would embody nearly all of these qualities. He would become living proof of what Sewanee imparts to its alumni; it was as Percy says, "a place to be hopelessly sentimental about and to unfit one for anything except the good life."

Frank seems to have left college for one of the universal reasons: discontent with the arduous life of studies while outside there was the world of excitement and success. There is no evidence of academic, financial, or personal reasons for leaving the college. Perhaps it was wanderlust or theatrical ambition, the latter inflamed by the favorable reception to his singing and acting. In any event, he left Sewanee in December 1904. He had participated in the college dramatic club; the last note about his theatrical activity at Sewanee was that he played in Shakespeare's *Twelfth Night* in June 1904. He said good-bye to his friends and the faculty and especially to his best friend, Henry Gass, who would later become a Rhodes scholar professor at the school and the first dean of men there. Frank took his last look at the campus Percy later described as "so beautiful that people who have once been there always, one way or another, come back." Frank Gumm was one of those. As the aspiring performer left Sewanee, he was not only fit for the "good life" but was young and handsome, carefree and confident, as only an 18-year-old can be.

3

A THEATRICAL BOND

He met my mother, Ethel Milne, when
he was singing in a Wisconsin theater.

Until he arrived in a Northern city around 1912 there is little known
of Frank's life. Several years of this period are accounted for when he
settled in Tullahoma, Tennessee, a little town midway between Murfreesboro and Sewanee. Economic necessity and perhaps frustration in vaudeville attempts caused him to revert to his provincial background; he took
a job as office manager and bookkeeper for Walter D. Fox in Tullahoma.
He lived on Lincoln Street where he shared a house with his brother and
sister. He contributed his musical talents, "helping out at different occasions," according to Floyd Mitchell, a former mayor. His was a conserva-
tive and well-ordered life, in the rural manner. Frank could be found
directing the church choir, as well as being a soloist, and intermittently
appearing in variety shows at the Citizens Theater.

But with an impetuousness that was becoming characteristic, after
having led an apparently model life, assisting Mr. Fox in founding a
boy's orphanage for the region and singing at social events, Frank
terminated his job and residence after almost six years. His reason for
leaving is not known. Residents recall only that he headed north and
that his brother and sister left town at the same time.

Frank made an irrevocable break with the South, heading for the

Great Lakes area. In the sedentary day-to-day routine of Tullahoma, he may have felt that life was passing him by and realized his potential as a bachelor and wandering minstrel, the unique self-sufficiency of being able to sing for one's supper. So at age 26 he headed for the boards of vaudeville.

In 1912 he arrived in the lake port city of Superior, Wisconsin, walked down Tower Street, noting the names and locations of the resort city's various theaters—the Orpheum, Alcazar, Bijou, Parlor, Lyric, and others. Being one of the favorite spots of the Midwest, each spring and on through the late summer, the town was full of vacationers. For a town of about 45,000, there were a lot of theaters and jobs for entertainers. He got a room in one of the boardinghouses or small hotels and made the rounds of Superior's silent moviehouses.

Going from theater to theater he met Ray Hadfield who was to become the "father of the movies" in Superior. Frank met him at the Orpheum, which was on Tower Street, and quickly learned that Hadfield was the local impresario of moviehouses, having opened his first one in Duluth in 1905. Now he had several theaters, one right down the street and a couple in Duluth, and he needed reliable performers. Hadfield's theaters were often filled to capacity; he had been given many "gray hairs," to use his words, by his employees, especially inept movie projection operators and vaudeville pianists. Of course, neither of these jobs concerned Frank; his forte was vocal solos of popular and traditional songs.

They hit it off well, and Frank got a job, starting at the Orpheum. Hadfield soon discovered that Frank really could sing, and he was rotated every few weeks to other Hadfield theaters. Although he did occasional straight vaudeville, Frank became primarily an "illustrator," or song leader, of the short-lived illustrated-song craze.

With his angular good looks, emphasized by dark brown eyes flecked with green and a quick Irish smile, he became an asset to Hadfield's theaters and seemingly could have worked there indefinitely. He liked the work, which gave him room for expression, as well as being an outlet for an increasingly nervous impulsiveness.

The illustrated song was a species of vaudeville, albeit perhaps the lowest-ranking. These shows, which had originated over a decade earlier in dime museums, vaudeville, and silent moviehouses, consisted of a dozen or more colored slides which re-created the images of the lyrics of current songs. Promoted by music publishers, each line of the songs was shown along with a handcolored, melodramatic photograph. The first slide announced to the audience: "All Join in the Chorus." Frank's job was to lead the audience in the songs during intermissions as fillers while the reels were being changed for the featured movie. It was his job to sing the lyrics—usually two verses and a chorus—of a new tune being offered the public in hopes that it would catch on and sell sheet music.

The audience enjoyed looking at the colored slides, which inevitably diverted attention from the song leader. In addition, the illustrator had to overcome the apathy of most of the audience, who were not interested in singing along. It was considered a thankless, discouraging job, Hadfield was lucky to have the confident Frank Gumm in his employ. It was common knowledge among theater owners that enthusiasm more than talent was needed, and to the delight of Hadfield, Frank had both. His relaxed, outgoing ardor and good, strong voice entertained as well as elicited a better than usual response in the sing-a-long.

Frank also participated in the straight vaudeville programs and could be heard singing current hits of 1913 such as the hymn, "The Old Rugged Cross" or his lifelong favorite, "Danny Boy." He was content while singing, and the audience responded appreciably. Whether singing solo or trying to lead the audience in song, Frank was pleased with himself. He wasn't fiercely ambitious like other artists who had also been song illustrators, such as Eddie Cantor and Al Jolson. Even Jack Warner as a boy had led the singing in his father's moviehouse. Frank was more self-contained; he also enjoyed music as an end in itself.

Superior had long been a good theater town. In 1905, during the height of the nickelodeon craze, it had 22 movie-vaude houses; it still had about a dozen. In the summer of 1913 Frank moved to another Hadfield house down the street from the Orpheum, at 1115 Tower Avenue. This was Superior's first real movie theater, with a sloping floor, opera seats, and a stage with scenery at the far end. As opposed to the more makeshift moviehouses of the period, this one had an ornate, theatrical appearance, with its ornamental-frieze facade over the entrance and two signs, one horizontal across the front and the other a suspended marquee running perpendicularly over the sidewalk, reading:

SAVOY

THEATER

10¢   Vaudeville   10¢

But now there was even a greater bargain: "summer season" prices. Matinees were advertised in the *Evening Telegram* at 5 cents, including vaudeville and pictures. Frank received no billing in the ad and perhaps only anonymous mention in this newspaper item: "The Savoy with its combination of vaudeville and high-class photoplays . . . noted for the distinctive quality that is offered to patrons . . . for the Fourth of July . . . there will be an extra special bill . . . one of the classiest holiday bills that it has ever offered. . . ."

A typical show at the Savoy at this time consisted of three or more vaudeville acts, together with a four-piece orchestra, a feature picture, a short subject, and an illustrated song—all for 10 cents. Hadfield had previously used a large phonograph, which was called the Victor Auxetophone and was run by compressed air. He attempted to have the illustrated songs sung by this machine, in addition to its providing accompaniment to the film. But the Auxetophone failed, and Hadfield went back to live talent. Thanks to the inefficiency of the phonograph, Frank had his job.

At the Savoy, although he got the spotlight for his efforts, Frank noticed that the real work each night was being hammered out by the house pianist, a determined and energetic 17-year-old girl named Ethel Marion Milne. As he got to know Ethel while going over the songs for the slide show, he realized that she could read music well and keep a tempo perfectly. He became one of Ethel's favorites, whom she liked to play for, in contrast to others such as one male soloist who couldn't remember the lyrics to any songs and had to pin them inside the proscenium arch. She was also taken with the appearance of this talented and independent young man from Tennessee. They became friends, and this seemingly perennial bachelor found himself captivated by Ethel.

Savoy Theater in Superior, Wisconsin, where Frank Gumm met Ethel Milne in 1913. *Courtesy* Evening Telegram, *Superior*

They rehearsed and performed together and went around town, stopping at the local beer garden for hot dogs and draught beer. Soon they were infatuated with each other.

Ethel was tiny, pretty with long dark hair, and heavy but handsome features, deep intense eyes with full eyelashes and full rounded lips and a healthy, steely grin. Frank admired her vivacity and openness. She was quite sophisticated and possessed a talent derived from a musically inclined family. Her job at the Savoy would appear to have made her a kind of bohemian for the day if a member of her family had not usually been nearby, since they all lived in Superior. They had moved around 1911, coming from northern Michigan where Ethel had been born, one of the older of the Milne children who numbered four boys and four girls. Frank visited the Milne home on Hammond Avenue and quickly took a liking to Ethel's family—her Scottish father, John Milne, and his Irish wife, Eva Fitzpatrick Milne. John Milne was an engineer and a tough-thinking atheist, quite a contrast to his effusive Irish wife. They came to Superior where John for a while went into the motion picture business by opening a moviehouse on Waterman Street, the original location of the Savoy.

All the family now went to the theater to watch the musical endeavors of the two young people who were in love. Most of the year, and especially during the peak season, the Savoy was filled to capacity twice each evening. The audiences were not aware that in addition to the vaudeville show, they were watching the classic show business story of two young performers meeting and forming a bond offstage and onstage.

Even the hits of Tin Pan Alley and Broadway were more romantic that year. "My Wonderful Dream Girl," "Sweethearts," "Where Did You Get That Girl" were all part of the atmosphere at the Savoy. Frank sang the big hit of 1913, which would ironically always be associated with his family: "You Made Me Love You, I Didn't Want To Do It."

Frank proposed, and as the new year began, they planned to wed. With all the Milnes present and with a newly ordained Episcopal minister, J. J. Crawford, officiating and a mutual friend, Alfred Street, as best man, they were married on January 22, 1914. The Gumm enterprise had begun.

4

SET FOR THE DURATION

We lived in a big white frame house . . .
the thing I remember most about it was
the laughter and fun we had as a family.

"The awful thing about show business is you have to lay it on the line again the next night, and again the next season. It takes its toll. Take, for example, 45-year-old Frances Gumm of Grand Rapids, Minnesota." So ran an insightful Associated Press review of a Judy Garland concert in 1967, more than a half-century after Frank and Ethel had arrived in Grand Rapids.

The toll was only too real. Just as people always recalled Judy's origins in the heartland of the United States, she was always haunted by the golden memories of this time and place which appeared to be like a fairy tale. She believed in perfection, an ideal that gave her sustenance and, later, cause for regret. It was there in Grand Rapids that she began to receive a lot and to give a lot. It is there that one can see an extraordinary, special child beginning to emerge.

In Grand Rapids began the odyssey of a talented and poetic individual, of a soul, for this, as unlikely as it may seem in the synthetic world of show business, is what drew people to Judy—"the vulnerability of a soul."[1] We see the bittersweet ingredients of family life, with its surface tinsel but also with undercurrents of drama and pathos. Underneath the corniness, optimism, ebullience of American home life were more pathetic elements—love, fear, pain, heartache. This is the enigma of American family life, an illusion that has had a longer twilight than most other illusions about American life and by which Judy was cursed as much as by fate. No one was more quintessentially rooted in America and family and their respective illusions than Judy Garland was.

Frank and Ethel did not have a lengthy vaudeville career. They continued to play in some of the same theaters in Superior, in the lake area where Frank had worked, and in numerous little towns nearby. Despite a warm reception of their works, they decided to settle down. They went up the road from Superior to a small town in Minnesota to raise a family.

They had passed through Grand Rapids before and knew a few people there. Less than a hundred miles from Superior along the Great Northern Railroad, it was the county seat, with a population of about 2,000. They took a liking to the village with its pine- and spruce-laden air, nourished by the Mississippi, green half the year and bare and soft white the other half when engulfed by the freezing winter temperatures.

They arrived in Grand Rapids in the spring of 1914 and for the first three months lived with the Aiken family, friends who were willing to help the young people. Both Frank and Ethel had the same high spirits, nervous energy, and talent that endeared them to their new friends and neighbors. Frank found a job that grew logically out of what he and Ethel had been doing to earn a living up until then. Perhaps at the suggestion of his father-in-law, he would do what thousands of other entrepreneurs across the country were doing—becoming movie exhibitors. He became manager of the only moviehouse in town, the New Grand Theater on Pokegama Avenue, a block away from the Mississippi River.

So the Gumms entered the glamorous movie industry the same way that other families were entering the business which would immortalize their names. From the early 1900s on, unknowns like the Foxes, Skourases, Warners, Mayers, and Graumans were converting town halls, burlesque houses, empty offices, and stores into silent moviehouses, which were originally called nickelodeons. Sam Rothapfel, who later became famous as "Roxy," opened his first moviehouse in the back room of his father-in-law's tavern in this same American scene. The industry, based on Edison's invention of the vitascope and which began in 1896, was prospering. Many of these pioneers would fan out through the various levels of the industry—exhibition, distribution, and production. Although medical experts warned that the moving images on the screen might cause permanent squinting for the viewer, by 1910 there were over 10,000 nickelodeons in the United States.

Frank's business motives would remain much more practical than some of his soon-to-be-famous contemporaries. He just wanted to find a respectable occupation that would be in keeping with his and Ethel's temperaments and talents and that would support a family. They went into partnership with Fred Bentz. Bentz ran the projection machines while Frank handled admissions and promotion and Ethel supplied what she called the "hearts and flowers type of music" on the piano below the stage. The New Grand was on the main street of town and had a seating capacity of 450.

From the very beginning of the moviehouse boom, vaudeville was used to lure customers in, and the Gumms' and Bentz' New Grand was no exception. It exuded a wholesome, family atmosphere, with live talent and movies. At the Grand, silent stars such as Theda Bara and Rudolph Valentino competed with Frank and Ethel Gumm who sang such songs as "By the Beautiful Sea" and "Back Home in Tennessee" on stage between showings.

Frank and Ethel were considered an admirable pair, an asset to the community. By the end of summer of 1914 they had rented a house of their own and had a full range of activities, including weekly dances and church. They had frequent visitors, mainly from Ethel's side of the family, as well as their new friends in Grand Rapids. Marriage and now a business had given more direction to Frank's previously undirected life, and he was pleased. By their second year in Grand Rapids, the business was thriving. They took a six-week pleasure trip to Chicago and other points in the Midwest. But Ethel became ill in Chicago, and they had to cancel the trip, going instead to the Milne home in Superior where she recuperated for several weeks. When they returned home the

Grand Rapids Herald Review wrote that the now familiar husband-and-wife team had been missed: "That Mr. and Mrs. Gumm have lost none of their former popularity during their absence was evidenced by the large house that greeted their return and the enthusiastic reception of their songs and playing."[2]

Frank told people that he and his wife had seen many towns and places during their trip, but that none compared to Grand Rapids, and they would "hereafter be content to remain here." This was an appropriate sentiment since, soon after their return home, Ethel found out that the cause of her illness on the trip was that she and Frank were going to become parents.

Reacting to his impending fatherhood, Frank decided to buy a half-interest in the theater, becoming manager-owner along with Bentz who bought the other half. As the winter of 1915 in Grand Rapids came to an end, with an endless succession of the latest hits like "The Port of Missing Men" showing at the theater, they were content to await their first child.

The baby was expected in the fall, but Ethel would not use the excuse of "confinement" to withdraw from her varied activities. In March she and Frank sponsored Grand Rapids' first style show at the theater. The merchants in the town provided the latest fashions for men and women. According to Frank, they drew the largest crowd that had ever attended the theater. Also drawing the crowds in were the latest Mary Pickford movies such as *Tess of the Storm Country*. She was one of the first idols of the screen, becoming a household word as the new film industry learned to promote itself in magazines such as *Ladies World,* whose April 1915 issue featured Mary Pickford on the cover: "The Most Popular Girl in the World."

The Gumms felt themselves on a par with all these competing events, and they began a publicity campaign to promote their own stage act. In a local news column in the *Herald Review,* called "Village and Vicinity During the Week," the first item simply stated: WHO ARE JACK AND VIRGINIA LEE? Townspeople didn't have to wait long for an answer, for Frank and Ethel unveiled their new act on Thursday and Friday, April 15 and 16, 1915, at the New Grand Theater. The *Herald Review* commented:

The entertainment given by Jack and Virginia Lee at the Grand theater last Thursday and Friday evenings was one of the best and most highly appreciated singing acts ever witnessed here. Jack and Virginia Lee are the stage names of Mr. and Mrs. Frank A. Gumm. Their act is one of piano playing and singing, southern melodies being the numbers favored. The tiresome dialogue and questionable repartee depended on usually to put an act of this kind over were conspicuously lacking, the performers contenting themselves and pleasing the audience by permitting nothing of this kind to creep into their meritorious performances.[3]

This earliest review of the Gumms is the only known theatrical notice of the Jack and Virginia Lee act.

They rented a two-story, white frame house at the corner of Second Avenue and Fourth Street, in anticipation of the family addition. This was to be the permanent home of the Gumms in Grand Rapids. It was a roomy, midwestern house, with plenty of windows in the front and an upstairs balcony. Another step, supposedly coincidental, was an increase in admission at the theater from 15 to 25 cents. Although the reason cited was increased costs due to improvements and better quality films, people couldn't help but associate it with the impending arrival of another mouth to feed in the Gumm home.

Mary Jane Gumm arrived on September 24, 1915, "to pay a lengthy and indefinite visit." According to the *Herald Review,* "the young lady— their first child, proceeded to make herself at home and Mr. Gumm, the well-known moving picture man, immediately opened the best box of cigars he could find, for his friends." Most of the Milnes came to see the new arrival, including the grandparents, Ethel's brother, Fred, and sisters, Cevila and Norma. In early November, Ethel and Frank took the baby to Superior to her grandparents and stayed a few days. Ethel returned to her piano duties at the theater, and soon Jack and Virginia Lee were appearing again on the New Grand stage, singing the hits of 1915, "The Old Gray Mare" and "There's a Broken Heart for Every Light on Broadway."

The business was doing so well that Gumm and Bentz considered moving to a new location, but they couldn't find a suitable building nor the capital to build a new theater, so, instead, they opened another

The Gumm home (as pictured today) at corner of Second and Fourth streets in Grand Rapids, Minnesota, where Frances was born. *Courtesy of Robert O'Farrell*

theater in nearby Cohasset. Times were prosperous for the Gumms, and soon they had a maid who lived in the back house on their property.

Frank was well liked in town as a theater man, churchman, and now a family man. It was soon apparent that he was a good and loving father who would give his child much attention and a sense of security. At the theater he greeted people in his genial and gregarious manner. He loved the limelight and the audience liked his spontaneity and wonderful voice. They grew accustomed to seeing Ethel at the piano below the stage. Most remembered them as "nice" and Frank as "very friendly," the more talented of the two.

Family and theater life flourished in the next few years. Frank and Ethel added to their family with the birth of a second child who, like George M. Cohan, arrived on the Fourth of July. She was born on a Wednesday morning in 1917 and was named Dorothy Virginia. Her arrival not only caused a flurry in the Gumm home but a commotion in town, since Dr. Hursh, who delivered her, kept a crowd waiting in the city square where he was supposed to deliver an Independence Day speech as well. When he was finally introduced at the park, he apologized to the audience, telling them that Mr. Gumm would have to explain his delay.

By the end of the decade Frank was in his mid-thirties, very dapper, the epitome of the smooth, polished, Protestant-educated Southerner, glib and witty, a good dancer and speaker, an all-round citizen who was good at everything he did. No self-doubt was evident. His few inadequacies were well integrated into his personality. But there was a nervousness in his character—the edge of the promoter, if not con man, the show-off concealing an inner strife. Occasionally it flared into a fit of temper, a low tolerance for criticism or being thwarted. His life was ordered around things being just the way he liked them; only Ethel would ever penetrate this order.

It was natural that after almost five years of marriage Ethel would be the first to see the defects in Frank's impressive veneer. Intimacy, familiarity, and love often breed an uncompromising, but necessary, real- ism between husband and wife. But Ethel now perceived more than just the ordinary advance of marital compromise; the disturbing thing about

Frank, which she would only gradually and painfully understand, would make her senses reel and eventually test her sanity. For the time being, though, she rejected the hint of a nightmare, of what her unborn daughter would one day recall from overheard conversations between her parents —her mother's strident, despairing accusations to her father.

The family was now seemingly complete. Frank and Ethel were pleased with its size. They had enjoyed the gentle changes in their lives of the past three years and saw the promise of a full life in Grand Rapids. They were in an enviable position as new parents, already prospering, and they felt an affection for the heavily treed, pastoral town with its warm summers and picture-postcard winters. They were set for the duration.

On a passenger car of the Great Northern Railroad in 1918 there was a group of men obviously of the same occupation who were engaged in brisk, outgoing conversation. The men used the train, which went through Minneapolis, St. Paul, Superior, and other, smaller cities, in pursuit of their daily occupations. They worked in the sales end of film distribution in the now-flourishing motion picture industry. Since the beginning of the decade, the movie business had increased geometrically, and these men worked at the grass roots level. Among them was a youthful, attentive medical student whose father was a theater owner and had dealt with film salesmen. This summer, the boy, Marcus Rabwin, decided to try his hand at selling and became a distributor of Zane Grey movies.

The more experienced men were filling him in on sales techniques, knowledge of the territory, and sales potential. One of them warned him to avoid Grand Rapids, that it would be a waste of time; and the others concurred. He was told: "There's only one theater in town, run by a fellow named Frank Gumm. He's difficult to deal with, won't sit down and talk to you, and won't buy because he says he buys his film in Minneapolis." The more he heard about Gumm, the more curious Rabwin became. It became a challenge to see if he could sell films to Frank Gumm.

Rabwin got off at the Grand Rapids depot and went down Pokegama Avenue to the New Grand Theater. He met Frank Gumm and found him just as described: he wouldn't sit down, pacing the floor and saying that he bought his films in Minneapolis. But to Rabwin's surprise, he did buy

from him. They immediately took a liking to each other. Soon Rabwin
met Ethel and the two girls and went to the Gumm house on Second
Street for dinner. He and Frank became friends. Over the next couple of
years he was a frequent house guest, staying for a few days, going to the
theater, and being entertained by the family, with Ethel at the piano and
Mary Jane and Virginia performing some of their first duets. He liked
being there and enjoyed the home entertainments, which were not awkward or embarrassing, as one might expect, because in the Gumm family
such improvisations were encouraged and always seemed natural.

The corner house was about four blocks from the theater, two blocks
from the Central School, and four blocks from the church. Frank was the
most ardent churchgoer. One lady in the local Episcopal church of that
day recalls that he had an "excellent and loud voice." Because he knew
the church service perfectly, people, not knowing of his Sewanee background, thought he must have gone to church school as a boy. He was
the lead singer and "about the only one who could really be heard."
Frank had a certain charisma, an occasional flamboyancy and temperamental quality. In church plays and at the New Grand, he wore a big
diamond ring which flashed while he was performing. Once he came to
church late. Not at all self-conscious, he put on his choir vestments and
walked right in, singing at the top of his voice and taking his place in
the choir.
    Frank and Ethel were firmly attached to Grand Rapids. The theater
prospered, and they busied themselves with their two children and with
the social and cultural life of the town. They took part in civic activities
and school events, with Janie now at the Central School, and they performed at the theater, where Jack and Virginia Lee revived their act.
Janie and Virginia made their debut as part of the new act—the Four
Gumms. Having practiced and performed at home, the two girls were
ready for the stage and by 1921 were a song-and-dance team. Grand
Rapids responded even more enthusiastically to the talents of the Gumm
family.
    In the early twenties Ethel found that she could channel her energies
into becoming, along with her theater-owner husband, a small-town

theatrical entrepreneur. Other than this endeavor, however, Ethel was typical of her times; she dressed in the style of the day, with her hair now short or bobbed. She sewed and cooked for her family; she made good use of her time. Like many women of her day, she was articulate and may have had some artistic pretensions. But she was not without taste and was certainly not a dilettante. She was unusual in that she was at once moralistic and tolerant. Underneath her external primness ran a current of romantic sentimentality. She was sort of a pioneer, strong, with fixed ideas and an ability to overcome odds, to turn a disadvantage into an advantage. She was a frontier woman with no frontier to conquer.

They entertained lavishly. Their friends were treated to Frank's hospitality and impromptu singing in the living room. Ethel started giving the girls basic musical lessons and made costumes for them. Janie and Virginia (now nicknamed "Jimmie") spent many evenings at the theater while Frank took the tickets and Ethel played the piano for the pictures. The girls felt at home there because it was so close to their house and because their parents spent so much time at the New Grand. Like most moviehouses of the period, the New Grand was not a real theater; that is, it wasn't an old legitimate theater or custom-built one. It was simply a large storefront or commercial building that had been converted into a moviehouse during the first moving-picture boom. Until a new theater was built in the early 1930s, various buildings on Pokegama Avenue served as theaters. During Frank's tenure he made the showcase as theatrical-looking as possible, with special effects and live talent in good family vaudeville. In the summer of 1920 Frank and Ethel and the two little girls posed for an apparently serene family portrait.

In late autumn the chill that announced winter was already in the air. Ethel's anxiety was piqued by the knowledge that she was expecting another child. It became a matter of contention between Frank and her, and this made her feel all the more helpless. Her suspicions of him had hardened. His immorality was substantial enough for Ethel to confront him with it and for him to offer embarrassing explanations. She expressed her hurt and revulsion, as she would many times in the years to come, by acting decisively. The revelation of Frank's sexual degradation led her from one unspeakable situation to another—abortion. Frank tried

Portrait of Frank and Ethel Gumm and Mary Jane and Virginia, Grand
Rapids, Minnesota, 1920. *Courtesy Mr. and Mrs. Allen Doran*

to calm her, but her conviction and apprehension were unmistakable. She did not want the child.

Ethel's mortification could be exceeded only by her humiliation at the public knowledge of Frank's philandering. From then on, no one could share her motives. For now—whether for moral, physical, or emotional reasons—she would attempt a resolution.

Bypassing their family doctor, they drove to Minneapolis to seek the help of a friend, Marcus Rabwin, who was a medical student at the University of Minnesota. Unaware of their real reasons, Rabwin saw them as wanting to undo what was simply a mistake. They told him that a third child was unacceptable to both of them. They also mentioned their surprise, that they hadn't planned to have more than two children. They gave Rabwin the impression that they were prudent enough to believe in the two-child maxim ahead of its time. They appeared to be in agreement on this point. They didn't ask Rabwin to do anything; they just wanted to know whether there was any way not to have the baby. Even Rabwin was taken aback. In 1921 abortion was illegal, and such an alternative was unsafe and scorned. He advised them to go home and have the child.

They drove the 150 miles back to Grand Rapids, Frank earnestly trying to cheer Ethel up. Minimizing his transgressions, he resolved to avoid anything that would threaten their happiness. Now they knew that what had been only an impulse was impossible. They accepted their friend's advice.

The crisis that preceded the birth of their third child is reminiscent of Norman Mailer's statement about Marilyn Monroe's formative struggle to live: "Any human who begins life with the debt of owing existence somewhat more than others is thereby more likely to generate an ambition huge enough to swallow old debts."

They returned to life in town, reconciled to the impending event. Frank envisioned a boy, which they wanted. This made it better, although it had been irrevocably decided that the third Gumm child would have its chance at life.

Winter ended as the lakes thawed and the waters of the Mississippi, at the source of the great river, warmed and turned from dark gray to deep blue. The Gumms were ready for their new arrival, their last child, an unknown quantity, an unknown energy source.

Ethel continued to play the piano right up until the week before the baby was due, which was at the beginning of summer. Jimmie went to visit her Aunt Norma and grandmother in Duluth, to give her mother a rest; but she returned before her mother went to the Itasca Hospital.

That Saturday evening the advertisement at the New Grand was appropriate: *The Three Musketeers*. But the movie was advertised for June 12 and 13. On the night of the arrival of the last Gumm child, a smaller ad read:

TONIGHT

HAROLD LLOYD in "An Eastern Westerner," a screaming two-reel comedy, and CONSTANCE BINNEY in "Room and Board" a five-reel Realart production.

The ad showed an increase in admission from 25 to 35 cents. As the show went on the night of June 10, 1922, Ethel had, according to two local newspaper editions of the next week, already given birth to "a new baby girl born Saturday morning" and delivered by Dr. H. E. Binet of Grand Rapids. "My parents had hoped for a boy, but I don't think they were too disappointed with another girl. They named me Frances— Frances Gumm."[4]

Frank and Ethel brought Frances home to the house on Second Street where her two sisters got to appraise her. Jimmie asked: "Is she an Indian?" because she was so red. Frank and Ethel laughed as they looked at their new child, distinguished only by her wide eyes and alertness. There was no doubt now that the third child was wanted; soon they would affectionately call her "Baby."

All the relatives and neighbors immediately noticed Frank's special pride in her. Some members of the family called her "Fanny," but the nickname didn't stick. A month later they went to the Episcopal Church where Frances was baptized by the rector, Robert Arthur Cowling. She had one godfather, Ted Toren, and two godmothers, Jenny Toren and Mrs. Arnold Wickman.

Before she was very old she was taken to the theater where she slept in a box backstage while her mother played the piano and her sisters performed onstage. "My first two Christmases I slept in a dressing room while the rest of the family was onstage performing," she later recalled.[5]

She was at the New Grand long before she was able to walk. When she was old enough, she was always running around the auditorium, through the lobby, backstage and onstage. Long before her formal, or informal, stage debut, Frank had to carry her off the stage several times when she interrupted a performance. A friend of the Gumms said that little Frances "just loved to be up there."

During her first year, until she got out of the cradle, Frances could only observe the New Grand. The year 1922 was a good one for theater and music, with songs like "Chicago, That Toddling Town," "Toot, Toot Tootsie," and "Who Cares?" These were the earliest sounds she heard at home on the phonograph or which were sung by her father, or sisters or played by her mother on the piano. She may have heard Frank sing the poignant spiritual, "Going Home" or Janie and Jimmie singing the hit, "Carolina in the Morning." The first movies she may have seen at the New Grand that year were *Blood and Sand* with Valentino, *Oliver Twist* with Jackie Coogan, and *Orphans of the Storm* with the Gish sisters.

Her parents and sisters indulged and petted baby Frances from the beginning. She was given plenty of growing room. The foundation of a confident and buoyant personality was being laid. "My father had a special kind of love for me; he always called me 'Baby.' At night before he went to the theater, I used to crawl up into his lap in a white flannel nightie and listen to him sing 'Danny Boy' and 'Nobody Knows the Trouble I've Seen.' Those two songs formed bedtime ritual with Daddy, and it was a ritual that I loved."[6]

Townspeople remember Frank driving in his old Ford, most of the time accompanied by Frances rather than by the older girls. They felt that he was much more protective of her than of them. From Frank on down, it was clear that Frances was privileged, that she would never be ignored.

The captivating baby became a soothing balm in the unresolved drama between Ethel and Frank. This is not to say that she was a pawn or object of emotional exploitation, but that her liveliness was more than welcome. Frank's love for her may have been partly reparation to Ethel and partly an indication that he would be all he appeared to be—father,

Portrait of "Baby" Frances, one year old, in Grand Rapids, Minnesota, 1923.
Courtesy of The Garlandia Collection of Wayne Martin

husband, and provider of security and stability. Ethel, too, embraced the child as her truly beloved, but she also saw in her a chance for their family's well-being. Both she and Frank knew they would have no more children.

Frances was assertive; things came to her naturally. She was so cute that people wanted to be around her and give in to her. Mary Jane and Virginia were always putting on neighborhood talent shows, and when Frances was a year and a half old they let her sing "Jingle Bells." "Then she wouldn't get off," Jimmie recalled. Later the two older girls put on a circus in the garage and let Frances be in the sideshow where she and another little girl were Siamese twins. But there wasn't enough action. Frances wanted to sing, so her sisters let her sing "Tie Me to Your Apron Strings Again." It was the last time Frances was put in a sideshow.

The four Gumms continued to perform in local shows, and Frances didn't know why she was being left out. Around Christmas time, 1923, when Frances was 18 months old, Ethel was producing a musical comedy for the church guild, called *Mary,* which was to include all of the family except Frances; she could watch but not take part. Frank had the lead, taking the role of "Gaston Marceau, the funny Frenchman." The next day the *Independent* reported:

Misses Mary Jane and Virginia Gumm in their "Hello" song provided a riot with the audience and did their work creditably. . . . Being unable to obtain printed copies of some of the numbers, Mrs. Gumm cleverly composed melodies that fit the words. The "Money" song, sung by the male quartet, was a composition original with Mrs. Gumm.

In the spring the Itasca Dry Goods Company had its annual style show. There, at the age of two, in the store, Frances made her public-singing debut. Her theatrical debut was yet to come.

The next summer they went to visit Frank's family in the South and visited Sewanee and Murfreesboro. They stopped by Henry Gass's, but the Gasses were away for the summer. In Murfreesboro Frank's cousin, Anna Lee Mirtz, recalls meeting the visiting Gumms and Frances who "was already a charmer, and even sang then. She met her grandparents and uncles and cousins there for the first time."

Formal portrait of Frances at about 18 months in Grand Rapids, Minnesota.
Courtesy of Mr. and Mrs. Allen Doran

During Christmas 1924 the Gumm house was full of the magic of the holiday for Frances's third Christmas. House and snow merged in the heavy winter as Grandma Milne and Aunt Norma, now living in Marquette, Michigan, arrived for the holidays. The Christmas tree was already surrounded with gifts.

At the theater there was also fun. No special holiday show was planned at the New Grand before Christmas, but there was some spontaneous fun at the theater during the holiday. Frances later recalled differing versions of the story, but it went something like this. A few days earlier, perhaps Christmas Eve, although no one recalls exactly, Janie and Jimmie were doing a duet on stage between movies. Frank was in the box office, and Ethel was at her usual place at the piano. The theater was crowded. Frances was running around backstage or sitting in her grandmother's lap while her sisters sang. She was envious of their being allowed to perform onstage, and she now saw them enjoying themselves, as well as capturing the attention of the audience. To her way of thinking, there had been enough family shows without her. Her family loved her, but they wouldn't allow her on the stage. She decided that this would be remedied, and right then. Of her own volition, and possibly with a little neglect on Grandma's part, she got on the stage. Her sisters, who were finishing their song, saw her coming and headed for the wings. Frances paused, looking at the audience as they tittered. Ethel yelled at her from the piano: "Get Off! Get Off!" Frances knew her sisters didn't just stand there, so she sang the only song she knew—"Jingle Bells"—over and over again. All she had going for her was volume and mettle. The audience laughed and sighed and applauded the irresistible performance. No one recalls how long she was up there; they only remember that she didn't want to get off. Frank had to go on stage and get her after her sixth, seventh, or eighth round of "Jingle Bells." It was exhilarating; she had gotten her way. The audience clapped and laughed as her daddy carried her off into the wings.

Although embarrassed, Frank must have been amused while carrying off his baby who told him: "I want to sing some more!" It was the last time she was left out of anything.

Never mind how she had gotten up there. It was clear to Ethel and

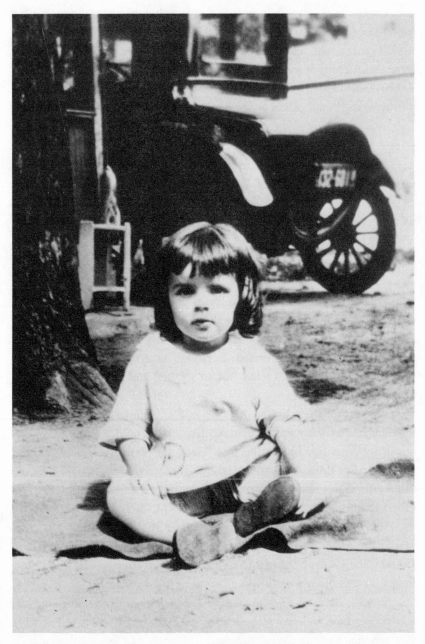

Frances at two in yard of home in Grand Rapids, Minnesota. *Courtesy of Bill Chapman*

Frank that she belonged; besides, a trio wasn't a bad idea. "A few days later I became the third member of the singing and dancing Gumm sisters," Frances said. Her recollection later was correct. The only thing about her debut that Christmas 1924 was documented in the *Grand Rapids Independent* which recorded the first billing and advertisement for the young vaudevillian as she began her career:

AT THE NEW GRAND
Thursday and Friday
SPECIAL FOR CHRISTMAS, "Through the Back Door" with MARY PICK-FORD, America's sweetheart, in the leading role. One of the nicest pictures Miss Pickford has appeared in. You will enjoy every bit of it. A two-reel comedy "Motor Mad" will also be shown. Added attraction for Friday evening: the three Gumm girls will entertain in songs and dances featuring Baby Frances, two years old, Virginia seven and Mary Jane nine. The little girls will appear between the shows at 9 o'clock.[7]

Frances's impetuous debut followed by her formal premiere engagement were incidents, not great events, in the lives of the Gumms in the early 1920s; her joining the family act merely endeared her more to everyone. To Frances it seemed as though everyone in the world had come down to the New Grand just to see her, and she wanted to do it again.

Aside from their life at the theater, the Gumms were remembered for their more commonplace qualities. Passersby could see the girls playing in the sand box or chasing their large dog about the house. During thunderstorms Ethel would become so frightened that she would take the three girls down to the cellar, one of the few hysterical quirks they recalled about her. On Sundays they attended church and listened to Frank sing the lead solos. The girls never joined the choir, although Ethel played the organ there. Frances attended Sunday school with Janie and Jimmie. She always appeared to be a "darling" to churchgoers—a chubby little girl who often wore a white fur coat.

Frank took a job with the *Grand Rapids Independent*. With his college background and general articulateness, he was well qualified to serve as a reporter in town. With the theater, church, family, and newspaper, he was busy. He was also involved in civic events as president of the

Earliest picture of the Gumm trio in Grand Rapids, Minnesota, 1924–1925.
Courtesy of Bill Chapman

Pokegama Club. He ran the Wednesday night dances at the Pavillion where he and Ethel occasionally provided the music. And he was sought after as one of the town's best dancers. On one occasion he was "induced" to sing a song which a Mr. Peterson had written about Grand Rapids: "Grand Rapids, Grand Rapids, where piney breezes blow, / We love your hills and ridges, your river and your bridges / . . . we're with you for Grand Rapids' sake." And so on—life was simple and pleasurable.

Ethel's family came frequently. Her brother John, who had a good tenor voice, sometimes sang solo at the New Grand, and he and Frank performed duets. Grandma Milne often came to visit, sometimes before she and Norma went west where Eva accompanied her younger daughter who was pursuing a career in the theater. Norma was a singer and dancer, and for many years Eva traveled around the country with her. On the Milne side of the family there was a tendency toward being overweight, and Norma had a robust figure. One contemporary said that Norma performed as a part of a group called the "beef trust," that they were "all fat and had no talent." Norma later appeared in a chorus line in Los Angeles.

Marcus Rabwin, who had finished medical school, now visited the family often and saw the musical work of the three Gumm sisters after dinner at the house. Around this time Frank lost a lot of weight. Marcus referred him to the Mayo Clinic where a goiter was removed. The goiter must have accounted partly for his nervousness, for he now became much calmer. That year, 1925, they said good-bye to Marcus who was to intern at the Los Angeles County Hospital.

At the theater Frank showed such memorable hits as *Tiger Rose,* extolling the virtues of the film and its immortal star in an ad:

AT THE NEW GRAND

LENORE ULRICH, the original "Bird of Paradise" in "Tiger Rose" her new production that is startling, pretentious and magnificent from every viewpoint. One of the outstanding specials of the year that is just now being run in the big city houses.

Meanwhile the efforts of the Gumm family singers were more modest. With Frances part of the act, the entire family became a staple of

Saturday and Sunday night showings. Although Janie and Jimmie had gotten some newspaper notices in Grand Rapids, there were no reviews of Frances's early performances, good or bad. But already her singing elicited a personal reaction. A native of Grand Rapids recalls her artistry even at the age of three or four; she was "quite an actress," able to remember words to songs well and who performed with absolutely "no stage shyness." According to the music teacher at the Central School, Frances "could carry a tune as well or better than an adult" by the time she was four. "Cute as a bug's ear," she loved the stage and being in front of audiences and was something of a show-off on stage but always in a cute sense. The die was cast, however, for what would become a lifelong dissenting view of her musical abilities. A friend who saw her frequently on the stage at the New Grand Theater said that "everybody got a big bang out of her, but she couldn't sing worth a hoot."

"My father gave me my first singing lessons," Judy said. "They started about the same time I learned to talk. When I began playing vaudeville engagements with my sisters, he helped coach us. He told me to put all my enthusiasm into a song. Doing that would make the audience like me, he said, even if they didn't like the song." Her brassy, uninhibited enthusiasm, which would repel many later, was influenced by Frank's extroverted song-leading style. In addition to this, there was what has often been described as the naturalness and beguiling innocence of her voice. Henry Pleasants sums up his impression 50 years after her birth: "She had the most utterly natural vocal production of any singer I have ever heard . . . it was an open-throated, almost birdlike vocal production, clear, pure, resonant, innocent . . . a viola-like voice . . . the warmth, the tenderness, the radiance, the exuberance."[8]

What was not hereditary can be traced to Frank. Her later plaintive and heartrending version of "Danny Boy" can be related only to her father's bedtime lullaby of it when she was a baby in Grand Rapids. Indeed, the wistfulness and richness of Judy Garland's voice is probably best described with the appellation of her parents' vaudeville act—"the sweet Southern" sound.

This, then, was the agreeable atmosphere that contributed to Frances's concept of herself. Attention and excitement swirled around her.

Frances at about two and a half years in this original family photo with the early nickname "Fanny" in corner, Grand Rapids, Minnesota. *Courtesy of the University of the South*

How can one describe the stimuli that make a child feel special, other than to say that the total aura meant two things to Frances: she was totally accepted, and she sensed that it was all for her. How tragic that the adult Judy Garland lost the trust and security that were the foundation of her personality.

In Grand Rapids there was nothing but confidence in her makeup. It is evident as she eyes the camera, dressed in a velvet gown and white bonnet at age two or in a low-cut, white dress with the petticoat showing at age three. She had nothing to fear from anything or anyone. There is mischief in her impish smile, with its come-hither look.

In 1925 Mary Jane starred in *Cinderella,* assisted by Virginia in the part of a page. Frances could not be in the play since it was a school play and she wasn't old enough. But at the New Grand, Frances made her first planned solo debut:

This Week's Picture
ATTRACTIONS
Sunday and Monday
WANDERING OF THE WASTELAND, a Paramount special done in natural colors throughout. An all-star cast . . . BABY FRANCES, the two-year-old daughter of Mr. and Mrs. Frank Gumm, will entertain between shows and there will be a vocal solo by Frank Gumm. The little girl will appear only Sunday evening.

There was nothing backward about Frank's promotion of his girls. Even during other shows he managed to squeeze them in, as can be seen in this advertisement from the *Independent* just before Frances's third birthday:

TONIGHT
EXTRA ADDED ATTRACTION. MISSES DORIS SMALL AND PEARL TROMBLEY OF NASHWAUK IN "THE VALENTINO TANGO" and other novelty dances and song specialties. These clever girls present a neat up-to-the-minute VAUDEVILLE attraction which will surely be a big hit. Between their changes MISSES MARY JANE, VIRGINIA and FRANCES ETHEL GUMM will entertain with a novelty song and dance skit.

Between 1924 and 1926 they began to make appearances in neighboring cities. On weekends they would travel to Cohasset, Hibbing, or

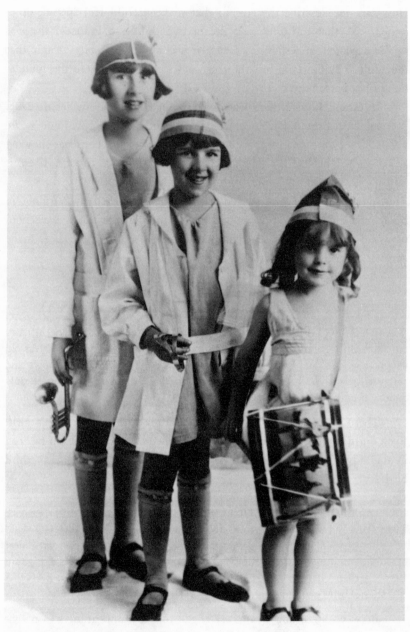

Mary Jane, Virginia, and Frances with drum in Grand Rapids, Minnesota.
Courtesy of Bill Chapman

other nearby towns. Some suspected that Ethel pushed the girls in organizing these little tours, but the girls obviously wanted to perform. It gave Ethel a chance to use her talent for writing songs and arranging dance numbers, as well as to get other than just local reaction. In addition to her pride and industry, there were business motives. Frank was a promoter who wanted to attract customers from the outlying regions. Given a momentum by necessity and their fascination with the theatrical life, this pattern that he and Ethel established later became irresistible. There was every indication of the Irish "laughter and fun" that Frances spoke of later, as the Gumms could be seen on summer evenings closing up the New Grand and walking up Pokegama Avenue toward Fourth Street and their house under the spruce trees, the three girls playing with one another as their parents watched from behind.

This picture of family happiness was soon to be disrupted. It was already threatened by what was surfacing in Frank again. He thought that family life would resolve it, but in his late thirties, after 10 years of marriage, he was unable to transcend a basic part of his nature. By late 1925 talk of his homosexual activities had filtered into some limited, but credible, conversations in Grand Rapids. Accounts of his advances toward some young men, as well as other behavior with some of his theater employees were recounted.

In the context of small-town America in the 1920s and in light of Frank's position as a married man and father, the dilemma was staggering. The gossip was greeted with disbelief at first, then with caution and restraint. After all, Frank was a highly regarded leader of the community and a family man. He and his wife mingled with the best in town, and Mr. Gumm had contributed much as a prominent churchman, town booster, and theater manager. His talents as a performer and his personal charm and friendliness made it hard for townspeople to suspect, much less censure, him; to them it was unbelievable that Frank Gumm would be doing such things.

Naturally the small town of Grand Rapids could not, in 1925, understand or condone such behavior. Most of the men were employed by a large paper mill. Most of their pursuits were built around hard work, family, and church. They had welcomed the entertainment offered to

Baby Frances, two and a half to three years of age, in Grand Rapids, Minnesota. *Courtesy of Bill Chapman*

them by the Gumms, perhaps forgetting that they had learned that show folks had often been considered loose in their morals. Recalling her youth in her last years, Judy said that her family was shunned by respectable people because "vaudeville people were always considered sort of wicked. . . ." His connection with the theater was a good cover for Frank and may have gained him a little more toleration, but it wasn't enough to quiet the talk. The persistence of it, which they at first discounted, caused some of them to question Frank's fitness to greet their families at the theater.

Fifty years later, close friends reminiscing about the Gumms said "it was too bad about Frank and his problem." His habits had destroyed his family's life in Grand Rapids, Minnesota. Another man, in recalling Frank, referred to his blatant behavior in Grand Rapids and remembered his homosexuality.

Ethel's innocence had slowly faded. Now her first instinct was to try to minimize the humiliation to the family. There is no calculating the effect of such a revelation on this 30-year-old mother who looked into what was now the abyss of her love for her husband of a dozen years. During the past five years she had been forced to face what to her were unthinkable horrors—perversity, abortion, and now banishment. So she turned to her children, not with a vengeance, but with a zeal to protect them.

By the spring of 1926 Frank and Ethel had decided that they must leave Grand Rapids. They didn't share their decision with anyone, keeping it to themselves until more definite plans were made. Early that summer they would take a pleasure trip west, during which they would look for a place to settle. Contrary to later belief, that Ethel was responsible for uprooting the family, it was Frank who was responsible. There were no business reasons for leaving; the theater was thriving. Nor was Ethel interested in Hollywood and its need for child stars, as was later believed. In 1926 she was not driven to make stars out of her children. She wanted to remain in Grand Rapids and raise her family.

These years were "tinsel and gold" for Judy Garland. Soft and warm recollections of the big white house under the pine trees and the fun and laughter ringing through it; the secure nights bundled up with her sisters

in the long Minnesota winters; her father singing ballads to her at bedtime; the glittering New Grand Theater where she had her first tantalizing
encounters with the funny assortment of faces propped up in their chairs
waiting to see what she would do.

Suddenly, for no apparent reason, a blissful way of life ended. Of
course, Frances is too young to inquire; for her there was only the promise of better things ahead. Only later would she realize that Grand Rapids
had been her first loss. With the family's departure, broken dreams are
being institutionalized for her and her family. Their success had become
a failure.

Judy would relentlessly wonder why they left Minnesota and what
her life would have been like if she had stayed there and grown up like
anyone else. She didn't understand their strange farewell. In later years,
when she blamed her mother for most of her problems, she would especially rail at Ethel for abandoning their wonderful Grand Rapids life:
"Mother's ambition to make movie stars of us really took possession of
her. She uprooted the whole bunch of us. . . . Daddy sold the theater and
our lovely white frame house, and we headed for California, where Jackie
Coogan and the Our Gang comedies had inspired Mother."[9]

Ethel died before telling Judy the truth, and Judy went to her grave
without understanding that it wasn't entirely her mother's fault. Frank
was never able to tell her that he was responsible for their departure
from Grand Rapids, Minnesota.

It was not Ethel's obsession with movies or making stars out of her
children, nor was it Frank's health, as one story goes. It was a stress that
now became a part of the whole family's life and impelled them to end
their serene existence in favor of a mercurial, gypsy one of sudden departures and unhappy endings. They left simply because of Frank's homosexuality which, though it wasn't a subject of general gossip, was sufficient for the Gumms to decide to move away when word got around
town about Frank's sad frailty.

Frank began to tell a few close friends that he believed they could
do better elsewhere. First they would take a vacation out west. They
mentioned to their close friends that in the back of their minds was the
possibility of settling there. Grandma Milne and Norma had been to

California where Norma had performed and had sent back favorable reports. So had Marcus Rabwin. Now they would see for themselves.

Their resolve to leave Grand Rapids did not change the outward appearance of their daily lives, though; life at the New Grand and 403 Second Avenue continued as usual. Family appearances at the theater varied. Ethel played the piano, Frank sang between shows, or the trio tried out a new song or performed out of town. Ethel and Frank tried to get extra exposure for their act and got a booking in Virginia, Minnesota, at the Garrick Theater. They wanted to try out their act away from Grand Rapids and their diversionary three cute kids, in order to polish it for what was to be a working vacation. It had been a while since they appeared before an unfamiliar audience. By early June the act had to be in shape, as they announced their plans in the *Grand Rapids Herald Review:* "Mr. and Mrs. Frank A. Gumm will spend the month of June touring through the West and playing at theaters to help defray their expenses. They will go from here on the Great Northern to Seattle, Washington . . . to Los Angeles. . . . On their return trip they will go through Denver, Omaha and back home."

Mary Jane, Jimmie, and Frances had been lobbying to be included. They had a one-track mind about it, and soon their entreaties were successful. The night before they were to leave, Frank and Ethel were thinking about how they had never been away from the kids before. This sentiment, combined with the pleadings of the girls, led to their flipping a coin to decide the matter. The girls won. As Frances later said, they all "piled into the old touring car and spent three months on the road, playing one-night stands in just about every city between Grand Rapids and Los Angeles."

5

VAGABONDS ADRIFT

*I cried and applauded all the way
to California.*

"Those are the days I'll never forget."[1] Judy never forgot the warmth
and closeness, the adventure and fun, of traveling with her family, a
troupe of wandering minstrels working their way across country in the
summer of 1926. The four-year-old was touched by her family's together-
ness, a family adrift in the world yet safe and secure because of their love
and devotion to one another and because of their common endeavor.
Frances cried and applauded for them as they crossed the American West
in the old touring car.

They took the northernmost route, along Highway 2 across Minnesota, North Dakota, Montana, Idaho, and Washington. They performed
along the way and rewarded themselves with a vacation at Glacier National Park. Although the engagements were necessary to pay for the
trip and the anticipated expenses of the move from Grand Rapids, it
wasn't real work. An agent-friend of theirs arranged some bookings for
Jack and Virginia Lee who now had an extra bonus for their bookers.
But for the most part Frank had to make arrangements as they entered
each town. He carried 11-by-14 photos of them in performance, which he
presented to local theater owners. The photos, along with the girls, were
hard to resist, and local vaudeville drew some extra customers into the

theaters. They played the Orpheums, Arcades, Strands, and Lyrics across the western United States. Some towns such as Grand Forks, North Dakota, or Havre, Montana, had three or four choices, but in the small villages most of the moviehouses didn't advertise in the newspaper, relying merely on their marquees or billboards. Because variety performers were in demand, they played almost every town on the route. It is likely that Frances performed at the "Palace," the 100-seat one in Saco, Montana, a town of 300.

They sang, danced, and visited friends in Kalispel, Montana, and Seattle, Washington, took in the new countryside, and laughed and sang reprises of "California, Here I Come"—Frank behind the wheel, joining in with the girls. They were on the road for more than six weeks before reaching Washington on the West Coast. The trip was unabashed fun, a frolic. Performances that didn't go well were as memorable as the successful ones. The occasional mishap became part of Frances's vaudeville tradition which would in later life demonstrate her perennial quest for spontaneity.

On this tour Frances was featured in the trio's act in an Egyptian costume with balloon pants, ankle bracelets, and spangles, "while Janie and Jimmie wore Spanish costumes," toreador pants, and what Frances called "funny hats" with little balls hanging from the brims. They did the latest hit of 1926, "In a Little Spanish Town." It went smoothly until Shelby, Montana, at the Liberty Theater. The two older girls were singing the chorus while Frank dressed Frances in the wings. Ethel was at the piano. It was to be a quick costume change, but he couldn't get her into the balloon legs. He started all over again, yelling to the girls to sing another chorus. They kept singing. They'd sneak a look, seeing that he was having an awful time, and Baby Frances was standing there naked, while Frank, with a flashlight in the dimly lit wing, was trying to untangle the baubles, spangles, and beads. He kept telling the girls to sing another chorus, and Ethel kept playing out the chorus until the girls finally gave up after eight rounds. The audience never got to see Baby Gumm's acrobatic Egyptian bellyroll. The girls squealed and laughed over this for the rest of the trip and for years to come. Ethel eventually got the costume untangled on the way to Kalispel.

The family act was a simple one but subject to human error. A typical show started with Frank doing one or two songs and a dance. He often sang "I Will Come Back," which Judy said was one of his own composition. Then Ethel followed with one or two songs while Frank played the piano for her. The performance was capped off with the singing and dancing Gumm sisters, featuring "Baby Frances" whose impish vitality entranced audiences.

When there were no costume-change snags, family loyalty extended to the part of the family not on stage; they sat in the audience and applauded the others. When Frank finished his number, he would introduce Ethel who came up from the piano, a ritual that always moved the impressionable Frances. Frank would introduce Ethel as "a tiny, pretty lady with pretty, tiny hands," which, Judy said, "brought a catch to my throat and tears to my eyes."[2] Also, the song Ethel sang, "I've Been Saving for a Rainy Day," made Frances cry. Later the poignant memory of this song would elicit the contradictory description of her mother as "terribly untalented but very touching."[3]

Leaving the state of Washington, they went down the coast toward California, reaching Los Angeles in late July and seeing the splendors of southern California, including Hollywood, for the first time.

Los Angeles in 1926 (there were no freeways, smog, tall buildings, Griffith Observatory, or Union Station) was as pristine and sunny as it was claimed to be—an expanse of small communities connected by long avenues, blue skies, palm trees, and green-ochre foothills. For about a month they stayed in Hollywood in a hotel near Sunset Boulevard and Van Ness and saw enough to know they wanted to come back.

They renewed their friendship with Marcus Rabwin, who showed them around Los Angeles. He and Frank looked around for a theater opportunity, but none was available. They returned to Grand Rapids, limiting the performances in order to get back and make plans for returning to California.

Back in Grand Rapids, Frank told his partner of their plans. Without delay they sold the theater, Bentz deciding to quit the business too. There were rounds of farewells for the family as they said good-bye to their friends and neighbors. The *Independent* announced: NEW GRAND

Virginia, Frances, and Mary Jane on the porch of their first Los Angeles home on Glen Manor Street, 1926. *Courtesy of Mr. and Mrs. Allen Doran*

SOLD THIS WEEK—FRANK GUMM TO LEAVE SOON FOR THE WEST. The decision and preparations made, their life in Minnesota came to an end.

Some have wondered what their life would have been like if circumstances had been different and things had taken another course. Judy continually speculated about that, just as she wondered how people would react to her death someday. Both concerns are understandable in such a perplexing life. After her death it was said that she would have been pleased by the quantity and intensity of the news coverage of it. She did remark once: "But if we'd stayed in Minnesota, my life might have been very much happier."

All day long and deep into a humid night they stood, waiting as long as four hours for a few seconds glimpse at the tiny and terribly fragile figure in the white steel coffin. Judy Garland was at her death a sad ruin, all her incandescent talent ravaged by too many drinks and too many pills and too many adoring audiences. Yet something in her drew them still, 21,000 strong, to the little uptown Manhattan chapel where Judy met her public for the last time. And it was difficult to say whether the thing they saw and mourned in her, and in themselves, was that shining-eyed rainbow girl of so many years ago—or the bruised and vulnerable woman of 47 who had struggled to the other side of the rainbow and found nothing there. . . .[4]

Newsweek, July 7, 1969

Judy Garland, who paid a tragic price for the life of the show business superstar, died in London Sunday. She was 47. It was a quiet end to a stormy career. . . . She had suffered from hepatitis, exhaustion, kidney ailments, nervous breakdowns, near-fatal drug reactions, overweight, underweight, and injuries suffered in falls. Her previous four marriages had ended in divorce and her life was a chaos of unhappy love affairs. Her career was a series of soaring highs and plummeting lows. In between she was sued when she backed out of performances, fired for contractual failures, and booed off the stage when she couldn't remember the lines to her songs. . . . But, throughout her crisis-ridden career, she refused to quit fighting. . . . When her career—and, usually, her personal life—hit rock bottom, she would stage a spectacular comeback and again hit the bigtime . . . was under psychiatric treatment by the time she was 18. By the time she was 23 she had had three nervous breakdowns. When she was 28 she slashed her throat in a suicide try. . . .[5]

Dial Torgersen, in *Los Angeles Times,* June 23, 1969

The obituaries of Judy Garland cast a cold light upon the golden era of M-G-M mythologizing. The prematurely professional children of hard-bitten vaudevillians, doped like race horses for their twelve-hour days in front of the grinding cameras, were fed into the gigantic escapism machine geared to the pious simplicities of a rural, puritan, mostly imaginary past. Small wonder that these children, grown older, sought in drink, pills, and frequent marriage the real self they had been cheated out of. The food of millions, they were themselves fearfully hungry. Dream figures, walking and singing through the dreams of anonymous multitudes, they woke to private lives cursed by something like sleeplessness. That Judy Garland contained a real person, no one doubted, perhaps, but herself; she was there to the end, twitching the microphone cord, vividly beset by the awkwardnesses of performance that most performers hypocritically suppress, forgetting lyrics to remind us she was human and not a rerun, disarmingly *there* in the very totality of her confusion, her croaking voice the nearest thing we have had to Piaf. . . .[6]

New Yorker, July 5, 1969

The Scarecrow came to her funeral; so did Andy Hardy. So, in spirit, did the countless legions of Judy Garland's fans, 21,000 of whom appeared in person and jammed the streets of Manhattan's Upper East Side last week to file past the bier where her body, dressed in the ankle-length gown she had worn at her fifth wedding, lay in state. . . . Judy Garland never really had a backyard to call her own. Born Frances Gumm . . . [she] was a vaudeville trouper at the age of five. . . . The nearest thing to a home that Judy had was the MGM lot in Hollywood. . . . To her studio, Judy was not a child but a box-office property with rare natural gifts. Rarest of all was the instinctive, trembling vocal style that somehow managed to combine womanly pathos and childish innocence. . . . "She was so sweet," recalls Jack Haley, who played the Tin Man. "I would say, 'Well, Judy, if you ever become a star, please stay as sweet as you are,' and she would say, 'I don't know what could change me, Jack. Why would anything change?' ". . . . At 21 she was visiting a psychiatrist regularly and living on pills: pills to put her to sleep, pills to wake her up, pills to help keep her weight down. Eleven years, two husbands, and 20 movies after making *Oz,* she had established herself as the best of a bevy of girlish filmland warblers. . . . But she could no longer handle the pressure of stardom. She began showing up for work late or sick, then did not show up at all. She was suspended once, twice, and finally, in 1950 fired for good. . . . Judy had too much talent and too much voice to stay down for long. . . . There were also memorable personal appearances . . . Manhattan's Palace . . . London Palladium. . . . Garland was never a pioneer, just a music-hall balladeer who liked to sing love songs. . . . She belted them out in a high throb-

bing, no-holds-barred soprano that sounded as if it came from a near-to-
bursting heart. . . .[7]

Time, July 4, 1969

She sang and she sang and she sang. The Yellow Brick Road turned into
a treacherous path of mean curves and cruel bumps. But little Dorothy was
one tough dame; she fought hard. Now Judy Garland has gone somewhere
over the rainbow for the last time. It seems somehow impossible that she
won't make another of those dramatic comebacks; that people won't cheer
her, mesmerized by her talent and surprised that this vulnerable lady made it
through still another tumultuous time. She didn't really entertain. She went
out there looking to be loved and she used her voice and fluttering hands to
clasp people by the thousands to her wanting heart. She returned the affection by putting on one helluva show. . . . The word to remember is legend;
bigger than life, twice as talented and much more vulnerable. She wasn't indestructible after all. Those were real tears in her voice. . . .[8]

Wayne Warga in Los Angeles Times, June 1969

The night of her death, June 22, 1969, on the CBS Sunday News, Harry
Reasoner ended his broadcast with these comments:

Reasoner: The first thought of many people when they heard that Judy
Garland had died before her time was that it must have been some kind of
tragedy; she had so many tragedies. Partly, maybe, because no adult life could
have satisfied either the girl who sang "Over the Rainbow" or the people who
heard her sing it. The thing about Judy was that after that people forgave her
a lot and always hoped for her and liked her. One who liked her was Ray
Bolger, who was the scarecrow in The Wizard of Oz. Bruce Morton talked to
Bolger in New York today.

Bolger: I walked on that set the first day when we were making The
Wizard of Oz, and I looked over and I—I said—I saw the most beautiful
child . . . and I said "That's Dorothy!" and I remember what a beautiful person she was inside, what respect that she had for her fellow performers. She
didn't try to upstage you, as they say, or steal a scene. She worked with you.
Making that picture of a year—took a year to make it—she had all those
qualities. She had a brain, she had a heart, she had courage, she had love for
her home. But Judy never had a home. Not the Judy Garland that toured,
that played the Metropolitan Opera House, the Palladium in London, the
Palace in New York, in nightclubs, theaters—one-man, or one-woman, concerts wherever she went—this Judy Garland never had a home, and I think
this is the saddest, saddest part of her life. I think that's why she had always

wanted that one thing that she never really got. She reached for it. She married enough times to try for it. But she couldn't. I don't think she could ever live in a home because her duty was, in her own mind, to her public, her audience.

Reasoner: She certainly did marry enough, most recently in London three months ago to Mickey Deans. In five marriages she had three children —one of them Liza Minnelli, now a substantial singer and actress on her own.

Toward the end Judy looked like this, awfully old for Dorothy, old maybe even for 47.

Not everybody liked Judy Garland. There were people of her generation who did not think she was the world's greatest singer, who found her adulthood embarrassing, who didn't like the kind of silly people who were her coterie in later years. But if you were born in 1923 or some old year like that, Judy Garland was once the picture of innocence for you, and now innocence is dead, one year older than you are.[9]

Judy always remembered their last night in Minnesota. Frank and Ethel returned from Birmingham, Alabama, where they had said good-bye to Frank's brothers, Will and Bob. They drove to Duluth for a farewell party with Ethel's relatives. There at Uncle John's the three girls frolicked with their 14 cousins and a menagerie of cats and dogs. In the shady twilight in the backyard there was a little singing, mostly talking about the West with its sun and oranges, cowboys and movie stars, desert and palm trees. Their cousins were envious. Ethel's sisters and brothers were confident about their future in California, although they themselves were secure in their established, protected lives, in contrast to the glamorous but unknown. As they embraced and the relatives gathered around the departing car, it was those left behind who appeared the saddest. Although the Gumms found it hard to say good-bye, they were cheerful and bouncy as they left.

The family didn't perform along the way this time, since Frank was eager for them to get to California and establish themselves before their savings were exhausted. They spent about two weeks at a hotel in Hollywood until they found a small house to rent at 3154 Glen Manor in the Atwater district of Los Angeles. It was nearly Thanksgiving and they would live there just six months. "We moved into a green

The five Gumms pose in front of their California home upon their arrival in Los Angeles, 1926. *Courtesy of the University of the South*

stucco bungalow for about six months while my father went shopping to buy a new theater," Judy remembered 40 years later.[10]

It was difficult for Frank to find a theater. This was one time when some extra income would be welcome. Ethel began to get the act in shape, but in Hollywood there were already plenty of precocious child entertainers. She enrolled Jimmie, Janie, and Frances in the Ethel Meglin Dance Studio. The studio was a training school, as well as booking agency for the movies and stage.

In 1926 it was still an asset to have a connection with vaudeville, since the decline in real vaudeville began that year, not coincidentally with the premiere of the first talking motion picture—*Don Juan* with John Barrymore—a process that would culminate in all-talking, all-singing movies by 1929. By chance, the Gumms arrived in Los Angeles during the year of the greatest changes in vaudeville and motion pictures. Vaudeville appeared to be prospering in downtown Los Angeles, especially at the flagship of vaudeville theaters, the Orpheum. Up and down Broadway and Hill streets, vaudeville was featured as an adjunct to movies such as *Beau Geste* and *Ben Hur*.

As the Gumms got their bearings they could see the contrasts in Los Angeles in 1926. They saw the Angelus Temple in Echo Park and the real-life drama and theatrical evangelism of Aimee Semple McPherson. In Hollywood they saw the public extravagances and eccentric hullabaloo of its inhabitants. In the same vein, typical of the exploitation of this era, was the death of Rudolph Valentino that year and the histrionic funeral at Campbell's Mortuary in New York where hysterical crowds viewed the body.

The three girls made local appearances on their own. It was around this time that they performed at the Biltmore Hotel and for their efforts earned 50 cents each.

Ethel and the girls toured the downtown and Hollywood area, more as sightseers than performers, while Frank looked for a theater. But by Christmas there were still no prospects. The girls appeared in their first Meglin production as three of the "100 Clever Children in the Twinkletoe KIDDIE REVUE" at Loew's State on Broadway where the Duncan Sisters were headlining with their "Topsy and Eva" act.

By March 1927 Frank was forced to look in outlying areas. He found a theater in a small town outside Los Angeles in the Antelope Valley. It looked like it would have to be that one, and Frank expounded on the virtues of the area to the family and the fact that the theater was the only one in the area. "Mother was disappointed when we moved up to the desolation and heat of the desert."[11] Ethel knew they needed to settle down before the savings ran out, but she could not conceal her anxiety at having to move to another small community. They had planned to live in Los Angeles but were now going to move to Lancaster.

6

A BARRIER FROM THE WORLD

*So we settled in Lancaster and grew
up watching movies.*

By the summer of 1927 they had settled in the small California desert town of Lancaster. Frank took over the operation of the only theater in town, and the family gradually slipped into the tempo of life in their new home. They "grew up watching movies."[1] This was no exaggeration, at least when they first arrived. School was out, and the long, hot Mojave summer was beginning. In a town lacking shade or relief from the heat, Frank's theater afforded a built-in feature for the residents. It was, as advertised, "the Coolest Spot in the Valley."

The Antelope Valley, once the home of roaming antelopes and now more noted for its rabbits, was at its most beautiful when the wildflowers covered the rolling hills. The spectacle brought people from all over southern California. The Gumms found themselves driving through the sparsely settled high desert, not as barren as the girls had imagined, but dotted with Joshua trees and expanses of desert flowers. The beauty of the area was heightened by the surrounding mountains.

The provincial half of Frank had found a home in keeping with his rural, Southern life. Lancaster was about 80 miles northeast of Los Angeles, separated from the city by the San Gabriel Mountains, bordered on the northwest by the more imposing Tehachapi Mountains and on the east by the Mojave Desert. It was a good three-hour drive from downtown Los Angeles.

Although they had not wanted to move again, they had little choice. In over six months this had been the only business opportunity he had found.

To children any change has an air of excitement to it. The only thing that counted was that they were all together and their father had finally found a theater. There had always been a theater, and the last year had seemed strange without one.

In Lancaster they were greeted by Mr. Claman, the manager and an ex-vaudevillian. Claman had become dissatisfied with running a moviehouse and was anxious get rid of his lease. While their parents talked to Mr. Claman, the girls explored the theater, running up and down the aisles and onto the stage. They all liked it, but on Frances especially, the rich glow of the bronze-colored interior made a deep impression.

After Frank had finished his business with Claman they drove the two blocks to Cedar Street to look at the two-story wood-frame house they had rented. The house was more like their Grand Rapids home than the bungalow in Los Angeles. The school was half a block away, the theater a few minutes' walk. Everything in Lancaster was within walking distance; in a few months the Gumm girls would know every square foot of it.

They lived in the second house from the corner of Newgrove and Cedar streets in the heart of town. Lancaster was the hub of the valley, a typical western desert town of about 1,000 population, including out-lying farms and ranches—a small American town whose center covered several blocks. The business district centered around the train depot. The theater stood prominently on Antelope Avenue, later called Sierra Highway, since it was the main road through town.

The arrival of a new family was news, especially since the head of the family would be the new theater manager. In Lancaster the theater was no mere makeshift house or old nickelodeon in need of remodeling. The Lancaster Theater had opened only the previous Christmas with

Cedar Street as it was in the 1920s with a glimpse of the Grammar School, Lancaster, Calif. The Gumm home was located just behind the school. *Courtesy of John Reber*

A Cheerful Fraud, starring Reginald Denny, and had become an object of both ridicule and pride. The theater was dubbed "Carter's Folly" by the townspeople because they thought the ambitious enterprise of the owner, Whit Carter, was doomed to fail. After all, how many towns in that day, with a population of only a thousand, could boast a modern, custom-built theater with a seating capacity of 500?

There was a lively curiosity about the family. The word had spread that not only was Mr. Gumm a showman, but he and his wife were musicians and singers as well, in addition to their three young daughters who formed a singing and dancing trio. This abundance of musical ability in one family inevitably was an object of interest and skepticism. The arrival of a family of minstrels seemed strange, strange, too, because awaiting them was a new theater that had been designed with vaudeville in mind, but with the exception of some local talent shows had featured only movies.

The still handsome and dapper Frank Gumm now found himself managing a family and theater in California on the edge of the Mojave Desert. From the outset Frank made changes. He installed a new cooling system. He featured gift nights, or "china nights," and introduced discount theater ticket books and other innovations designed to attract moviegoers. Regular theater advertisements to appear in the local newspaper, the *Ledger-Gazette,* describing the latest movies and invariably proclaiming either "Added Attraction on Stage" or "Vaudeville Between Shows," which, for Lancaster, came to mean the Gumm sisters or a revival of Jack and Virginia Lee.

In 1927 the hedonism of the Roaring Twenties and its "flaming youth" was not evident in Lancaster. Throughout the United States prohibition and bootlegging continued side by side. Charles Lindberg won a $25,000 prize for his nonstop flight across the Atlantic and immediately became a legend. Babe Ruth hit 60 home runs that year. Entertainment and communications captured people's attention. CBS inaugurated its national broadcasting system, following NBC's example of the previous year. Live opera was broadcast for the first time, and television was demonstrated by the Radio Corporation of America. The Academy of Motion

Picture Arts and Sciences was founded and gave its first Oscar to Emil Jannings, Janet Graynor, and the film *Wings*. Musicals triumphed on Broadway but not in films, which had just introduced its earliest example of the "talkie." Comedy and drama dominated the silver screen.

Popular songs of the day reached Lancaster through sheet music and radio. "Bye Bye Blackbird" and "My Blue Heaven" were the hit songs when the Gumms entered town. The girls were already music crazy. They quickly memorized the lyrics to new hits and knew scores of songs. Frances learned them, too, following the example of her sisters.

The Gumms were eager to ingratiate themselves; acceptance was important. For family and business reasons, Frank and Ethel wanted to make a good impression. Lancaster was as clannish as any other American small town, and Frank was chiefly concerned about winning acceptance for his girls. Aware that show people were sometimes regarded with suspicion, Frank did not want any aspersions cast on his girls and always tried to convey a sense of privilege to them, insisting that others do the same. He bolstered their confidence and sense of security without indulging them. Like most fathers who love their daughters, he tended to spoil them but not unreasonably. But beyond Frank wanting this permanence for the children, he wanted to regain the lost stability that he had cast away in Grand Rapids.

As it turned out, they had no more to fear from the town than the town had from them. Frank remedied what skepticism there was with a large advertisement in the local paper:

Extra Special
LANCASTER THEATER
Sunday and Monday May 22–23
Mr. and Mrs. Frank Gumm and Daughters will present a cycle of songs and dances between shows each evening at 9 o'clock and also at the Sunday Matinee. Having purchased the theater, I am taking this method of introducing the family to the good people of Lancaster and Antelope Valley. It is my intention to continue presenting the high class picture program as given by Mr. Claman and I cordially ask the support of the public in keeping the entertainment up to the highest possible standard. Your co-operation will be appreciated.

Respectfully, FRANK A. GUMM[2]

The weekend of the twentieth was spent in preparation. Ethel selected and made the costumes, and the songs were rehearsed. This show was important, and they took it seriously. In the coming years such shows would be a routine part of Lancaster life. The Gumms would long be remembered performing on the stage of the Valley Theater, the name with which Frank would rechristen the theater in late 1927 and by which it would always be remembered.

A substantial number of townspeople came to greet and look the Gumms over. The movie was at 7:15 that evening, and they came on at 9:00. Frank and Ethel were first, reviving a ballad and spiritual from their old act. Then they spotlighted the three girls who sang "Bye Bye Blackbird," "When the Red, Red Robin Comes Bob, Bob Bobbin' Along," and their standard from the cross-country trip, "In a Little Spanish Town," with Frances doing her dance in the second chorus. This time everything turned out all right.

About all that could be said for the Gumm sisters was that they were loud and brassy. Occasionally they managed to harmonize, making up in confidence what they lacked in technique. To the people of Lancaster this family was a novelty, and they greeted them with much applause. The following week the *Ledger-Gazette* announced on page 1: "GUMM FAMILY WINS LANCASTER APPROVAL. Mr. and Mrs. Gumm are accomplished musicians and gave two very pleasing songs while the little daughters completely won the hearts of the audience with their songs and dances."

They had broken the ice.

In later years residents recalling the Gumm sisters did not discriminate between the girls' individual talents; they didn't single out the youngest as the most talented but simply as the one "you noticed." Frances just had more energy and vitality. Many would say that if they were judged by their voices alone, Virginia had the best voice and was the prettiest. Others liked Janie's voice. But all agreed that somehow the "little one" always stood out, maybe because she was the smallest or the cutest. All agreed, too, that Frances was the loudest. The volume coming from her was most noticeable when the girls weren't harmonizing correctly, which in those days was frequent. There would be time enough

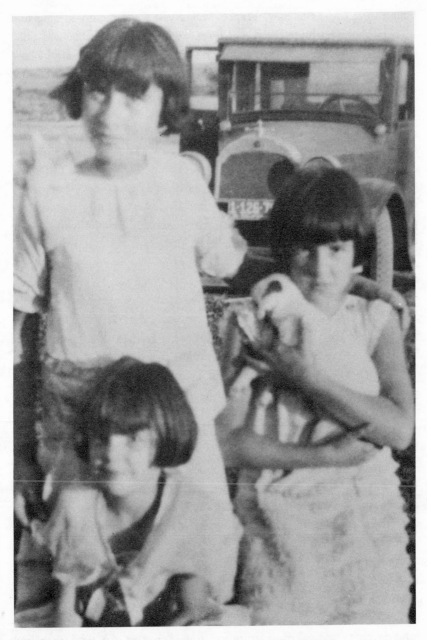

The three sisters on the lawn in Lancaster, California, about 1927–1928.
Courtesy of Bill Chapman

later to improve. For now, Frances was given the freedom to sing and shout without restraint. Trial and error would teach her what was good and bad, what people liked and didn't like. Her innate sensitivity and eagerness to please would eventually help solve the aesthetic problems, as would her mother's lessons and perseverance.

An important factor in the early stage training of the girls was the continued support of the local audiences. Many of them were country people, ranchers and farmers who liked music. Lancaster already supported many local musical endeavors. The residents were originally attracted to the naturalness of the family and were appreciative and understanding of the girls' inadequacies. They were simply grateful for the live, spontaneous entertainment. These uncritical people, who saw the Gumm children as normal, healthy kids, just like their own, made Janie, Jimmie, and Frances feel welcome on the stage. The intensely loyal audience was the beginning of a pattern Judy Garland would pick up again in the last two decades of her career—the reliance on loyal fans, on a cult. She knew that her listeners were on her side, that this loyalty to her was portable. In 1927, at her father's theater, Frances Ethel Gumm was beginning a long run as the center of attention.

There was something about this child that set her apart from her sisters and other girls of her age. A charisma was evident; an extraordinary personality was developing. Aside from her being the youngest member of the act and its being her father's theater, there seems to have been something about her that struck a responsive chord in others.

That "something" did not go unobserved by local residents. In the first weeks of summer many in town had not yet seen the Gumms perform. Some, especially the children, called the singing and dancing sisters the "three gumdrops." The girls began to appear regularly on Sundays and special occasions, and gradually people made it a point to go down to see them perform. Mrs. Abbott kept exhorting her neighbor Mrs. Story to go see the show, finally taking her down herself, telling her that she must see "how exquisite that little one is."

Years later Ethel would say she didn't know how they ever lasted so long in that "sun-baked little desert town," but at the time they had little difficulty in adjusting to their new home. It took awhile to make friends. The girls may have thought this was because they were show people. It may be that some did not befriend them because they *were* show people, but Frank and Ethel would soon remove these objections.

At the time of Frances's fifth birthday they didn't know enough of their neighbors to have a party for her, so they celebrated her birthday by themselves. On Virginia's birthday a month later, things were different. In a new party dress Jimmie opened her gifts as Janie and Frances led everyone in singing "Happy Birthday." At seven o'clock a dozen or more children could be seen marching, running, and shouting down Newgrove Street to the Lancaster Theater for a party. This was a ritual that would make a party at the Gumm home an envied occasion in future years. Ethel went to the theater in time to play the piano accompaniment for the still-silent movies as Frank calmed down the children. They settled down to watch Richard Dix in *Paradise for Two* and a western, *A One Man Game.*

To mark the first movie selected by Frank under his new management, *The Yankee Clipper* with William Boyd, Frank and Ethel appeared between shows, singing popular songs. On the Fourth of July, the family appeared together, singing a song written by Ethel: "Rocky Mountain Moonlight." Then in mid-July occurred the first single billing in Lancaster of "Baby Frances Ethel Gumm," singing songs between showings of *The Poor Nut.* Two weeks later Mary Jane and Virginia were billed in "A Song Specialty" accompanying the John Gilbert movie, *Twelve Miles Out.* A short time later Ethel and Frank again sang, preceding Lon Chaney in *Tell It to the Marines.* At all these performances a striking characteristic of the family was noticed: when some part of the family finished their act, no one was more enthusiastic than the rest of the family, sitting in the audience cheering and applauding from the front row. Many in Lancaster were at first taken aback by this.

The first summer in Lancaster went by with the girls watching and competing with movies. This was their life; they had no great theatrical ambitions. All summer long, the girls sang and danced between movies and became reacquainted with the bigger-than-life images on the screen— Bessie Love, Norma Shearer, Lon Chaney, and others.

Frank quickly became known as a friendly and congenial theater

Mary Jane and Frances in California about 1927. *Courtesy of Bill Chapman*

man. Ethel was the small woman who played the piano at the theater, as accompaniment to the movie show. She was liked but was recalled from a distance, thumping away at the piano.

The girls were remembered for more than their singing and dancing. Classmates thought of them as just normal kids who grew up together with them. Virginia was the prettiest and from the beginning was probably the most popular. Janie was considered more introverted and serious. But neither girl had Frances's energy. The most frequently mentioned picture of Frances was that of a skinny, elflike kid—tiny, with "nothing to her"—playing on Cedar Street or running down the street in front of the theater. The father of one of her playmates remembers a "common, ordinary little girl, dandy-looking and good natured" who used to sit on his lap flirting and joking.

The other memory of the family was that over the years Mrs. Gumm was regularly seen behind the wheel of the Buick, pulling out of town, heading toward the city or other destinations, on weekends or summers or whenever possible. In September Janie entered the seventh grade and Jimmie the fifth at Lancaster Grammar School. Frances was not old enough for school yet. By the end of summer the trips out of town alone with her mother began.

7

THE MINT CANYON HIGHWAY

*But she'd bring us down to L.A. every
weekend.*

At 31, Ethel Gumm, who had always been active and energetic, began
to show a compulsiveness that was to affect her family deeply. To others
her appearance was now that of a woman whose prettiness was becoming
obscured by her plumpness. She still impressed people as being charming
and vivacious, though. In whatever she did, she was hardworking and
talented—always caught up in a flurry of activities, concentrating on
the task at hand, while setting her sights on the next one.

Aside from running the household, Ethel taught the girls new song
lyrics and how to sing them, in addition to dancing, related physical
exercises, and piano. She also made their clothing, including theatrical
costumes. She was writing songs and playing at the theater. Soon after
their arrival at Lancaster, she began to contribute her singing and piano
talents to local events—recitals, Kiwanis meetings, PTA, school plays,
Saturday night dances, fairs, Christmas shows, weddings, and funerals.

Ethel was never the kind of stage mother that flourished in the
waning years of vaudeville and early ones of the movies, the ruthless
mother pushing her children with no apparent regard for their feelings
or appreciation of their talents or interests. Thousands of them descended
on Hollywood with their children "like flocks of hungry locusts."[1] Ethel
wasn't one of these, although she followed a similar course.

77

She never overestimated Frances's talent, however. At five, the wide-eyed, good-natured, trusting Frances began to notice her mother's determination. A feeling of dread overtook Ethel after they left Grand Rapids, and she tried to insulate herself from further vulnerability to past events recurring. She was scarred; the mother Frances would see from then on was more calculating, less spontaneous, someone who could not commit herself totally to her home and family.

In later years, Judy could never understand Ethel's motivation and tended to blame her mother for the direction her life had taken. Judy's bitterness notwithstanding, there is no question that Ethel acted ruthlessly or unkindly toward her youngest child. When they took the first of those hundreds of trips in the old Buick, neither Ethel nor Frances knew where the long, curving Mint Canyon Highway would lead.

Ethel renewed her contact with the Ethel Meglin Dance Studio on Glendale Boulevard. Mrs. Meglin had established her studio in Los Angeles in 1924 at the end of her career as a ballet dancer in New York musicals which were staged by Florenz Ziegfeld and Charles B. Dillingham. Ethel saw the need to seek out responsible people in her theatrical dealings. She recognized in Mrs. Meglin the integrity she wanted. In addition to providing dancing lessons, the Meglin Studio was a clearinghouse for youthful talent, the latter being what Mrs. Meglin built her reputation on. Actually she was a booking agent whom theatrical and film producers relied on. "Meglin Kiddies" was destined to become an institution in Los Angeles. In a few years young Shirley Temple, with her mother, would enter the studio for dance lessons and a couple of years after that became the country's main box office attraction.

In Ethel Mrs. Meglin saw a sincere woman and in Frances a normal, unprecocious little girl. At this time, however, there weren't many opportunities, so Ethel agreed to keep in touch. Frances, Janie, and Jimmie took dance lessons at the studio, which advertised "Results Guaranteed," and they appeared in Meglin shows.

Ethel became familiar with the theatrical district of Los Angeles. Frances liked the excitement of Los Angeles, although she came to dislike the long drive to and from the city. She liked the contrast of the city with Lancaster and the flurry of activity connected with the trips.

Although she was always glad to return home, the trips gradually accustomed her to being away from home and appearing before strange audiences.

Los Angeles was the biggest city Frances had ever been to, and it captured her imagination. As Ethel made contacts, they walked by or went into some of the vaudeville and movie theaters the girls would eventually play: the Biltmore, Hillstreet, Loew's State, Pantages, Orpheum, and the Million Dollar. Most of them were on Broadway or Hill street, and the stars that dominated the marquees in 1927 were Fanny Brice, the Duncan Sisters, and the great Nazimova. These names became part of her theatrical heritage.

Ethel took the girls to the city on weekends, where they played luncheons, theaters, dinners, and other small events. She used her contacts with Mrs. Meglin and other agents or simply walked up to a band leader and asked him to let the trio or Frances sing. To Frances it not only seemed that her mother was very bold in approaching strangers, it stirred a certain feeling to know that she was the something special being offered in these encounters. Ethel seldom got the brush-off. She was good at what she did and became better during the next few years. The person she usually spoke to, whether a booker or theater owner, was curious about what this attractive trio sounded like or what this piano-playing mother and her little girl could do. Few were disappointed with either.

Most of the time the girls did not want to leave Lancaster. It was a wonderful place, much better than Los Angeles. These early years were lean though. Somehow the Gumms gave the appearance of being well off even though neighbors claimed in hindsight that they weren't as rich as they seemed. They lived beyond their means, with little regard for thriftiness.

Frank was creating goodwill by using his family on the stage and with his promotional schemes. For the girls, the performances weren't a hardship or a chore; they loved it.

Frances was literally between the screen and stage eras, in one of transition. As a child of both movies and vaudeville she was to move back and forth between the two. In the sanctuary of the Valley Theater she casually observed the luminous ghosts whose faces were revealed on the screen. She met the great ones here—Swanson, the Gishes, Pickford, Garbo, Gilbert, and Barrymore. She learned about expression by imitating them at first. She later told her daughter, "I stole from the greats." What she didn't learn from the early screen stars she picked up on the stage, at home and on the vaudeville circuit where she saw Tucker, Morgan, Lewis, Jolson, and the Foys, although her peers were the talented, but "small coin," acts of small-time vaudeville. This was a high-spirited milieu she would be fond of throughout her life. But it would take the movie world to bring to the fore the nuances of her personality and the emotional range that was within her. While this career may have masked some of her sheer uninhibitedness, the camera revealed her deeper, more touching, qualities. Perhaps the repression of MGM and the medium was responsible for the poignant actress. When she sang on the screen, with the two traditions merging, viewers could see that never has a more superb voice flowed from such a lovely face. This was fitting because never has one's whole life been more invested in singing.

The hot summer wore on, with the temperature rising to over a hundred degrees in late September. But inside, in the world of movies and vaudeville, Frank kept the temperature an even 70 degrees. No wonder Frances and her sisters preferred it on stage and watching movies every night.

Frank grew fond of Lancaster. It would be a good place for the family. He was a true believer in the "good life," an optimist who believed that things got better and better, that everything turned out well in the end. With his religious background, Frank believed in redemption and perfectability; he saw Lancaster as a blessing, a chance to recapture the sweetness and light of the past, a chance to start again.

Being a theater entrepreneur suited his bucolic personality; running the moviehouse was a leisurely way of life. Once Mary Jane, when asked by one of her teachers, what her father's occupation was, replied: "Oh, nothing . . . he just goes to the show everyday." For Frank and the girls, if not Ethel, life was tranquil.

The Valley Theater was part of a new brick building containing other businesses—a tire shop, a barber shop, and a pool room were on the main street in town. The house on Cedar Street and the school were directly behind the theater, two blocks west. Around the corner from the moviehouse was another major street, Lancaster Boulevard, which was sprouting some new stores and featured the Old West Hotel, built in 1874. A few buildings down from the theater were the Jazz Cafe and Candy Shop which, along with the theater and hotel, were local gathering places.

The Gumms became friends with the Charles Wakefield family, the owner of the Candy Shop. The girls grew up with the Wakefield children. Janie, Jimmie, and Frances were in the shop every day. Frank and Ethel often had coffee or ice cream there after the theater closed, and Frank sometimes took the girls there for lunch. Soon he and Charles Wakefield were exchanging services—candy and movie shows for each family. At Christmas, Wakefield would supply the candy canes for the special children's matinee.

The Gumm house had an all-American, almost Andy Hardy, quality to it. It is a cliché to say that music filled the house, but in fact it was common to hear Frank's Irish tenor, Frances's blaring vibratto, or Ethel's playing on the baby grand, rehearsing the trio or playing one of her own compositions. Grandma Milne spent most of the year with them. A neighbor recalls that she made donuts and that the house was filled with the aroma of her baking.

In late afternoons Frances practiced upstairs and Ethel worked on the costumes for the act. Ethel was so productive that for future Halloweens, friends got their costumes from her collection. The girls, with Frances and the other kids, would go out in the dark, deserted streets and scare each other.

Frank joined the Episcopal Church, and Ethel and the girls attended occasionally. Frank was choirmaster. He was faithful about his duties and kept the Sunday school going by purchasing all the Sunday school papers.

When Frances entered school she made friends with a little girl called "Babe." Frances would run down Cedar Street and around the corner to the Story house. On one of her early visits the family offered her raisin cookies which she refused, saying she didn't like raisin cookies. The Storys recalled that Frances "was very cute, and knew she was cute."

The Jazz Cafe, Lancaster, California. Scene of numerous impromptu performances by Frances in late 1920s and early 1930s. *Courtesy of Mr. and Mrs. Arne Wirta*

Mr. Story never forgot the day when Frances climbed on his lap and told him: "I'm going to be a movie star someday." They noticed that Frances preferred men, "fatherly people."

Irma Story taught the kindergarten Sunday school at St. Paul's Mission. Frances and Babe were in her class. At that time a Negro family came to church every Sunday all the way from Rosamond, some distance north of Lancaster. One Sunday the family's little boy was seated next to Frances who later told her father that she didn't want to sit next to him. "Mr. Gumm, who was a Southerner, became very angry" and discussed it with the minister who would see to it that it didn't happen again. He talked to Mrs. Story who at that point quit as Sunday school teacher. She never discussed the matter with Frank, and they remained friends.

Frank may have just been indulging Frances who probably had never seen a Negro child before, or at least close up, but his giving in to his children was consistent. It was observed over the years that he thought his children were better than the other children, that his kids could do no wrong.

Mrs. Story said that Frances had "a sparkle to her." Although aware of her charms and talents, she was not self-centered. Frances was attentive to people, captivating them with her lovely brown eyes and expressive face. Mrs. Story also remembered that Frances had no figure and was "chicken-breasted." Her cloths never fit her, which was a constant problem for Ethel. Irma Story, as did most of the townspeople, thought Frances inherited her voice from her father. When asked if her voice was distinct or loud in those early days, a friend of the family replied: "Loud! It blasted out in that theater without a microphone . . . we loved it."

Lancaster was treated to several previews of Frances's maturing voice. The trio was in the limelight enough for them to have their partisans and their critics. Occasionally they were booed by the audience which thought they were getting too big a dose of the Gumms, but for the most part, people swore by the family and liked their shows.

The Gumms were considered fascinating and "sophisticated," moreso than anyone else in Lancaster. It was a source of pride to have such a family; it was different to have the kind of shows they put on. Frank's was the only movie theater around, the only place in the valley that had live singing and variety on stage. It was an extra bonus to people who otherwise had to go into Los Angeles to see vaudeville. So, despite a little jealousy, Lancaster embraced the Gumm family.

In mid-October 1927 the town held its first fair since 1919, and out of the 2,000 people at the fairgrounds, the five musical Gumms stood out. Playing to their largest audience yet, Frank and the girls sang and danced while Ethel opened the show with a "pianologue."

. Before Christmas they put on a show they would remember for a long time. Janie and Jimmie had been mimicking the Duncan Sisters since they had seen the act in a downtown theater the year before. The Duncans were known for their song "Rememberin'," from *Topsy and Eva,* and the girls had been polishing their imitation.

On a Friday night that December Frank featured *Topsy and Eva,* starring the Duncan Sisters. The Gumm girls called their show "The Kinky Kids Parade." They performed in blackface, the accepted vaudeville fashion of the day. Frank didn't advertise that title for the girls' act, perhaps because it was too obviously a racial slur in a community that had some Negroes. After the movie Janie and Jimmie gave a clever imitation of the Duncans. Originally Frances wasn't to be in the show that night, but as usual she didn't want to be left out, and the older girls realized that a show without their kid sister would be incomplete.

Ethel applied the blackface for Frances, a mask she would become more and more comfortable behind over the years. She followed her sisters on stage for a solo, and the footlights caught the fragile little minstrel girl, five years old, doing a version of "Mammy," in imitation of Jolson. "The sun shines east," she yelled, "the sun shines west," holding her arms in minstrel style as she danced one way, then the other. Stopping to face the audience, she shouted: "but I know where the sun shines best." Ethel kept up with her in the pit as she bellowed "Mammy . . . Mammy."[2] Her diction wasn't very good, but she was sassy and boisterous. Nothing could contain her high spirits as the audience cheered and cheered. When she came off stage Frank, surprised at such an exuberant performance, embraced her. Janie and Jimmie were taken aback at the explosive display. Ethel was pleased. Frances, of course, was delighted

Frances at age six in theatrical pose in Los Angeles, 1928. *Courtesy of Wide World Photos*

that she was beginning to do something onstage that not only pleased people but upset them a little as well.

She was becoming an individual who aroused strong reactions in people and even then was aware of her ability to do so. It would have a narcotic effect on her. And she was controversial; some people called her "leather lungs," and a music teacher in town thought that the young Gumm child had a raucous voice.

In Judy's childhood were the seeds of strength and courage for the times when the going would get rough—provender for the lean years. People always wondered why she continued to sing in public toward the end, displaying a skeletal talent devoid of nearly everything that had once made her great. This endurance had a lot to do with her unpredictable quality. When all seemed lost, she, by sheer will power, would surprise audiences and peers with her ability to recover. She had inherited her mother's perseverance and her father's irrepressibility. Despite insecurity and diminishing power in her last years she went on and on because her spirit demanded an encore.

This resilience was pathetically evident during the last decade of her life. She was still upsetting people and eliciting polarized opinions from admirers and detractors alike. In 1965 Ralph J. Gleason found her "efforts to recapture her vocal powers painful and pitiful and embarrassing." He asked of her performance in San Francisco:

What other performer could get away with forgetting what song she was singing, forgetting lyrics and then leaving by the wrong exit and still have her faithful applaud rapturously? In fact, her entire performance had a dream-like quality to it as though she were sleep-walking, a puppet in red stretch pants and a striped blouse, hung there on strings. . . . Only occasionally was she able to summon the strength to belt out one of the famous Judy Garland tones in the upper register. . . .[3]

Even her friends at *Variety*, who had followed her career from the beginning, had to label her singing in 1965 as "pathetic":

Miss Garland's voice was like sandpaper grinding, often missing the notes completely, often touching them for a split second then falling away, often wanting them so badly that her air-clutching motions seemed to take on new meaning all of their own . . . this was a sad Judy to watch. . . .[4]

She had begun to run into trouble again in the late 1950s:

At 160 pounds she was a sad caricature of the real Judy Garland. It was surely during this time that her audience began to feel compassion and pity for her, as well as admiration for her courage and sense of identity with her anguish. It would seem as though this were actually the end of her. And then, with the mercurial change so characteristic of her, she came out for the second half of the program [at the Metropolitan Opera] in her tuxedo, with her legs in long black stockings, and she proceeded to dazzle her audience with a display of the Garland talent at its peak. The audience found it a moving, almost unbelievable experience. Many wept. . . .[5]

After her comeback at Carnegie Hall in 1961, which perhaps exceeded her return at the Palace in 1951, at least in terms of emotional satisfaction, she again toured the world with mixed success:

Three hours out of a London nursing home, Judy Garland stepped into a spotlight at the Palladium theater today and literally stopped the biggest charity show of the season. . . . The Beatles and a host of other British entertainers faded into the wings as Miss Garland brought the house down with her famous version of "Over the Rainbow" and an encore rendition of "Swanee." The audience cheered so hard, so loudly and so long that the show was forced to close. . . .

Opposite results were achieved in Australia in 1964:

Judy was hooted off a Melbourne theater stage . . . her Australian concert tour ended in a chorus of public indignation . . . crowd of 70,000 yelled "You're late, have another brandy." Miss Garland replied, "I love you too." . . . "Sing, sing, get on with it," the crowd yelled. Heckling continued as she sang several songs. "I didn't like it," said Judy, "I sang a song called 'I'll Go My Way by Myself,' put the microphone down, and got the hell out of it. . . .

Time magazine reported on her in 1967:

As the pit band strikes up the overture, the now capacity crowd begins to peer anxiously toward the orchestra section entrance. Will the star make it?

Many rise in anticipation. Then, dramatically, the spotlight splashes against the lobby door. She has made it. In a sequined paisley pants suit, a fragile and unforgettable figure jogs down the aisle, hugging admirers, shaking hands and just plain shaking. She is—who else?—Judy Garland, now 45, and making her third Palace "comeback" in 15 years. "This is going to be an interesting performance," she begins hoarsely, "because I have absolutely no voice. But I'll fake it. . . ."[6]

Of this last run at the Palace, a little more than a year and a half before her death, *Hi Fi Stereo Review* commented:

. . . year by year her public appearances become trials by fire. How long will she be able to continue. . . . Granting that part of the excitement nowadays is the rather sadistic one of an audience waiting to hear what part of the voice will shred next, in all fairness it must be said that when Garland is Garland, she truly is a theatrical presence who verges on the sublime. . . .

Burt Korall reviews a recording of this Palace opening in 1967:

. . . the Garland voice is unstable . . . there is strain . . . as you listen . . . a strange thing happens: the ragged voice and forgotten lyrics become progressively less important. For all the technical insufficiencies of the performances, she still gets across. Like an aging fast-ball pitcher, Judy Garland makes her experience and know-how pay. . . . Hard, cold evaluation of a fading voice is easy. To go below the top layer of a performance is another matter. The sharpness and excitement of youth may be gone from Miss Garland's efforts, but the intrinsic spark remains. . . .[7]

In 1969 Vincent Canby remembered Judy Garland's last Palace performance:

. . . at the Palace Theater here not quite two years ago, there was displayed the kind of magic that has very little to do with the fun of being fooled. The voice was gone. The figure was not only slim, but vulnerably thin, and yet the performance was full of energy, transformed and shaped by her intelligence into a momentary triumph of style. It was also a somewhat nerve-racking experience, since you knew it couldn't last. It was rather like watching an extraordinary light show, and being aware that no longer was there a power source for all that electricity. . . .[8]

In 1928 there was no inkling of the trials by fire to come. Frances could be seen running the streets of Lancaster and conning her lessons in theatrical "magic."

Janie and Jimmie were doing the things most girls their age were doing—setting their sights on local boys and playing on the streets, along with Frances who was enjoying her last year of preschool freedom. They went to the theater and the Jazz Cafe every day, and Frank made occasional trips to the city to book films and make other arrangements. Ethel was on the go all the time. They were preparing for their first holiday season in the valley. They were even told that they might have a white Christmas, which they had missed the year before in Los Angeles.

It was indeed an age of innocence for the Gumms, as well as their neighbors. The concerns of most people were immediate ones. Local newspapers reported the small events of the day. A juvenile joyride in a stolen car was reported with this headline: "YOUTHFUL OFFENDERS MEET SWIFT JUSTICE, A mistaken desire to see the world led John Fields and Harvey Johnson into the strong arms of the law." Or a turkey flock theft before Thanksgiving: "A Palmdale man reported the loss of his flock Monday night . . . the only safeguard is eternal vigilence . . . by ranchers . . . many of whom literally sleep with their birds." Or a sad tale of local interest: "The vicious dog that bit Mrs. Jacoby in the face a week or so ago is reported to have bit Mr. O'Malley in the face on Sunday morning. The dog has been sent to Palmdale, according to reports, all of which is a sad blow to our neighbors to the South." Generally it was a safe, idyllic time.

It was in Lancaster that Frances got her first public notice. In 1928 the local newspaper reported that Frances Gumm, who in later life would have every personal detail and private mishap of her life chronicled in print all over the world, experienced her first personal tragedy. The paper reported: "The youngest daughter of Frank Gumm had the misfortune of falling from a swing at school and hurting her neck quite badly."

Frank had noticed some film activity outside Lancaster on the way to Palmdale, the next town. Many from Lancaster went over to watch

Hollywood stars on location. They saw the director, King Vidor, and Marion Davies shooting scenes for her last silent movie, *Show People*. It was a story in which Hollywood was parodying itself, the tale of a normal young girl trying to crash the movie business, who storms the gates of MGM and finally succeeds in the business but only after much hard work and great personal sacrifice. She is told that she must be willing "to take it on the chin." She does, until the time when her father comes to see her and is at a loss to understand what has happened to his darling, innocent daughter. The Gumms eventually saw the movie at the Valley Theater; the movie and its moral seemed to have no bearing on their lives, though.

The outside world that penetrated their lives was only comprehensible if closer at hand. In a nearby California mountain gorge the St. Francis Dam broke, and the stories of the destruction of towns and schools and the loss of over five hundred lives inflamed the imaginations of Lancaster children and adults.

Around this time the Gumms had a sudden interruption in their own lives. Frances, who was strong physically, suddenly became ill. Her condition worsened for several days, until Frank called Marcus Rabwin, now a resident surgeon at the Los Angeles County General Hospital. Frank and Ethel were concerned about her condition, and Rabwin had her admitted to the hospital, although they didn't qualify because they weren't poor. He had her admitted to the pediatrics ward as if she were a member of his own family, with the special permission of Dr. Oscar Reiss, the head of the hospital. The illness lingered for several weeks, becoming a crisis in the family. Ethel and Frank took up temporary residence in Los Angeles, with Frank commuting to Lancaster. The unwanted child six years ago was now the object of an anxious vigil. Rabwin and the other doctors didn't know what was wrong with her; it was simply a mysterious childhood disease. For three weeks this went on. Then she suddenly showed signs of recovery. When she got home, Frances remembered every detail of her hospitalization. Dr. Reiss, later connected with the famous Reiss–Davies Clinic, had taken over her case, and Frances never forgot his face and his constant attention. Two decades later she would ask him to deliver her first-born child, Liza.

Back in Lancaster the Gumms returned to normal, cherishing Frances more than ever. Marcus Rabwin followed her steady recuperation. He remarked years later that her basic physical constitution always was strong, that she had innate stamina and energy. Indeed, it would be almost 30 years before she had another serious illness.

Rabwin was an occasional visitor at the Gumms' home, as he had been in Grand Rapids. He would drive out, have dinner, and go to the theater. Rabwin didn't notice any outward change in the family or between Ethel and Frank. His visits were reminiscent of those a decade earlier. On these trips he couldn't help but notice that the admission was 50 cents for adults, while in Los Angeles it was only 35 cents. Frank pointed out that people in the area were willing to pay that price for entertainment; it had been the price when he arrived, but he would lower it before long.

During this second year in Lancaster, Frances and her mother began the regular trips to Los Angeles and other distant cities. She would sing before any group of listeners if Ethel could wangle an engagement. She and her mother would arrive in town and have lunch or dinner, after which Ethel looked for a booking. They weren't unpleasant trips, although years later a bitter and disillusioned Judy claimed that her mother had been uncharacteristically cruel, threatening to leave her in hotel rooms alone if she didn't cooperate or perform well. It is more likely that Ethel used psychological threats instead of corporeal punishment (which she didn't believe in), so such incidents may have occurred, making an indelible, if exaggerated, impression on Frances. But these were temperamental and blurred recollections, not in keeping with Frances's contentment during those years as a child entertainer. It was what followed that distorted her memory.

By the summer of 1928 the girls had gained sufficient exposure in their Los Angeles performances to get a break. Ethel had put together a good act and had established enough contacts to secure an audition for a radio show. The audition succeeded; the Gumm sisters were going to sing for the first time on radio.

Before their first broadcast over KFI in Los Angeles, the girls told everyone they knew to listen to the show. This added a thrill to their new professional venture as the five Gumms drove to Los Angeles for the appearance of 12-year-old Janie, 11-year-old Jimmie, and 6-year-old Frances. The Wednesday of the broadcast, and the following Wednesday, their Lancaster neighbors tuned in "The Children's Hour" and heard the Gumm sisters singing such songs as "Avalon Town" and "You're the Cream in My Coffee." They were beginning to have a glamorous childhood.

In September 1928 Frances joined her sisters at the Lancaster Grammar School. Further excursions into the world would now be prevented by school attendance. Ethel kept busy with numerous activities. There were still the Sunday night shows on the Valley Theater stage. Frank and Ethel became socially active, playing bridge regularly and entertaining neighbors at home.

They prospered, associating with prominent people in Lancaster. This social activity came on top of all of Ethel's other endeavors, but she still had room for more. She seemed to run on nervous energy, never satisfied with doing nothing. Ethel's drive was part of her charm. The family was used to it. When there was a void, Ethel would busy herself with knitting, saying that it gave her something to do. Townspeople remembered Ethel's traits even if they didn't fully understand them. Many recall today, to their amazement, the scene of Ethel down in front of the stage of the Valley Theater, plunking away at the piano and reading a book at the same time. This is how automatic her job as accompanist had become. One man, incredulous at hearing that Mrs. Gumm read a book while playing the piano, went down to the theater and confirmed the fact for himself. One woman who remembered Ethel at the piano, said that it was "like she had two minds."

This was typical of Ethel. The dissatisfaction with the present, the inability to relax, would be transmitted more to Frances than to the other girls. This amazing stamina, and her comeback power as a "lady Lazarus," would be noted frequently during Judy's career. Her mother had a lot of energy, which Frances inherited. Ethel believed that people were happiest when busy and would often quote the old saying, "the devil finds uses for idle hands." In her perpetual motion Ethel used the proverb as a credo. Like many before her who believed in the work ethic, she equated industry with virtue and idleness with sin.

Most agree that Ethel's piano-playing was better than her singing, which she admitted, saying that the girls inherited "the fine voice of their father." Although people describe Ethel as "pounding" or "thumping" away at the piano, the fact is that she was a first-rate pianist. Her soprano voice, Janie and Jimmie later said, wasn't "so bad," while Judy recalled it as terrible, "but very touching." The music teacher at the high school remembers Ethel as a "very good musician with a good sense of rhythm." She also recalled Ethel as a woman with a lot of fire, not overbearing, but nonetheless opinionated, with definite ideas on most things.

There were occasional weekend bookings that fall and early winter, and Ethel took the girls to the city. Even though Frank didn't always approve, he would drive into the city to catch their show. He was in a weak position. Ethel was asserting herself. She began to get the upper hand. After all, no one liked the vaudeville atmosphere more than Frank. Despite his intermittent disapproval of these trips, this was his way of keeping the family together, assuring his girls that they would find him in the audience at show time. By this time, they had two cars.

Ethel was determined to give Frances some experience on the stage of a big downtown theater during Christmas 1928. Ethel Meglin was planning her biggest children's revue yet. The *Los Angeles Examiner* heralded it as the greatest revue in which children ever had taken part. The revue was to play the Loew's State Theater during Christmas week and would be previewed at the Shrine Auditorium as a part of a bigtime, all-star charity benefit sponsored by the *Examiner*.

Ethel took one performance at a time, and Frances was readied for the charity show. On a Thursday evening in December the whole family traveled to the city to the recently built Shrine Auditorium. At show time Frances and the other Meglin moppets took their place among the great stars of the day—Dolores Del Rio, Tom Mix, Joan Crawford, Billy Dove, Myrna Loy, and 400 other attractions, including Hal Roach's "Our Gang." The 100 Meglin Kiddies were swallowed up on one of the world's largest stages. All the newspapers could say of the Kiddies was that they "poured out upon the stage." But no special recognition was given them or Frances; all she got out of it was a moment's exhilaration at gazing at the near-capacity crowd of 6,500 people.

This show offered an entree to Ethel. She decided that Frances would appear Christmas week at Loew's. Frank didn't want her to do it, but Frances was eager. He insisted that Ethel and Frances return to Lancaster each night. Frances had already gotten used to overnight stays with her mother at small hotels in Los Angeles.

The Christmas show at Loew's State was a Fanchon and Marco show, a type of stage show that was fast becoming distinguished by dynamic vaudeville and choreography created by the two producers. It is said that Frances's solo, "I Can't Give You Anything But Love, Baby," brought down the house. Reviews didn't single out the talents of the Kiddies, but perhaps she helped inspire these reviews: "The children perform like tried and true troupers . . . they more than make up for occasional mistakes in the breathless, do or die manner in which they work,"[9] and "The Meglin Kiddies range in size from babes who haven't the strength to do the stunts required of them to young ladies who are about ready to take up chorus work professionally."[10]

It had been fun, and Ethel and Frances knew the solo had been a success. The engagement ended, and they drove home. The daily rides had been tedious; Frank and Ethel would compromise this year.

One thing Judy excelled in was expressing ambivalent emotions on screen. Even in the corniest and most trite of her movies, she was physically or socially torn between people and things while always being good-natured, giving her all, pleasing everyone. In *Andy Hardy, Little Nellie Kelly, For Me and My Gal, A Star is Born,* and others, she was called on to convey these torn feelings and divided loyalties.

At the age of six this diminutive girl was fast becoming the object of a subtle, deep-rooted conflict between her parents. Frail and delicate, pretty in an unusual way, she was sensitive to this stress, but her outward appearance belied her feelings. Frances was playful and good-natured, receptive and spontaneous. Everyone, especially adults, liked her, which she reveled in. She wasn't conceited or spoiled. The ideal

Loew's State Theater, Los Angeles. View down Seventh Street at Christmas time, 1928. *Courtesy of Terry Helgesen Collection*

child. Women liked to look at her, and men wanted to put their arms around her in a fatherly gesture. She was, in short, irresistible. No wonder Frank idolized her. The qualities that drew people to Frances grew out of the experience of her friendship with her father. In this way, perhaps, she was spoiled. Frank, although perfect only in Frances's eyes, was setting a standard for her to seek in all things in life.

She knew that the one thing her mother and father had in common was a love of show business. Here was a mutual ground where she could please both parents, if ultimately for different reasons.

The new year 1929 brought little change in Lancaster. The newspaper reported that the town of Lancaster could boast one dog for each family, and the Gumms were no exception; they had a Pekinese pup.

Travelers passing through Lancaster could stay at the Western Hotel for a dollar a day, compared to two or three dollars in Los Angeles. Bacon was 19 cents a pound, prime ribs the same. Tomatoes were 25 cents a pound, and a two-pound jar of peanut butter cost 17 cents. Since most people in town were poor, the stock market crash later that year wouldn't be a big shock; they would be less affected by it than many others. A seat at the Valley Theater was still 15, 25, or 50 cents. Business at the theater was brisk. Frank was exhibiting a new, all-electric phono-graph-radio in the lobby, as well as announcing "the first synchronized sound picture ever shown in the Antelope Valley, *Sonia, A Melody of Love.*" He was also featuring a stock company play, *16 and Saucy,* a comedy by the Spence Theater Company. The Gumms exhibited their prosperity with a large dinner and theater party for friends. The trio entertained in the living room after dinner.

One local event Frances always remembered with disdain were the regular rabbit drives in the valley. Much larger than the dog population, the rabbit colony rampaged through the alfalfa and other crops. The paper that year reported: DAMAGE BY RABBITS ESTIMATED 140,336 FOR PAST SEASON. To solve the problem, rabbit drives were advertised, and trainloads of hunters came in from Los Angeles and other points. Although guns were sometimes used, more often they were prohibited. The men, on foot and on horseback, would surround a field and chase the rabbits into an improvised corral where they would beat them to death with clubs. The unpleasant memory of men carrying rabbit carcasses through town remained with Frances throughout her life.

The new year brought another first for the family. Frank would be the only Gumm not involved in the grammar school play *Cinderella in Flowerland*. Ethel provided the music for the play, which included the three girls, Virginia getting the lead as Cinderella, Mary Jane stretching her thespian talents to play the prince; their little sister was listed in the program as "the Bonnie Bee, Frances (Baby) Gumm." It was added that "the above characters are supported by a cast of Sunbeams, Raindrops, Butterflies and Blossoms, in attractive and colorful costumes."

It was a very cold evening. Afterward they all went over to the Candy Shop where Frank treated the members of the cast to refreshments and convinced his three girls that they couldn't have been better. Despite his praise, the girls could tell that he was upset about something. He was disturbed; he and Ethel had argued since Christmas over differing goals for the girls. They walked home against the chilly, now windy, evening.

A few days later Frank and Ethel hosted a dinner party at their home while the girls visited friends. They were entertaining some of the town's most prominent people—the owner of the theater property, the local doctor, and others. Frank was particularly concerned about appearances this evening; there was no evidence of strain between him and Ethel. They played bridge after dinner. Their friends didn't know it yet, but within the past few days a decision had been made.

8

A NAME IN THE WORLD

My father didn't want us to perform,
but whenever we worked anyplace, he'd
come and watch.

Ethel and the girls were living in an upstairs apartment at 1814½ S. Orchard, an area near Washington Boulevard and Vermont Avenue, adjacent to the downtown Los Angeles theatrical district. Ethel's plan was to remain there indefinitely.

Ostensibly they were in the city to enlarge their theatrical experience. Neighbors in Lancaster were told that the girls were going to Los Angeles to "pursue special studies." It was a legitimate reason, considering their background. They told their friends that they would be back on weekends to visit their father, and for Ethel to play the piano at the theater. But it was clear now that Ethel, after 15 years of marriage, was no longer dependent on Frank.

At this time there were some opportunities for the girls, and Ethel, stranded in Lancaster like an artist without materials, had to be near Los Angeles. Ethel Meglin saw promise in the trio and wanted to use them in some productions.

The girls were torn by the move. They had noticed the strain between their parents. They were afraid of a separation from their father. Janie and Jimmie's interest in entertaining was mercurial; Frances, though, took it all to heart. The two older girls liked entertaining together and knew that there would be good opportunities in Los Angeles, but still they would miss their friends in Lancaster. They threw themselves into their activities in the city while hoping for a quick return home. Ethel enrolled them in a professional school for theatrical children, with academic classes in the morning, which freed them in the afternoon for show business. They went to Mrs. Lawlor's Professional School on Hollywood Boulevard.

Their performances consisted of whatever Ethel could find for them. Pickings were slim, and Ethel entered Frances in the *Los Angeles Evening Express*'s "Better Baby Contest." The term "baby" was defined loosely, and six-year-old Frances, among thousands entered, rose to the occasion and won honorable mention in the talent division. With it went a prize—a $10 gift certificate from the Broadway Department Store.

Judy recalled the unusual nature of the life of the children she ran into backstage and of the unusual, exciting days in vaudeville. She met young Donald O'Connor who with his family played many of the same theaters. She recalled playing tag and hide-and-seek and learning how to play jacks from him. Later on, at the Lawlor School, she would meet 12-year-old Mickey Rooney, whose first career in the Mickey Maguire series had ended and whose second career would soon begin at MGM. Although she would become very familiar to vaudeville, Frances's experience differed from such kids as O'Connor and Rooney, in that her background was rooted in the family theater, on her father's stage, and not in vaudeville. It was on that stage that she gained a privileged attitude about the stage. She could always be herself, and she knew that she could do things on the stage that others couldn't. This attitude would never desert her. Even in one of the last performances of her life she remarked: "There's nothing like aristocracy in vaudeville."

That year, a decade before she became famous in movies, she made her unassuming film debut. Ethel Meglin had mentioned to Ethel the possibility of using the girls in a movie. That spring she had finally arranged with Warner Brothers to supply talent for a film short which would feature the Gumm sisters. Warner's was making hundreds of short subjects at the time, many of which were fantasy and fairy tales, and the Meglin Studio was a logical source of talent. The first short was

The Gumm Sisters, 1930. *Courtesy of the* Chicago Tribune

going to be called simply *The Meglin Kiddie Revue*. They spent weeks rehearsing while word soon drifted back to Lancaster that the girls were going to make a movie.

The movie was a natural for them. It was a singing, talking, and dancing show. When the time came for the final shooting of the scene, the trio appeared in matching, two-tone satin outfits, with polka-dot top hats. Frances announced the act as she faced the lights and rolling cameras for the first time. "Now you will see us," she said in a babyish, halting voice, "in a dancing and singing number by the Gumm Sisters, *not* [with gleeful emphasis] the Wrigley Sisters." After the pun about their name, the Meglin Kiddie Band played brassy ragtime accompaniment to "The Sunny South" which the girls harmonized on. They were interrupted in several spots by Frances who was heard yelling over her sisters and the 20-piece band. The performance was "raucous." It's easy to see why a local theater owner supposedly told Frances about this time: "You may sing loud kid, but you don't sing good."

The preparation, rehearsal, and making of the movie lasted several months, until the summer, a period that was also marked by other appearances in the city. The film would not be shown until later that year and would do little more than bolster the girls' confidence.

Frank lived alone in the house on Cedar Street. His daily routine was occupied by running the theater, having meals at the Jazz Cafe, getting his daily shave from John Perkins, the barber, and playing some occasional bridge. He was left with little to do.

He frequently made trips into Los Angeles, though. In early April he saw the girls appear in another large Meglin revue at the Figueroa Playhouse. In a four-hour show which included 500 kids, the trio sang, with Frances again featured in a solo. In a ruffled, low-cut dress ballooning from the waist down and with a bonnet on her head, she sang with clarity and bounce, getting the most rousing applause of the afternoon. What was becoming apparent when she sang were a sad expression and mournful eyes; her face was as vibrant as her voice. People were compelled to notice her.

After the show they celebrated with dinner. As always, the girls' activities were enlivened by the presence of their father. They talked of the arrival of their Uncle John and of their return to Lancaster for the Minstrel Show to be presented in May.

The arrival of Uncle John was cause for celebration in a house where they celebrated and sang on almost any occasion. Frances was used to the fact that in her house people launched into a song at any given moment. She or any member of the family was perfectly at ease whether singing by the staircase next to the baby grand or at the theater. These gatherings were the times she liked best. Before leaving, Uncle John made his customary appearance at the Valley Theater where the audience was treated to his "silvertone tenor," as he was known in Duluth and where he had appeared on radio.

The local paper announced that "Frank Gumm will abandon all dignity to cavort as an end man" in the annual Minstrel Show and that Mrs. Gumm would be on the piano. "The Gumm Sisters will close the vaudeville show with the latest song and dance numbers."

Thursday evening at eight o'clock, the second annual minstrel and vaudeville show had drawn a capacity crowd in the Valley Theater. The Antelope Valley Band, tightly assembled in the pit, with Ethel at the piano, brought the chatty audience to order as they played "Officer of the Day." The final bars of the march reached the settling audience as the house lights dimmed. The footlights came on, and the red velvet curtain rolled up to reveal the entire company, including the four Gumms, singing the opener, "When We Turn Out the Home Town Band." As the march concluded, the curtain descended to applause, and Frank and his nine cohorts quickly took their places in the "circle" which opened the traditional minstrel presentation.

Banjo-strumming, with bass and piano accompaniment, introduced the circle of wise-cracking end men wearing blackface and trading quips with the straight man. Frank sat on the far left, surrendering his usual composure as he raucously delivered his repartee to the laughter of the audience and the jangling response of tambourines.

Several of the men in the circle offered a song or dance. "Kansas City Kitty" was a rouser and caused some foot-stomping, while "The Songs My Mother Used to Sing" hit a sentimental chord. But it was

Frank's polished tenor that got the most applause with "Here Comes
My Ball and Chain," apparently not dedicated to Ethel who was down
in the pit smiling and plunking away as the audience roared their
approval.

The "olio," or vaudeville half of the show, opened with "Those
Banjo Boys," Weir and Martin, two gentlemen in town who had been
making the rounds for years but who never failed to strum a little frenzy
into the audience. Next was the "Community Quartet," followed by "The
Girl with the Guitar" and two other acts, which brought the show to its
anticipated highlight—the Gumm sisters. The girls, presenting "Popular
Songs and Dance Specialties," scored a knockout with "Ol' Man River"
in costume and blackface. Frances threw herself into it as usual, with her
slender legs and long arms taking on the appearance of a large marionette
as the charcoaled face bounced around stage with arms flying and legs
kicking. The audience applauded enthusiastically as the girls took their
final bows and merged with the entire cast for the finale, "Hello Sun-
shine."

They returned to Los Angeles to make several appearances at
Shrine events in early June. Back to Lancaster in time for Frances's
seventh birthday. At home and the theater, they had a small party for
her and an array of gifts. At the theater, along with Wallace Beery in
China Town Nights, was an "EXTRA ADDED ATTRACTION: THE
GUMM SISTERS appearing Sunday only with the act they presented
with the recent band minstrel show." Things seemed to be returning
to normal.

Three nights later, Mary Jane graduated from grammar school. She
sang a vocal solo, "A Perfect Day," at the graduation exercises. Frank
entertained the entire graduating class at the theater. The girls were glad
to be back with their father. Ethel had no reason to keep them in Los
Angeles any longer. She couldn't ignore the fact that they wanted to
stay home, and Frank wouldn't permit another prolonged theatrical
sojourn. So they resumed life on Cedar Street at the beginning of another
hot summer. In the hot desert summer Frances was a common sight
walking to and from "the plunge," the only swimming place in town.
A schoolteacher recalls looking out her window and seeing the young

The three sisters in a pose in Los Angeles about 1930. *Courtesy of Bill Chapman*

Gumm child walking by in a black bathing suit, right down the middle of the street, never on the sidewalk. She vividly recalls this scene, because at the age of six or seven, Frances still had "nothing to her, and was like a cricket with skinny arms and legs." Another lady, thinking back over 40 years, recalled the same sight, Babe Gumm in her black bathing suit looking "like a little spider."

That fall Frances would be starting second grade. About this time she made friends with a fourth grader who would become her best childhood friend, Ina Mary Ming. "Muggsie," as she was nicknamed, became fast friends with "Babe," as she always called Frances. Townspeople remember the two kids as being inseparable.

They had known one another since the Gumms arrived in Lancaster, but it wasn't until Ina Mary played a Butterfly to Frances's Bonnie Bee in *Cinderella* earlier in the year that they became better acquainted. "We just got along real good," Muggsie said, recalling how they did everything together—roller-skating, bicycling, yo-yoing, and swimming. Ina Mary was almost three years older, but that made no difference. In the hot Lancaster summers they went every day to the plunge. They could be seen running home without their shoes; "we never wore anything on our feet," recalled Muggsie. They'd have to stop in the shadows of the telephone poles and bushes, it being nearly a mile, with few trees and lawns, until they got to Cedar Street. They would arrive home together, where Frances would begin her late-afternoon practice.

Muggsie, of course, was aware of Frances's musical activities. She maintains that, aside from her lessons and performing, Frances, like herself, had a normal childhood. It is apparent, however, that a more disciplined pattern to Frances's life was emerging. Ina Mary's father remembered that Babe Gumm would come to play but then had to go home to practice. "Her mother was very strict about that." As they became closer, Muggsie became a unique observer of this early stage of Frances's career. She accompanied her on numerous out-of-town trips with her mother, either to audition, rehearse, or perform.

Muggsie's father was captivated by the little girl to whom he taught cartwheels in his living room. He remembered her as a youngster with "a good smile, dandy looking, with her black curly hair . . . who enjoyed life and was good natured, not stuck up." To him she was a "common, ordinary little girl, a darling little kid." Forty years later, Mr. Ming, thinking of the youngest Gumm child who played at his home almost every day, said: "I loved her then and I loved her later." Thinking of her untimely death and her expressed disdain for Lancaster and its people, he stated sincerely: "I know she never had it in for me." After 1934 he never saw her again and with regret said: "I always hoped that she'd come back to visit me."

Muggsie also had a theatrical act, with a friend, Ruth Gilmore, and they, too, performed at the Valley Theater. She instructed Frances in tumbling and other acrobatics. They would play each day after school and often stay overnight at each other's house. Muggsie thought Frances emotional and sensitive as a child, but as close as they were, Frances never confided any desire or dream of becoming an actress or singer to her friend. As far as she could recall, Frances was happy and had no unusual ambitions. But at a certain time each day the little girl would

Frances at about age seven in 1929. *Courtesy of John Ferjo*

Formal portrait of Frank Avent Gumm in the early 1930s. *Courtesy of the University of the South*

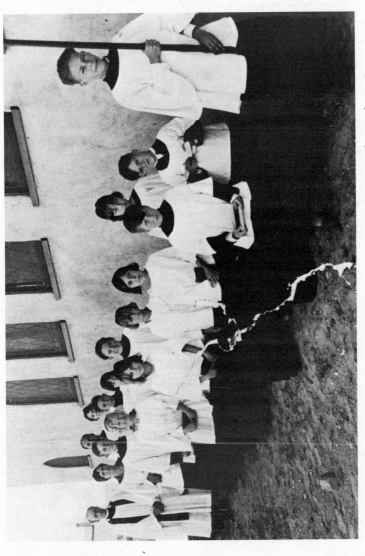

St. Paul's choir, Lancaster, California, in the 1930s with Frank Gumm (fourth from the left), Miss Kinnamon (next to Frank), and "Muggsie" Ming (fifth from the right). *Courtesy of Ina Mary Miller*

Bishop Theatre
Tuesday and Wednesday
JULY 16-17
EXTRA ADDED ATTRACTION

The Three Gumm Sisters

(IN PERSON)

now with the famous Meglin Kiddies of Los Angeles, and available only during vacation times, will appear in HARMONY SONGS, TAP AND ACROBATIC DANCNG.

A GUARANTEED ATTRACTION

On the same bill with Metro-Goldwyn-Mayer's 6-reel feature picture "A SINGLE MAN," starring Aileen Pringle and Lew Cody. Also two-reel comedy "Thundering Tupees" and M. G. M. oddity "The Persian Wedding."

A 1929 advertisement for the Gumm Sisters in the *Inyo Register,* Bishop, California, for the performance which earned seven-year-old Frances her first individual praise. *Courtesy of Chalfant Press*

110

leave the Ming home at Newgrove and Fig streets to go home for lessons and practice. Others on Cedar Street remember Frances upstairs in her bedroom doing her vocal lessons, the voice carrying far down the street.

Late in July the whole family drove up to Bishop for one of their only bookings that summer. Frank saw in these family tours the opportunity to maintain his influence over their life together. They reached Bishop in time to put an ad in the local paper. The wording of the ad seems to indicate an agreement between Frank and Ethel about the availability of the girls for "vacation times" only. On July 16, 1929, it appeared, along with a photograph: "Extra added attraction THE THREE GUMM SISTERS —In Person—now with the famous Meglin Kiddies of L.A. and available only during vacation times, will appear in HARMONY SONGS, TAP AND ACROBATIC DANCING—A Guaranteed Attraction."

Bishop, about the size of Lancaster, was also the center of a sparsely populated area. The Bishop Theater, like the Valley, was one of the few sources of entertainment; it seated 400. The girls did their current act, including "The Sunny South" from the Meglin movie, and Frances did an imitation of Ted Lewis, singing "Wear a Hat with a Silver Lining" and "Little Pal." They were a great success and for two nights got a rousing ovation. When they returned home, Ethel carried with her a review from the local newspaper. The girls had received their best review thus far:

The singing and particularly the clever dancing of the three Gumm sisters won the commendation of audiences at the Bishop theater last night and the night before. Mary Jane, Virginia and Baby Frances are the daughters of Mr. and Mrs. Frank Gumm of the Valley theater, Lancaster. They have certainly applied themselves well to their studies in the Meglin Dance Studio in Los Angeles, adding that advantage to their talents. All do so well in their specialties that the discrimination of special mention is hardly just: but the remarkable work of Baby Frances particularly appeals to hearers because of her diminutive size and few years.

The reviewer felt called on to mention the "remarkable" qualities that those around Frances had been noticing. As the 1920s came to an end, young Frances Gumm had not yet made a name for herself in the world, but in Bishop, California, she had garnered her first rave newspaper notice.

Up a dark alley to the stage door hurries a strange little creature bundled in mink from ears to ankles. In the dim light it looks like a fur shmoo wearing a top-knot of hair curlers.

Inside the jampacked theater tension hangs like a net between the audience and the big orchestra on stage. The overture begins, and one by one all the familiar hoped-for melodies come flooding back. Each time the musicians launch a new one across the footlights fans send back salvos of applause, and with every volley the emotional pressure inside the hall rises a few more degrees. Finally the vast space above the audience shimmers with visions of clanging trolley cars, men that got away and birds flying over the rainbow. At this point in the series of identical musical evenings which have taken place recently in 14 major U.S. cities, a plump little 38-year-old woman hiding behind furls of dusty curtain knows it is again time to go to work, and to deafening billows of applause, which drown out the orchestra's final crashing chords, Miss Judy Garland trots cheerfully to center stage.

The uproar subsides, the songs begin . . . "So keep on smiling, 'cause when you're SMILING. . . ." At first the audience cannot believe it will last. "You go to my head . . . I could cry—salty tears—" The big, sobby voice flows out unrestrained across the footlights, rich as caramel, solid as lava. This is the *old* Judy Garland voice. . . . "Who cares what banks *fail* in Yonkers, long as you've a kiss that CONquers?" She's strutting now balancing on the slender legs and prancing like a pony. At the end of Act 1 comes a performance of "San Francisco" so brassy, so sassy, delivered with such a full head of steam that one expects the whole theater to pull away from the levee and start churning down river under its own power . . . Then the Vesuvius of torch songs, "Stormy Weather," sung with tears in her voice, her eyes, her throat, running down her neck. . . .

By temperament she is incapable of holding anything of herself in reserve. This gives her performance an old-fashioned theatrical excitement. . . . This all-out quality, this determination to give everything she has, is a trait that Judy was born with. . . .[1]

This was Frances Gumm in 1961, as described by Shana Alexander in *Life* magazine 32 years after the Gumm sisters, with young Frances, wowed the audience in Bishop, California. Judy Garland nee Frances Ethel Gumm, had reached the peak of her artistic form at Carnegie

Hall and other concert halls throughout the United States. This was her vintage voice; her performance was truly a "glimpse of sheer perfection," to use Deans' and Pinchot's words. The fun, hard work, innate talent, and intense feelings of her youth as a member of the Gumm family singers was now manifesting itself in a display of "old-fashioned theatrical excitement."

The writer, Miss Alexander, attested to the fact that these shows occurred over and over in the early sixties. She watched Judy's entrance on stage:

By 8:50 p.m. at the theater, the overture is pounding forward and . . . without warning, Judy Garland suddenly turns her back on the watchers in the wings, sets her shoulders, takes what seems a 10-gallon deep breath and then—astonishingly as one looks out from the darkness directly into the footlights glare—she appears to glide away onto the bright lit stage like a child's pull toy, powered by the rising wave of applause itself.[2]

For 35 years she had been walking out over the footlights as if powered by the "wave of applause itself."

At the time of these tumultuous concerts Judy had been back performing on the stage for 10 years, the only alternative left to her after her movie career ended in 1950. But now she was on her own. Her mother and father's association with her career was now a poignant relic of the past, although what she was doing now (she called it giving the audience "two hours of POW") was clearly linked to her remarkable childhood when she began to stop the show as a young vaudevillian.

Ralph De Toledano, writing in the *National Review,* comes closest to analyzing the Judy Garland phenomenon of 1961 at Carnegie Hall:

There are some performers who have it, really have it. By some sort of empathy, they reach out over the footlights and merge with the audience . . . Alla Nazimova . . . Pablo Casals. . . . The performer who has it ceases to be himself. He is possessed of his audience, even as his audience is possessed of him. This is what makes a cult. And this is what Judy Garland has, what lifted her . . . to the joyous, tragic tears-to-the-eye bringing singer of America's living popular ballads. It is unnecessary nowadays to say "Judy Garland." The "Judy" is sufficient, as storming, cheering, shaken and deeply moved

Americans who have heard her in concert can attest. Judy is a cult. Even before she opens her mouth to sing, she has made her point . . . her triumphant Carnegie Hall concert . . . repeated in sixteen cities . . . left the usually glib critics groping for adjectives and feeling the inadequacy of their clichés. . . . Judy holds back nothing . . . She gives every song . . . everything, and takes everything from it. It is then that the heart discovers the secret of Judy Garland's singing. She has found the eternal verities buried in sweet or maudlin, rowdy or vulgar, melodies that the philosophers of Tin Pan Alley have given her. The full-throated open voice in overstating its penance, has in fact paradoxically reduced it to an essence. . . . There is none like Judy to cut to the quick of our emotions, to become the symbol and the song itself. . . .[3]

The sweet, commonplace girl from the country had long since become "the symbol and the song itself." Frances had become a woman and a performer of mythical proportions, as David Shipman depicts in his image of her achievement:

Indeed, if it can be measured by the pitch of excitement in the auditorium, Garland was the greatest artist of the century: no one who was ever at one of her concerts could ever forget the tiny stocky figure on stage, the huge, warm, dramatic voice and the hysteria invoked in the audience. . . .

There's no question that at the age of seven the true performing artist was emerging in Frances. She knew what audiences liked. She had learned to sing songs in that manner with her own gusto.

In August Frances and a fellow performer from the Meglin Studio, Eugene Taylor, appeared in a Sunday night program at the Valley Theater: "Last Sunday the patrons at the Valley theater were given a rare treat in the song and dance specialty presented by little Frances Gumm and Eugene Taylor. The kiddies sang and danced exceptionally well and created a riot with the audience when they finished their skit with the 'bowery number.'" The newspaper didn't elaborate on the "riot." It was just another indication of Frances's ability to stop the show, to stir people emotionally. The people of Lancaster were witnessing the birth of a theatrical phenomenon.

As the summer went on, the girls renewed their friendships while

Frank featured "country store" nights with prizes of groceries and meat and a "hot weather inducement" to keep cool by selling two-for-the-price-of-one tickets. There was one more performance out of town before the summer ended, and then school resumed.

They appeared again with the Meglin Kiddies at Loew's State in Los Angeles. This time it was with "56 clever tots" instead of the usual 500, and with Stephen Fetchet headlining the bill. The girls were featured but received no special notice. The *Variety* reviewer could only think of how many stage mothers were pulling the strings of these would-be stars:

How many mothers the management is struggling with isn't known, but the strain must be heavy—and it's hot besides. Can figure they were all out front on this first show. Couple of the tots must solo too. And always the same—those gymnastics and roll-overs which come so easy to limber babies. Once in a while all right but not every week. Don't parents ever figure they can burn a youngster out? Same as an athlete.[4]

9

A REPRIEVE

Maybe I fulfilled Mother's ambitions,
and maybe she fulfilled hers.

Ethel and the three girls walked down Fifth Street toward Walker's Department Store where, as everywhere in downtown Los Angeles, the store windows were shimmering with Christmas decorations. This was a busy day for them. They entered the bustling department store where Ethel had a booking for the girls. Babe, Janie, and Jimmie were joking about the fact that they had never played a toy department opening before, but the nature of the booking did not deter Ethel. Nothing could depress their spirits that day, because as the girls did their numbers for the Christmas shoppers, Dad was at Union Station, waiting for the arrival of Grandma Milne on the train from Minneapolis. The girls sang enthusiastically throughout the day to the distracted customers at Walker's.

Grandma's arrival to spend the winter signaled the beginning of the Christmas season for the Gumms. The girls quickly filled her in on their recent activities, including the fact that they were again appearing on radio each Monday afternoon with Big Brother Ken over KNX. They were even heard by their Uncle Will, Frank's brother, in Birmingham, Alabama, who sent a telegram congratulating them. But the big news was that they had changed their stage name to "The Hollywood

Mary Jane, Virginia, and Frances doing their act about 1930. *Courtesy of Maurice L. Kusell*

Starlets Trio" and were going to make a second film short for Warner Brothers, through their association with the Meglin Studio.

Their grandmother had arrived in time for all the festive activities at home and the theater. Frank was offering "six oil paintings of Lupe Velez" to "the first six women to enter the theater." At home Grandma went about making special pastries for Christmas in addition to renewing the ritual of tea and cinnamon toast every afternoon.

During Christmas week Frank gave his usual free matinee for the children in town, and candy canes were again supplied by Charles Wakefield. They ended the season with an elaborate Christmas dinner at the Munz Country Club, to which over 40 guests were invited. Janie, Jimmie, and Frances joined their father who was chairman of the Christmas carol program and, with other carolers, roamed the streets singing carols.

After Christmas Ethel spotted an advertisement in the theatrical section of the *Los Angeles Examiner*: "The KUSEL Theatrical Dance Studio—300 CHILDREN WANTED FOR JUVENILE REVUE." On her next trip to Los Angeles she introduced herself to Maurice L. Kusell. The youthful and urbane Mr. Kusell appeared to have something to offer her and the girls. Like Mrs. Meglin, Kusell had run a dance academy in Los Angeles since the early twenties and had been a dancing star of musical comedies and vaudeville. Later he was the choreographer of *Fox Follies of 1930* and *The Great Gabbo,* as well as stage productions on the East and West coasts. He could give the Gumm sisters the opportunity to polish their dancing—tap, off rhythm, acrobatic, buck and wing, waltz clog, soft shoe, eccentric, slow buck, high kicking, and chorus. Dancing was to be as important in Frances's career as her singing. Ethel agreed with Kusell's philosophy that the basis of musical comedy was dancing. "Today, anyone entering motion pictures as a profession *must* be able to *dance,"* he said.

Ethel asked about lessons for the girls and about Kusell's production involving the 300 children. He told her that it would be in July. Ethel said she would be back with her daughters.

In 1930 there was a dropping off in the number of their appearances in and out of town, which lasted until mid-1931. The drop-off

Maurice L. Kusell, dance director and Frances's instructor from 1931–1934.
Courtesy of Maurice L. Kusell

was to the girls' liking, since Janie and Jimmie were active in the social life of their friends. In addition, Janie's last year of grammar school had been broken up by the temporary residence in Los Angeles, and Frank didn't want that to happen to Jimmie. So all three girls got a respite from show business.

There was no lull for Ethel, however; she accepted the girls' lack of interest as a passing phase. There was a limit to how much she could understand them. She admitted that, like many parents, she didn't always understand her children. She frequently told friends about the time she had bought Frances a new party dress. When she gave it to her, Frances broke into tears, begging and pleading for another dress instead of that one. Ethel was at a loss until Frances said: "Oh Mama, it has ruffles." She knew Frances hated ruffles but either didn't think it was important or had forgotten Frances's dislike for that kind of dress. Characteristically Ethel acted impulsively; her way of doing things took precedence over other people's feelings. Ethel believed that she contributed to her daughters' happiness. She wanted the girls to enjoy their youth. She was a true innocent who never doubted herself but who often lacked insight.

For the next two months they did not leave Lancaster except for a few trips Ethel made alone to Los Angeles. Frances and Jimmie returned to grammar school while Janie started high school. Ethel turned her energy to another project. She became part of a local orchestra which included John Perkins who would become a steady friend of the Gumms. In the orchestra Ethel played two other instruments besides the piano. The group provided music for Saturday night dances, Kiwanis dinners and other affairs. At one of the Kiwanis dinners Frank was called on to sing "Pagan Love Song." At another, Frank was pressed into the program with a demand for "Swanee River" which was followed by an encore of "Sunny Side Up," Ethel accompanying. These occasions kindled memories for Frank and Ethel of their courtship at the Savoy Theater in Superior.

Frank and Ethel enjoyed sharing their prosperity. They entertained frequently, giving dinners at home or taking couples to Hollywood to dine. Ethel made occasional trips to the city with Mrs. Gilmore, a neighbor whose family had become close friends. Frank and Ethel shared many social evenings with Mr. and Mrs. Gilmore; their children grew up together, and their only child Ruth was the acrobatic partner of Babe's friend Muggsie. The closeness of the two couples would later become a subject of gossip in Lancaster because much later William Gilmore became Ethel's second husband, as well as a stepfather Frances never fully accepted.

One of the Valley Theater advertisements in 1929 heralded a coming attraction: "Saturday, Louise Fazenda in 'Finger Prints,' a mystery comedy drama picturing the adventures of a wise chick who lays for a lot of bad eggs amid the taut tip-top terrors of a $5,000,000 mail robbery. Lots of good comedy."

Hollywood was going into musicals in a big way. At first it was just to take advantage of the new talkie techniques. Later, as the Depression wore on, they became a means of escape. As soon as talkies arrived in Lancaster, Frank showed Metro-Goldwyn-Mayer's *Broadway Melody,* which was billed as an "all talking, all singing and dancing classic, starring Charles King, Anita Page and Bessie Love."

In Lancaster Frances continued to be the center of attention. The Wakefields, whose girls were playmates of the Gumms and who ran the Jazz Cafe, were reopening the store after alterations. Like a scene from a later movie musical, Frances assisted the master of ceremonies at the festivities marking the new look of the "well known palace of sweets." Standing by the soda fountain she sang one of her numbers. Her appreciative audience then went down the street to Haubrich's new music and radio department where Ethel and the newly formed orchestra were serenading customers. With Ethel at the piano the group played while Virginia and Frances sang three songs. The *Ledger-Gazette* reported that "a drawing of coupons for prizes was presided over by W. S. Mumaw, Baby Gumm assisting and winning the first prize."

The 1930s had begun; the full force of the Depression was just ahead. But the Gumms appeared as prosperous and as happy as ever. It didn't seem possible that circumstances could change that prosperity and happiness.

The new year 1930 found Ethel plunging into her latest project which, much to Frank's liking, was a local one. She rented a hall in town and enlisted her three daughters as assistants, and opened a music and dancing school. Initially about 20 students enrolled, more girls than boys, which was expected since boys were skeptical of dance lessons. The Gumm trio would be used for demonstrations and to set an example for the students. The townspeople liked the idea.

At this time Frank was touting the arrival locally of talkies which were making it necessary for exhibitors everywhere to invest in new sound equipment. The *Ledger-Gazette* announced: TALKIE EQUIPMENT FOR LANCASTER. Late the year before, Frank had begun promoting the coming change at the Valley Theater. He promised that the new equipment would be the same as that at the Los Angeles Hillstreet Theater. But by the new year the equipment still had not arrived, and Frank asked the public to be patient. In January the *Ledger-Gazette* reported: GUMM RECEIVES WORD TALKIES ARE EN ROUTE but later that month headlined: TALKIE EQUIPMENT SLOW IN ARRIVING.

In the meantime Frank hit them with more live vaudeville, with the presentation of "The Hollywood Starlets Trio," better known in Lancaster, of course, as the Gumm sisters. Because the sound equipment had not arrived, Frank could not show either of the film shorts the girls had made, so at this appearance they sang some songs from the most recently completed movie, introducing "The Land of Let's Pretend" and "When the Butterflies Kiss the Buttercups Goodbye."

Finally "the finest reproducing equipment" available was delivered and installed. Frank, who had brought vaudeville to the area, now would be its first impresario of the talkies. The *Ledger-Gazette* announced: THEATER NOW HAS TALKIE EQUIPMENT, and February 16, 1930, the people of Lancaster viewed the first talkie to be shown in the Antelope Valley—*The Virginian*, starring Gary Cooper.

Their introduction in the Valley was to free Ethel from her duties at the theater. She made good use of her time. It was almost time for another "Better Babies Contest" in Los Angeles. Even though Frances was now almost eight years old, she was entered. In March the local paper told its subscribers in a news item that "Frances Gumm was called to Hollywood Wednesday evening for a tryout before a director of the

Paramount film company in connection with the Better Babies contest being conducted by the LA Evening Express." She had her audition, but didn't even win a merchandise certificate, returning home as one of 50 finalists.

So two major companies, Warner's and Paramount, had ignored Frances Gumm, which was of little concern to Frances. She starred in the grammar school operetta *Goldilocks.*

In a self-pitying and theatrical pose during the last years of her life, she said that she had been relegated to the chorus in school plays in Lancaster because of bad grades, when, in fact, she was always the lead and on the honor roll as well. During her later years she viewed Lancaster not as a place of happy times but as the place where her childhood ended. This would explain why she later thought that she was not wanted and accepted as a child and why she said, "no one was allowed to play with me and my sisters. . . ."[1] She was "miserable" all the time; she had no friends. Although many in Lancaster were hurt by these remarks, more were incredulously amused when in later years they read such statements by the adult Gumm child as "the people in the town were like the countryside around them—barren and harsh." Frances was far from ignored in Lancaster; and on the contrary, as one said: "The whole town thought the world of her; they treated her like a queen."

Some of Judy's recollections of her youth would be humorous or merely theatrical if they were not, in fact, symptomatic of how disturbed she had become. The myths and distortions showed how much she was in pain:

Actually, Mother was no good for anything except to create chaos and fear. She didn't like me because of my talent. She resented it because she could only play "Kitten on the Keys" like she was wearing boxing gloves. And when she sang, she had a crude voice. My sisters had lousy voices too. My father had a pretty good voice, but he wasn't allowed to talk. . . .[2]

Her memory of her mother's piano-playing is both devastating and amusing, especially in view of the fact of Ethel's musical talent. Turning on her sisters was something new, since she did not ordinarily attack them, at least not as much as she did her mother. The remark about her father is the closest she came to unkindness toward him; she could never bring herself to blame him for anything. She went on to explain her treatment during these years and what it resulted in:

... I was put on the stage 2½ years after I was born. I enjoyed it because, while I didn't get any affection from my family, I got applause from strangers. . . . Then I became a thing instead of a person. And I never wanted that. I certainly didn't ask to be a legend. I was totally unprepared for it. Honest to God, I'd have been better off if I'd gone to school like other girls, attended the proms, and married some nice man. I've been a successful commodity for almost 43 years, but I apparently have yet to prove I'm a successful person—except to myself. . . .

This was the low point of her despair, expressed in an interview in 1967. It was part of a consistent pattern of anger which demonstrated how tortured she really was in her last years. Not coincidentally, it usually paralleled a low point in her professional life, when she was unemployed and considered a high risk as a performer.

But people believed these statements. Others took their cue from her. "Ethel Gumm was that most intriguing figure of the entertainment world, a stage mother who chose to fulfill her own dreams and fantasies through the careers she planned for her daughters. . . . Ethel Gumm's obsession became ever more resolute and all-embracing, and the mother love she felt expressed itself through that enactment." This description by Norman Zierold in *The Child Stars,* given tacit approval by Judy in her own comments about her mother, became the accepted view of Ethel. In countless accounts of Judy Garland's life, Ethel took the blame for Judy's problems; Judy's version prevailed. She succeeded in covering the tracks of the real story, as well as perpetuating the untruths she may or may not have believed herself.

It is no wonder that close friends of the Gumms were stunned at Judy's recriminations against her family and that Judy became estranged from her sister Jimmie during the last decade of her life. Only a handful of people knew the true story of Frank and Ethel Gumm and the tragedy that engulfed them and their daughter.

Even Judy's last husband picks up the theme, telling us, "in most families love and adulation are given to the most gifted child, but not in the case of the Gumms." This is nonsense; the source and author of such a contention is none other than Judy herself. She left this impression with everyone, repeating the stories of neglect, repressing the truth she found impossible to recall. It wasn't all self-pity; she was cursing a fate which she traced back to Frank and Ethel. But the facts were painful and paradoxical. If there was any deprivation in her youth, it was one of excess—those years were too rich, there was too much indulgence. It would have taken a Herculean effort on her part to satisfy these needs for the remainder of her years. This is why she looked back in such anguish. Her childhood psyched her up for a life of adventure, unconditional love, and undivided attention, the spotlight always on her.

Judy's mercurial nature allowed for many different poses. It is comforting to think that this often splendid woman knew all too well that there wasn't the slightest hint of cruelty during her formative years. When she was lucid about those years (and happily riding another wave of success), she would admit, as she did to Shana Alexander in 1961: "I had great fun as a little girl. We played backstage. Then I went on, sang, took bows, came off and had my mother do my ringlets up again. People always applauded and it was all rather pleasant."[3] When asked by Adela Rogers St. Johns in a 1945 interview (a good period of her life), about how her career began, Judy responded: "I think it all just came about sort of naturally, you know."

She never really knew. She could only express her loss obliquely through her intuition and her art. Deans and Pinchot tell us that in her last years she read books such as *Citizen Hearst* and *Nicholas and Alexandra*. She "brooded over the tragic fate" of the protagonists in them. Was there a light of recognition in such tales? Did she see a parallel between Orson Welles' film fascimile of Hearst's life in *Citizen Kane* and her own? Could she, who gained everything and lost everything, see a similarity between herself and the character who became a great person but who was forever at a loss to pick up the thread of his blissful life and the love he thought was denied him? Judy, too, searched.

In February 1930 the grammar school in Lancaster loaned some of their students to perform as extras in a high school production of the *Gypsy Rover,* in which Mary Jane starred. Frances was one of the "little children" in the play. In one scene in which the children climb up on the lap of "Sir Toby Lyon, a society butterfly," she upstaged the others. During one scene, as the children clambered into the lap of Sir Toby, who was played by a six-foot-four-inch student, Frances climbed up his legs, fell down; and to the delight of the audience, climbed right up again undeterred.

The music teacher at the high school, Miss Kinnamon, who directed the show, was an occasional visitor at the Gumm home. She was taken with the vivacity of the family, finding them "fascinating." She considered Ethel an admirable woman with much stamina, who kept a tight rein on the girls. Miss Kinnamon felt that Ethel was a good mother, one who kept her daughters fashionably dressed, particularly with their lively, colorful hats. After the *Gypsy Rover* show Miss Kinnamon came to the Gumms' house to talk to Ethel about an upcoming show which was to include Frances. Ethel was rolling some dough for baking, and Frances was helping. Ethel corrected Frances about something, and Frances pouted for quite a while, intermittently smiling at Miss Kinnamon and then returning to her pouting.

Miss Kinnamon thought Frances would have a good voice for opera, "a long voice, with great volume and capacity," but she realized that the Gumms were not interested in such music, so Frances would not be given the opportunity to find out. Frances was "assertive, not spoiled, and not backward. She knew what she wanted as a child, and she had great spirit and vitality."

She recalls Ethel rehearsing Frances and complaining about "Baby's Scotch wrists"—large, long, awkward wrists, and ugly, according to Ethel who felt they detracted from Frances's performance. Ethel advised Frances, whose use of her hands would become a hallmark of her singing

Frank Gumm with family friend in early 1930s, Lancaster, California. *Courtesy of the Tropico Gold Camp Museum*

style, to "leave your hands out of it, keep them quiet, let your voice and face tell it all."

Miss Kinnamon remembered Frank as quite a charmer. He was very talented, she thought, with "an uninhibited style, always at ease when singing." She compared his voice to that of Al Jolson, feeling that Frank could have been a success in the popular music field if that had been his goal.

Frank could be persuasive. He was an excellent dancer whom every lady in the valley wanted to dance with on Saturday nights. Miss Kinnamon said he would sometimes ask her to dance, especially when he wanted a favor such as playing the church organ the next day. She also witnessed his occasional bursts of temper, as once when he proclaimed: "I've had it with this town, the way they treat my girls."

These outbursts were Frank's way of venting his agitation about both the renewal of his homosexual urges and the apparent loosening of family bonds. Other than these quirks of temperament, Frank wasn't yet a subject of scrutiny in Lancaster. Although he recognized his pursuits to be self-destructive, in light of his relationship with Ethel, they probably brought him some fulfillment. An understanding of Frank Gumm by the people of Lancaster would come gradually. Years later an acquaintance said: "Frank Gumm was a homo . . . most people knew it . . . although most of the time he did his thing in L.A." Another person who had fond memories of the Gumms 50 years earlier, said: "there were unsavory . . . unsavory stories about Frank Gumm. . . . [I] was glad they left town . . . they didn't fit in. . . ."

Another Lancaster resident remembers that "Frank Gumm could talk his way into or out of anything." One day when he, Frank, and several other men went into Los Angeles to play golf, Frank suggested going to Grauman's Chinese Theater to see the movie that was premiering that night. It was May 27, 1930, and Howard Hughes' Hell's Angels, starring Jean Harlow, was opening. Frank arranged to get them into the theater. When Miss Harlow arrived Frank went up to the car and opened the door for her. While his friends cajoled him, shouting "Who are you?" Frank yelled back: "I'm Rin Tin Tin's cousin."

In Lancaster, then as well as years later, there was the notion that the Gumms were Jewish, which had no basis in fact. Their ethnic origin was Scotch-Irish. Those who maintained that the Gumms were Jewish were merely connecting Ethel's ambition and determination with Jewish stereotypes. Whenever he was asked, Frank said enthusiastically: "We're Irish!" But notion persists; many townspeople still believe that the Gumms were Jewish.

That May 1930 Frances took a leading role in a musical recital with Miss Kinnamon, in which they introduced 36 piano students of another music teacher in Lancaster. Frances not only served as a mistress of ceremonies, but was enlisted to perform, saved for the last in order to keep the audience from leaving early; for it was already known throughout the valley that she was an attraction worth waiting for. When her turn came—after 35 piano pieces—she sang a ballad and did a dance.

Despite continued theatrical appearances, all of the girls did well in school. Virginia was on the honor roll in the sixth grade, and Frances made it in the second grade. When Frances was invited to a birthday party at Easter, she won a prize for finding the most Easter eggs.

The Gumms and their close friends, the Gilmores and the Goods, frequently played bridge. The Goods also lived on Cedar Street. Harry Good was a member of the school board, and Anna Good was a long-time employee at the Valley Theater. They would come to "swear by the Gumms," and years later, when Frances was famous, they "would never hear anything bad about Judy."

The second Meglin movie, a sound and technicolor featurette, was premiered in Los Angeles at the Warner's Downtown and Hollywood theaters; within a month Frank showed it at his theater. It was entitled "A Holiday in Storyland." The trio did a harmony number, "When the Butterflies Kiss the Buttercups Goodnight." Valley people saw Frances at the age of seven make her film solo debut, singing "Blue Butterfly."

On St. Patrick's Day, the Gumms celebrated at a local party. Frank led off with "Danny Boy" and sang other Irish ballads. In the spring Jimmie graduated from the eighth grade. Ethel was at the piano, and Virginia sang "Gypsy Love Song" and "Brahms Lullaby." The school term ended with a lavish party for Frances's eighth birthday; the local paper reported that "the little hostess was the recipient of many lovely gifts." It was also reported that Ethel and the girls would establish "summer quarters" at Ocean Park.

Since the Gumms were prospering, the family separation for the summer could be explained as one of fashion, a vacation by the sea away from the heat in Lancaster. Professional reasons were not given this time, although the summer would see such activity. The fact was, Ethel wanted to get away badly. Professional goals for the children, as well as a growing, if unspoken, distaste for the hot, isolated town, camouflaged the discord between Ethel and Frank. Ethel seldom put any of her feelings into words; instead she sublimated them through theatrical activities that required frequent absences from Lancaster.

There were many reasons now for Ethel's break with Lancaster. The absences concealed several motives. She kept the potential for, or the reality of, gossip from her children. She dreaded a repeat of the Grand Rapids experience. Had Frances begun to overhear her mother's harsh charges through the walls about her father's "immorality"? "My parents were separating and getting back together all the time . . . the trouble really had begun in our family in Lancaster . . . it was a great contrast to the green friendliness of Minnesota. . . ."[4]

Ethel had long since made her accommodation with conventional morality. At the age of 35 she was inclined to look for consolation in an affair outside her faded marriage. Frances was to see things in Los Angeles and Lancaster that would hurt her deeply.

They vacationed at the beach in Santa Monica where they rented a house which would also serve as their headquarters for the summer vaudeville activity. Frank came to visit for a few days at a time, and for the Fourth of July they all went to San Diego where the girls were appearing with a larger group of entertainers called the "Hollywood Starlets." This was a group the girls had appeared with before and from which they had taken their stage name, "The Hollywood Starlets Trio." Frank returned to Lancaster, and Ethel and the girls settled in for the rest of the summer.

The Goods, Gilmores, and other friends spent a few days at Ocean Park. In the afternoons and evenings the girls would go downtown to appear at various theaters, nightclubs, or hotels in Santa Monica. They were also at work on a third Meglin film short, while Ethel took a position as accompanist for the Hollywood School of the Dance. At the end of the summer, they returned to Lancaster.

There were few excursions out of town that fall and winter, not even for the Meglin Christmas show at Loew's. Somehow Frank managed to keep them at home for the holidays. Back in school, Frances made the third grade honor roll. At the Valley Theater the highlight of the season was the showing of *The Wedding of Jack and Jill,* another Meglin film made for Warner Brothers. In it, theatergoers saw Frances, aged eight, in a film musical solo, singing prophetically the featured song, "Hang on to the Rainbow."

Music again filled the Cedar Street home. That fall Ethel was working on a song she had written and was trying to get published. It was a simple, but pretty, waltz entitled "Deep, Deep in My Heart." It would be nice to think that Ethel had some prescience about how apropos the lyrics were to Frances's emerging career; but she was thinking about her own life—her needs, her marriage. This combination of self-pity and resolve was typical of her and would become typical of Judy. In the song Ethel is clearly absorbed in herself:

> Did I hear you sigh little girl?
> Life's too short to cry little girl.
>
> Let those eyes of blue just keep
> smilin' thru and, remember I love you.

Judy's life was so full of drama that Liza's statement that she lived 80 lives in one almost seems accurate. Her first comeback—at 29 a return to the stage she left in the mid-1930s, to the Palace Theater in New York —was one of the most dramatic and stirring events of her life. The event had such an impact that it is now a part of New York City cultural history and an American show business legend.

Was this real pathos or merely "show business?" Was Judy Garland great because the name slides off the tongue so easily, or was the come-back at the Palace an achievement of the human spirit? In light of everything that happened to Judy, "The Palace" seemed inevitable.

Her spectacular film career at MGM, where she sang strongly and clearly for 15 years, was finished. Illness, temperament, recalcitrance, ex-ploitation by the studio, lack of personal satisfaction and peace of mind— all led to the dissolution of this association. Her life was shattered, and in a symbolic, but nonetheless serious plea for help, she acted out her utter despair. On June 21, 1950, a few days after MGM suspended her, a headline in the *Los Angeles Times* read: JUDY GARLAND SLASHES THROAT AFTER FILM ROW. The news account went on to say that the attempt, a superficial wound to the throat with a broken glass, had to do with "career troubles." "The actress made her stage debut at the age of 3 with her parents, vaudeville performers, but most of her life and educa-tion has been at MGM. . . ." Tragically this was true. More than half of her life had been spent under the auspices of the studio. The days of her youth were merely a dim memory. The two lives did not balance out.

The qualitative difference was still evident as MGM released their version of her suicide attempt, saying that after the incident, "she emerged weeping, remorseful and repentant." This was her last suspension from MGM; with the ensuing publicity of the suicide attempt, the spell of the studio was finally broken. Her film career over at the age of 28, Frances Gumm was on her own.

As early as the late thirties, when Frances was a rising MGM star, Ethel Gumm said that Judy "liked the stage" better than the movies "because of the audiences." Ethel, who had always geared her dream for the girls more toward vaudeville and radio, had once asked L. B. Mayer to release Judy from her contract. Ethel believed that Judy would be happier on the stage.

It is ironic that the MGM period, which was responsible for Judy's great success and international fame, was recalled as a grim, unhappy time for her. "Before MGM," she said, "I enjoyed being myself."

Whatever happened during those Hollywood years—fame and riches, love and marriages, divorces and breakdowns, hedonism and addiction—the fact is that her childhood as the center of attention onstage and off left her with unquenchable emotional needs. A friend commented: "Judy must be wanted every minute of every hour of every day —not just when she's on the stage. It's her lifeblood." During the years as a movie star these needs couldn't be met, the personal contentment and emotional satisfaction of her childhood could not be matched. The work schedule as Hollywood's most prolific and popular musical star soon took its toll. Judy became unhappy, nervous, and recalcitrant, while fighting a hereditary weight problem and subsequent pill addiction. When she performed she did it splendidly, but in the long run, working for a corporation with millions of dollars involved, the fun went out of singing and dancing; she was no longer doing it because it came naturally. The idyl of her childhood and the dream of success had turned into a nightmare, as it is in the fairy tale of the girl who wanted the red shoes and when she put them on, couldn't stop dancing. After saying "I just didn't want to live any more," looking back in anguish at her life, she still had too much will to live to just give up.

In an attempt to pick up the pieces of her career and life, she decided in 1951 to return to the stage as a solo performer. She had come full circle. She had returned to vaudeville.

It was as if the MGM years had been a long detour or hibernation. This new freedom to put on her own show would permit the apotheosis of Judy Garland. Her career seemingly ended, the years of her greatest triumphs were ahead. For two decades she would artistically transcend herself; as the *New York Times* put it, "something of an anachronism: a music hall performer in an era in which music halls were obsolete."

Thus she made her great comeback in 1951. People felt compassion for the singer who had cheered them through 30 movies. That she was as human and vulnerable as they thought she had feigned to be before the camera elicited a wave of sympathy and support for her. She said she felt this from audiences wherever she went.

The Palace Theater in New York, which had been the royal quarters and summit of American vaudeville, comprised of thousands of lesser houses during the peak of vaudeville, had yielded to movies in 1933. Now in 1951, after a successful tryout in London at the Palladium and some other European spots, Judy came to the Palace to reopen the theater. Robert Garland, the man from whom her last name was taken, said of the Palace revival: "It is as if vaudeville had been waiting somewhere for her to come along. And she, in turn, for vaudeville."

In her return to live audiences, she succeeded in blending her life and career more agreeably. Her opening at the Palace on October 16, 1951, was covered by the news media throughout the country. Sold out four weeks in advance, the opening night audience was stunned by Judy's 55-minute performance. On the streets reporters asked people for their impression of what had happened at the Palace that night and why there was all that nostalgia. With the reopening of the Palace as a vaudeville house and the subsequent breaking of all Palace records, which would not be outdistanced by any other performer, she had "begun to acquire that authority and command which were to make her the most potent stage performer of her generation."[5]

At the Palace, singing twice a day for 19 weeks, Frances Gumm redeemed herself in her own mind, and the basis for a legend was renewed. As she had in childhood, she gave the audience everything she had. Many critics perceived something more profound beneath the surface enthusiasm.

What young actress of serious drama excels the sureness and completeness of Judy Garland? . . . What Judy communicates all the time is a young-womanly wistfulness, an unselfconscious heartbreak which is not so much pitiful as disarmingly human. Even when her songs describe something missed, something lost, we feel that she gives more than we do, because she has experienced more. . . . Her power—and power is not too strong a word for the concentrated intensity of her delivery—lies not only in the sentiments she expresses, but in the fundamental strength required to be a really outstanding stage figure. It is the power of leadership over people through aggressive will. It is the power that rises from the desire and ability *to give.* . . . Judy brings her excitement right on stage with her: all she has to do is to appear before us and sing.[6]

Of the same show, Clifton Fadiman wrote:

I saw Judy at the Palace theater. . . . Where lay the magic? Why did we grow silent, self-forgetting, our faces lit as with so many candles, our eyes glittering with unregarded tears? Why did we call her back again and again and again . . . as we listened to her voice, with its unbelievable marriage of volume and control, as we watched her, in her tattered tramp costume . . . ? She was gaiety itself, yearning itself. She wasn't being watched or heard. She was only being felt. . . . The theater dead? I have rarely seen it more alive than when Judy Garland, crouched on the edge of the stage in a darkened vaudeville house that had seen a thousand animal acts and brassy comedians, voiced a lost child's pitiful lament. . . .[7]

As 1931 began, the Antelope Valley *Ledger-Gazette* published their front-page New Year's message, entitled THE BIRTH OF NEW HOPES:

And 1930 with all its heartaches and failures is gone, vanished forever; 1931 has dawned—like the good fairy that vanquishes the wicked witch. . . . We hope for great prosperity, for harmony, for success. And have them we shall. The finger of destiny points clearly. . . .

The first concrete success of the year was for Ethel, whose song was broadcast over a San Francisco radio station. Frank was showing movies such as *Let Us Be Gay,* with Norma Shearer, and *Little Caesar,* with Edward G. Robinson. His new advertisement read:

The VALLEY THEATER
"The Home of Better Pictures"
R.C.A. Talkie Equipment
FRANK A. GUMM Prop.
LANCASTER, CALIF.

In February he ran a western and touted the talents of a boyhood resident of Lancaster in his theater ad:

Feb 17–18–19 "The Big Trail" one of the greatest achievements of the screen, that enjoyed a long run at Grauman's Chinese. JOHN WAYNE, the hero of this masterpiece, attended Grammar School here in Lancaster, and is remembered by his classmates . . . YOU CAN'T AFFORD TO MISS THIS MARVELOUS SHOW.

Wayne had indeed attended the school a few yards away from the Gumm home, riding from outside town on horseback to attend classes where Baby Gumm was now in school. Frank was boosting local pride in this fact, as well as assuring good box office.

In Los Angeles the Gumms ended a professional relationship of some duration. At a Saturday matinee at the Hollywood Pantages Theater, the girls performed for the last time with the Meglin Kiddies. Ethel wanted to try vaudeville more independently now that the trio had shown its potential as a solo act. Coincidentally, about the same time Ethel severed ties with the Meglin Studio, Mrs. Temple brought her little girl Shirley in for dance lessons.

Judy remembered overnight stays when they made trips to Los Angeles. There was a stay at the Gates Hotel; from there they could walk down to Hillstreet or Broadway where Ethel arranged auditions and bookings. The Gates was associated in Judy's mind with some trouble between her mother and father. She recalled staying there with her mother for several weeks. When Judy resurrected unhappy memories of these days, she recalled the Gates as a symbol of discord, but if Ethel was unhappy during these times, she covered it up, burying herself in what was now becoming her life's work. The girls were becoming tired of the long, monotonous rides and did not want to go with their mother unless a definite booking or audition had been arranged, so Ethel, who never seemed weary of the trips, made many of them alone.

As far as the Sunday night performances at the Valley Theater were concerned, Frank never forced the girls to appear. There was one period of several months when they didn't sing at the theater. Some of Mary Jane's and Virginia's companions felt they often tried to play down their show business activities. A good friend of Jimmie's said that she hated performing. Janie and Jimmie were getting older; they were interested in what all young girls were interested in at that time. Frances, too, became weary, not of performing, but of the long trips and began to show signs of recalcitrance. Going on nine, she tended more toward childish pursuits, staying home and playing with Muggsie. She also had her eye out for the boys. Eddie White sometimes came by and walked to school with her each morning, and Buddy Welch, a classmate, was the object of an early crush. Another, Gayland Reed, whom Frances recalled having sent her a 25-cent valentine instead of the usual 5- or 10-cent ones, was always remembered as her "first love."

They moved next door to a large, beige, stucco house on the corner of Cedar and Newgrove, where there was more room for practicing, as well as entertaining. It was one of the biggest—and oldest—houses in town.

Frank could be strict with the children, and he wouldn't tolerate any misbehavior at the theater. Although he was effusive and indulgent toward his children, he would, on occasions, give spankings to both Frances and Muggsie. In comparison with Frank, Ethel did not appear to be as warm in Muggsie's eyes; she thought Ethel cold, not one to embrace or coddle Frances. On some occasions, when Ethel was in the city for prolonged stays and Frank was home alone, Muggsie recalled that he would play and sing love songs or sit on the front porch in the evening and sing lullabys to Frances and Muggsie.

That year Ethel compromised; they wouldn't have to perform during the school term. But she planned for them to take part in Maurice Kusell's juvenile revue in July. Within a month of Ethel's first visit to the Kusell Studio, he had met her daughters. He could see that they had enough know-how to participate in his revue. During the next few months they took dance lessons at the studio. Kusell soon became aware of Ethel's abilities; she would make arrangements for the orchestra in the musical extravaganza. Kusell found her charming, and a talented musician who was an excellent pianist. He recalled her at this time as being short and plump, not very attractive but nice and easygoing. He liked her, always thinking of her as a normal mother and not a stage mother.

Kusell would get to know the three Gumm sisters who would at times be in the studio almost daily, trained by the staff or by himself. He said they liked to perform and had a "first-class act." He remembers Mary Jane as a sweet girl and Jimmie as the prettiest. But Frances, he said, "was my most talented student." He thought that she was happy, never obnoxious, as many young stage kids were. He never noted any reluctance on her part to perform. Sometimes with an enrollment of a thousand kids, he recalled that Frances, the most talented, was never patronizing; she didn't call him "Uncle Maurice" as did many children prompted by their mothers. When she sang for him, she "belted out a song as strong as Ethel Merman."

With Kusell's studio as their new base of operations, their only out-of-town trips were to plan and rehearse for the July show, "Stars of Tomorrow," at the Wilshire-Ebell Theater. With the trio dormant for six months, Ethel concentrated on rounding up and rehearsing the orchestra. She was semi-employed and would be in the future either salaried by Mr. Kusell or performing services in exchange for dance lessons for Janie, Jimmie, and Frances.

For her ninth birthday Frances was given a party on the lawn of the house. Following that, rehearsals for Kusell's show increased. It was to run a week, but Ethel planned to stay in Los Angeles for at least six weeks to try and get in some other engagements.

On opening night all of the Gumms were in the city with some Lancaster friends to see the 25-scene show with a cast of 200 (instead of the originally planned 300). As the curtain went up, friends of the family saw Ethel doubling as pianist and conducter of the eight-piece orchestra. The capacity audience saw the Gumm sisters featured in a spectacular song-and-dance number, "Puttin' on the Ritz." Kusell recalls that they were "sensational." Frances shined. On this night her special talents did not go unnoticed, but it would be a few months before she reaped any benefits. The critics liked the show, including "the Gumm sisters in harmony songs."

After the show Kusell took them to a party at James Cruze's, a friend of Kusell's and a noted Hollywood film director. The girls sang at the party. Maurice also introduced them to George Frank of the Frank and Dunlap talent agency. Frank handled stars such as James Cagney and George Bancroft. He talked with Ethel and praised the girls, asking her to keep in touch with him.

They stayed in Beverly Hills after the Kusell show had ended, vacationing in addition to making appearances. The girls sang anywhere there was a booking, at vaudeville houses, at clubs and hotels such as the Trocadero, Beverly-Wilshire, Biltmore Bowl, and Cocoanut Grove.

In the valley late that summer the pear harvest was at its peak.

Ethel and the girls drove back to Lancaster into that pretty, high, desert setting. For Frances there was a feeling that she lived in two worlds. It took the return trip home to show her that the two worlds were compatible.

At a PTA event Frances earned more applause and a newspaper notice: "Little Frances Gumm captivated the audience with her two lively songs." She returned to Frank's moviehouse, sharing the bill with Marion Davies in *Five and Ten* as "An added attraction—FRANCES GUMM IN SONGS." She sang for nothing; it was fun to be on the family stage. This was her real world.

After the "Stars of Tomorrow" show closed, Ethel took Frances to see George Frank. Ethel didn't know it then, but Frances had been discovered on the stage of the Wilshire-Ebell; her big break had come.

Ethel had agreed to put Frances under contract with the agency, which would seek screen and stage work for her. A contract was drawn up, the first the agency had ever given to a child. This would mean prolonged stays in Los Angeles, since Frances was signed for stage, screen, radio, and television for five years. She was also rechristened Frances Gayne. She was nine years old.

What this would do to the family, what affect a career would have on Frances, was not discussed at home. Ethel, assuming Frances's success would be welcomed by all, took Frank's approval for granted, changed her name, and released the story to the local newspaper. On September 4, 1931 the *Ledger-Gazette* announced the news to its readers and printed a front-page picture of Frances. On the same page the columnist Arthur Brisbane discussed the exorbitant salaries of Hollywood performers, concluding that "nothing is cheaper, no matter what it earns, than the exceptional personality."

Only the ensuing stress and argument between the elder Gumms at home could alter the apparent destiny of Frances. Ethel was incredulous to find that her enthusiasm wasn't shared by the other members of the family, including Frances. None of them liked the thought of leaving Lancaster. Frances loved entertaining, but with the family, not alone and away from her friends. Frank thought she was too young for a career. Despite how good she was, none of the girls could imagine performing

Portrait of Frances at age nine in 1931. *Courtesy of Antelope Valley* Ledger-Gazette

141

View of Antelope Avenue with the Valley Theater on the right, Lancaster, California, in the 1930s. *Courtesy of John Reber*

without the others. As Jimmie said later, Frances "never liked to work alone. She hated it."

She was introduced to the valley people with the headline, "ON THE STAGE FRANCES GAYNE (FRANCES GUMM) in a group of song specialties." But two weeks later, family sentiment had decided the matter. Ethel had been told no, and on September 20, Frances reemerged at the Valley Theater: FRANCES GUMM WILL APPEAR AGAIN IN A GROUP OF POPULAR SONG NUMBERS, SUNDAY AFTERNOON AT 4, AND IN THE EVENING AT 9:30. Frank's victory would be a pyrrhic one, but for now, Frances had a reprieve.

10

FRIDAY AFTERNOONS

*I didn't particularly enjoy my life
as a child entertainer, but I can't
recall hating it. . . . I enjoyed being
on the stage.*

It was autumn in the California desert. Around Thanksgiving the annual
Alfalfa Festival took place, and townspeople engaged in three-legged
races, sack races, women's nail-driving, and greased-pole-climbing. RKO
provided the live vaudeville for the event, so the Gumms could relax
and enjoy the festival. There were cold winds that weekend. It might be
a cold winter.

Late that year Frances was again singing at local events, with one
show in Tehachapi where she performed at a ceremony of the Order of
the Eastern Star. Although it wasn't really a professional appearance, she
knocked them out again, singing "For You, For You."

Then she and Frank drove to Bakersfield where she sang before
1,000 delighting them with "Sweet and Lovely."

The audiences in Tehachapi and Bakersfield were seeing a preview
of a talent that would soon be set loose in the golden era of film musicals, a talent of almost mythical dimensions, ready to be unleashed as soon
as vaudeville expired and the age of innocence ended for the Gumms.

Judy Garland will always be an innocent. Much later Burt Korall described that quality, along with her MGM image and impact:

145

In the "Wizard of Oz" . . . as Dorothy, the wide-eyed innocent, Miss Garland
touched audiences deeply. . . . Once the studio realized the impact the girl
had made, the die was cast. Her image became fixed. Until the conclusion of
her MGM affiliation in 1950, she played paragons of virtue. Graciously
childlike, always seeking to please, she smiled bravely in the face of adversity,
cried glycerine tears, or bubbled over with candy-cane happiness. Lavish,
beautifully mounted musicals were her medium. Through a series of them,
all structured to make audiences forget daily cares and sing and pretend along
with the cast, Miss Garland sang vibrantly or with built-in sadness. She was
a plastic figure who could sing about *real* emotions.[1]

Critics and audiences would quite accurately describe Judy's "heart-
catching" aura, her singing as plaintive and poignant, and her acting as
sincere and convincing. Through the Metro films in which she consistently conveyed strength and gaiety, happiness and confidence, audiences
believed—and they were partially correct—that this was the real Judy.
They were not aware, perhaps because of the frivolous, light-hearted
musicals, that she was consciously polishing her special kind of artistic
expression.

This need for expression, which cannot be underestimated in a life
so thoroughly identified with the stage, was unmistakably linked to her
formative years. Virginia called Frances the "poet" of the family; there is
no doubt that her feelings began to be sublimated through her singing in
those years. With no knowledge of her early life, Harold Clurman intui-
tively describes the basis of her art in response to her show at the Palace
Theater in the mid-fifties, citing the metamorphosis of "the essential
purity of her performance" in contrast to her first appearance at the
Palace in 1951.

Her songs are often slushily emotional—that is, empty of specific feeling—
but she informs them with the anguished lyricism of a heavily laden experience. She is at bottom a sort of early twentieth century country kid, but the
marks of the big-city wounds of our day are upon her. Her poetry is not only
in the things she has survived, but in a violent need to pour them forth in
a vivid popular form, which makes her the very epitome of the theatrical
personality. The tension between the unctuously bright slickness which is
expected of her medium and environment and the fierceness of what her

being wants to cry out produces something positively orgiastic in the final effect. . . .[2]

She was the country kid. By the end of her childhood she would have an overpowering need to give out her highly emotional song. Another critic, Marjorie Rosen, concurs. Judy was "the girl next door who somehow strayed into unprotected territory."[3] In her first feature film, *Pigskin Parade*, she comes running out of a melon patch and announces to some passing sightseers: "I can sing! Do you want to hear me?", repeating it three times. She's going to show them what a country girl can do. No other clarion call could be more appropriate for the young vaudevillian who was to electrify audiences for the next four decades.

In her film career David Shipman notes what he calls "warmth poised on the brink of sadness."[4] This bittersweet quality is most striking in the movie *Meet Me in St. Louis*, in which Judy is seen in a story of American family life threatened by change. She conveys unrestrained emotion as she sings to her little sister "Have Yourself a Merry Little Christmas." Viewed today, her rendition of the song is so touching and possesses such a sense of loss that it is impossible not to associate it with 23-year-old Judy's piquant memories of her youth. In the movie she can be seen eyes heavy, her lips trembling, as she sings of hope, expressing the ambivalent emotions of longing and nostalgia.

At Christmas there was the usual caroling, the free show for the kids, and family reunions. A white blanket of snow covered the valley, and the Mint Canyon road was open only to cars with chains, as Ethel and Frances headed for Los Angeles where Frances was to solo for a week at the Warner's Theater downtown. It was Christmas eve.

Frances's strong "healthy voice," as she described it later, was becoming lyrical, full of rhythmic vitality. Although she was more in demand as a soloist, she was ambivalent about the stage. She felt accepted and comfortable while performing; she liked the applause and her life as a child entertainer, hating it only when it was no longer fun. All her happy memories of performing had to do with her family, but now her talents were becoming larger than those of the others.

Ethel got Frances an engagement at the Cocoanut Grove, singing with the orchestra. The skinny little nine-year-old with the "great big voice," with her large brown eyes and turned-up nose, became—at least for a little while—a big band singer of the thirties. Musicians began to notice her voice—its clarity, combined with instinctive emotion and conviction in delivery—as well as the way she physically threw herself into a song. Once she started singing, with or without her sisters, she loved it. To make it more relaxed and informal for her, Ethel took along Janie and Jimmie or some of the Gilmore children or Muggsie for the shows.

Performing wasn't the problem; the problem was leaving Lancaster without her sisters, to fill an engagement or audition. In 1932 and thereafter, the trips became more frequent. Frances began to dread the departures and sometimes all but refused to go. Everything was fine until the weekend. Frances "hated Fridays," according to her friend Ina Mary. Just when school was out, free to play for the weekend, it was time to leave for Los Angeles. Ethel would have the car packed with the music and suitcases of costumes and gear. As soon as Frances got home from school, they left. Muggsie often witnessed this scene. It upset the whole family to see Frances cry, complaining of a stomach upset while her hair was being put up in ringlets.

Her world was becoming fragmented. No wonder she later recalled Lancaster mainly as a place of constant departures and arrivals, separated by a long drive, to be repeated week after week. Her life was becoming more and more a dual existence, in which it was increasingly difficult to bridge the gap. If she had little regard for Lancaster later, it wasn't because she was unhappy there but because it was the place where her childhood was taken away from her.

Here was the basis, in part, of her love-hate relationship with her mother, the weakening of her father in her eyes, and a clue to some of her later ambivalence toward performing, especially under circumstances not completely to her liking.

Her resistance was not to show business but to the tide that was pulling her away from the ordinary lives of little girls: best friend, home, weekend play. This was not merely a childish tantrum against parental authority but an understandable sign of temperament. Perhaps

Frank could have prevailed, but Ethel had the upper hand in managing the girls' careers. On the other hand, since she was reacting to something that was so much in the family tradition—vaudeville—she may have appeared unreasonable.

To avoid the Friday-afternoon scenes, Ethel tried to get a booking for the trio or take a friend along to accompany Frances for the weekend. This was effective, for, on many trips, Muggsie went along. She saw those early days of her friend's theatrical indoctrination. Her companionship helped calm Frances. They played games such as License Plates to pass the time on the way to Los Angeles. Often they stopped at a restaurant in Saugus or Los Angeles. Muggsie would stay with Frances until show time and then sit in the audience and watch her perform. If it was an audition, she watched Ethel at the piano while Frances did her number.

In Lancaster many formed opinions of Ethel that never changed. They remember her taking the girls on tour, often staying away for long periods, and leaving Frank alone. Judging by appearances and the end result of these trips, people recalled Ethel with some disfavor. One neighbor of the family said she "had no use for her. Ethel didn't care about anything except getting one of those kid's names known." Another felt that she "neglected her husband" during the Lancaster years because of her ambitions. Others recall her "forcing those kids, Babe Gumm especially," to perform and tour. Another thought that "Babe was used" throughout her life, starting with her mother who "was a pushy movie-mother who thought she was better than the local yokels." Indeed, Ethel's objectives became more and more difficult to understand.

Frances's life was hard for her friends to understand, too, as she returned to school on Monday and told her friends matter-of-factly about how over the weekend she had sung with a big orchestra at the Warner's Theater or the Orpheum or some other Los Angeles theater.

Judy often thought about Ethel's motivations and the strange pattern of her youth. Years later she said of her mother's actions: "She was a lonely and determined woman, and I guess I'm the same way."[5]

In 1958 Judy played a two-week engagement at the Los Angeles Cocoanut Grove in another comeback, this time billed as "Miss Show Business." A reviewer commented that "the little girl who had been down so many times—but never counted out . . . proved again she is one of the great troupers of all time." In the family tradition she introduced her 12-year-old daughter Liza who joined her mother in a duet of "Swanee." Perhaps it was the presence of her own daughter or maybe just the nostalgia of playing the Grove that caused Judy to reminisce about her mother. With mixed emotions she mentioned Ethel each night during the performance. Now 36 she could look back almost 30 years to her childhood when her intrepid mother more or less dragged her little girl around Los Angeles looking for bookings and auditions. She told her audience: "a long time ago . . . I came down [to the Grove] one day with my mother, and she talked the orchestra leader into letting me sing a song."

It was a long time ago now, almost an eternity to Judy. So much had happened to Frances Gumm and to her relationship with her mother. When Judy achieved fame at MGM two decades before, she and her mother were very close and devoted to one another. But as time went on, and Judy was married and divorced, suffered from overwork and emotional crises, the chasm between them grew. She blamed her mother for most of her problems, and obviously this had a basis. She was unhappy, which in the Hollywood of the 1940s was well known. There were also rumors about a conflict between Judy and her mother. Rumors of an abnormal childhood and financial exploitation by her mother were circulated.

Earlier in the forties, when Judy's first signs of emotional instability flared up, Ethel could not see that there were serious problems ahead for her daughter. "Hollywood can't hurt my daughter! As long as Judy is the girl I know she is, movies or movie life can't hurt her. She is happiest when she is busy, and you know the old saying, 'the devil finds uses for idle hands.' . . . Judy wants to go on making pictures, minding her own business, developing her mind, building a sane and normal future for herself." Work had been a cure-all for Ethel; perhaps it had helped maintain her sanity. In saying what she did about the effect of Hollywood on Judy, Ethel was as resolute as ever in believing that what was right for her was right for her daughter.

In the early Hollywood years Ethel shared in the glory and riches of Judy's success. This apparently continued even after Judy married and Ethel had remarried. Ethel's second husband was William Gilmore of Lancaster, whose family had been so close to the Gumms during the Lancaster days. By the late forties that marriage had also failed, as had Judy's first two marriages, and the gulf between them became greater as Ethel moved to Texas to be near her daughter Jimmie. She became, of all things, though quite naturally, a movie theater manager. Judy was still the queen of MGM musicals.

In June 1950, when Judy was distraught and her movie career was disintegrating, she attempted suicide following a suspension from her latest movie at MGM; her mother rushed from Texas to be with her. The press reported that Judy wouldn't see Ethel. The controversy got a lengthy airing in the newspapers. Reacting to being kept from her daughter, Ethel said she'd "get in if I have to kick the doors down. I'm going to see my little girl." A friend of Judy's told a reporter that she would take Judy into her own home to give her "the loving treatment she should have had during childhood." Ethel replied that her daughter *had* been given "loving treatment during childhood," and that she wanted the world to know it. In a movie magazine article she protested, saying that Judy "was always a normal healthy girl . . . all that stuff is a lot of hooey. Judy had a wonderful childhood. She wanted to become an actress. It wasn't my idea. It was hers. . . . Her youth was fine and normal, and you won't find any trace of temperament or unhappiness there." Obviously Ethel was at a loss as to what had gone wrong.

Judy never really understood what went wrong either. During the controversy she never directly blamed her mother; it was her friends and associates who did. Judy later assumed this attitude toward her mother, when at low points in her career, she called Ethel "the real Wicked Witch of the West, who was no good for anything but to create chaos and fear."[6] But in an interview with a reporter who talked to both of them separately, Judy said: "nobody ever . . . forced me in any

Ethel with famous daughter, Judy, during MGM period, before their estrangement. *Courtesy of The Garlandia Collection of Wayne Martin*

way. I drove myself . . . it was my own doing." And Ethel, in turn, said Judy "was a sweet child, loving, generous, unselfish. . . ."

The relationship between them was obvious: their love for each other was obscured by bitterness, a bitterness that was unabated. "I always seem to be in my daughter's way," Ethel said about that time. Judy continually castigated her mother but admitted to her last husband that she "never really hated her." There is no question, however, of the powerful emotional influence her mother had over Judy.

In 1952 Judy married for the third time, to Sid Luft. It was the day after her thirtieth birthday. Soon after that, Ethel went to court, complaining that her daughter would not support her. She told a Hollywood reporter that show business life was not good for a child. "If you have a daughter," she said, "don't let her sing or dance. . . . We gave her everything she wanted. . . . Judy has been selfish all her life. That's my fault. I made it too easy for her. She worked, but that's all she ever wanted, to be an actress. She never said 'I want to be kind' or 'loved,' only 'I want to be famous.'" Ethel was in anguish over the course Judy's life had taken, although she never understood the events that had overwhelmed them and had led to this tragedy.

The extent of the tragedy was perceived by Paul Coates in his column in the *Los Angeles Mirror* in 1952:

In the early 30's Judy Garland and her mother, Mrs. Ethel Gumm, were a familiar sight at most of the vaudeville auditions around Hollywood. While Judy, a pert, wide-eyed child, sang, mamma accompanied her on the piano. Mrs. Gumm was a tenacious stage-mother. And it finally paid off. Her little girl became a big star. But yesterday I learned that Judy Garland's mother is working as a factory clerk now. The time card she punches at Douglas Aircraft in Santa Monica lists her as Mrs. Ethel Gilmore. . . . For many years Hollywood has been privately aware of the tragic rift between Judy and her mother. . . . Nobody can really know what has caused this obviously deep and terrifying resentment. Judy Garland's life has been marked by success and tragedy. Undoubtedly her mother's relentless driving was at least partly responsible for the success. But that same relentless driving could also be completely responsible for the tragedy this young artist has known. Miss Garland was never a child. At 3 years old she was already a "theatrical property"—first to her mother, then to Metro-Goldwyn-Mayer. It was a shockingly abnormal unbringing. And it was bound to have unhappy repercussions. Here they are: Judy Garland's net for one week's work at the Philharmonic Auditorium is $25,000. Her mother's take-home pay from the factory that same week will be a little over a dollar an hour.

But the results were even more irrevocable. The lonely and determined Ethel Gumm worked as a clerk at Douglas Aircraft. Her lawsuit had fallen through. Years later, Ethel's lawyer confirmed that Judy was at this time trying to make some arrangements to supply financial aid to her mother; but it was too late for a reconciliation. On January 6, 1953, the *Los Angeles Times* reported the end of the story:

JUDY GARLAND'S MOTHER FOUND DEAD IN CAR LOT. Mrs. Ethel Gilmore, mother of Judy Garland, was found dead yesterday in a Douglas Aircraft Co. parking lot at 27th St. and Ocean Park Blvd., Santa Monica. She apparently was the victim of a heart attack. The body of the 58-year-old onetime vaudeville performer, lately a Douglas employee, was found slumped in a half-kneeling position on the pavement between two cars. . . . Police said she had apparently driven to the plant yesterday morning, arriving at the parking lot at about 7:15 A.M. She was due to report to her $61-a-week clerk's job. . . . Police theorize that she was cutting between cars hurrying to work when she suffered the attack. . . .

And so the indefatigable Ethel Gumm died in a parking lot, characteristically "hurrying" to work.

On Thursday, January 8, 1953, last rites were given to Ethel Gumm at the Little Church of the Flowers in Forest Lawn Memorial Park. Mary Jane, Virginia, and Judy attended the funeral. The newspapers reported that the three sisters, who "were once known in show business as the Gumm sisters," arrived separately. The services were conducted by a family friend. Judy was deeply shocked by the loss of her mother. A family friend later told Judy that Ethel had recently told him that "she always stood behind her—in whatever she did." He said, "they always loved each other in their hearts."

Ethel's inability to grasp the events of her life or to perceive that her actions and their consequences might have created unhappiness for her and her daughter was evident in an interview with a Hollywood reporter. She tried to convey her bewilderment by telling the reporter about a conversation she had had with her daughter a few years earlier, about Judy's biggest contract signing at MGM: "Judy, think! You, Frances Gumm, getting $5,000 a week," Ethel told her. "Aren't you thrilled?" "Yes, Mama," said Judy, "but I always had everything I wanted."

Because of the Depression Frank lowered the price of admission at the Valley Theater from 50 to 35 cents for a "trial period." But most of the time, when someone came along who was out of work and didn't have the price of admission, Frank let him in free. With him, Southern hospitality always took precedence over business.

Even with a heavy professional schedule Frances found time for fun. In 1932 she did have everything she wanted. She was seen skating in front of the theater, looking "so skinny her legs were like pipestems." She was "happy-go-lucky." The trio still drew an audience in town, and many thought that the talents of the girls were about equal. Janie could put across a song with style, and Jimmie had a "good blues voice." But they had competition. Shirley Eyler, a former teacher who taught Janie and Jimmie, recalls that "Frances had such vitality, more life to her," adding: "the volume of her voice was unbelievable for such a small body." The two older sisters were "at times upset by all the attention paid to Frances," but they had to admit that Frances earned it.

One incident when Frances was 10 occurred while she was playing with some friends. She and her friends were running through some back lots in town. They ran through a vacant shack which housed some machinery, where Frances encountered her mother in what she later concluded was a rendezvous with a man all the girls knew. The man chased them off and was so angry that he referred to them from that day on as "brats."

This image could always be conjured up to intensify Judy's resentment toward Ethel, and surely it traumatized the trusting Frances who had witnessed her mother's indiscretion. In later life she assailed her mother for many things, always begrudging her this sin. Ironically she never became aware of her father's indiscretions. Ethel shielded her from them.

Before summer the weekend ads for the theater read: "Baby Gumm between shows" or "Baby Gumm will sing," with mama at the piano and dad standing in the back, smiling.

On one occasion that summer, Maurice Kusell, his wife, aunt, and her son came to visit. His aunt was Myrtle Stedman, a motion picture actress who would be known for her work in *Famous Mrs. Fair* and *School for Girls.* After dinner they all went to the theater to see Frances perform.

In May the PTA gave a musical. The Gumms, who were not scheduled to perform but were present, apparently in case of an emergency, were mentioned in the *Ledger-Gazette*:

Owing to a number of conflicting events, some of the numbers planned did not materialize, but those delightful entertainers, Mrs. Frank Gumm and Baby Gumm came to the rescue with "Only God Can Make a Tree" and "Cherie" sung by the little artist. Their music is always enthusiastically received everywhere, and is so graciously tendered.[7]

That summer would be a pivotal one for the trio. Ethel had secured an audition with an agent for the Fanchon and Marco shows, which was typical of the good vaudeville shows of the time. They weren't pure vaudeville, but instead were "unit" shows, or "presentations." That summer the girls appeared as a trio, which pleased Frances. This tour was a good example of the girls throwing themselves into their work, giving it their all. They had long said that, as a trio, their "main goal . . . was to headline the Paramount Theater in Los Angeles." They would soon realize part of this dream, playing the Paramount, not as headliners but as one of the featured acts.

They started the Fanchon and Marco tour at the Fox Theater in Long Beach and followed with three days at the Manchester Theater, an outlying movie-vaude house. Then they were ready for the move downtown to the gigantic stage of the Paramount Theater. There was a large ad in the major newspapers for the movie *Devil and the Deep,* starring Tallulah Bankhead and Gary Cooper, and the stage show called "Diversity," with six big acts, plus Georgie Stoll and the Paramount orchestra. For the three girls, now 16, 15, and 10, respectively,

Stage of Paramount Theater, Los Angeles. Scene of Frances's early triumph at age ten that earned her her first *Variety* review. *Courtesy of Adelaide Kinnamon Ladd*

this was the most exciting night of their professional lives. Many of their friends came to see them. They were third on the bill—"The Gumm Sisters–Blue Harmony;" others were Fuzzy Knight, screwball comic, headlining, Lester Horton and his Voodoo dancers; Three Jacks and a Queen, adagio dancers; Three Society Steppers, hoofers; and the Paramount Dancing Beauties. The girls sang two songs. In a long-forgotten review in *Variety,* the Gumm sisters got their first notice in a theatrical paper: "Gumm sisters, harmony trio, socked with two numbers. Selling end of trio is the ten-year-old sister with a pip of a lowdown voice. Kid stopped the show, but wouldn't give more."[8]

From that summer on, there was a consistent dynamism in Frances's performing. She was putting her eight years of experience into practice now. Her vaudeville know-how was beginning to show. She enjoyed being on stage exhibiting a gleeful vitalism and uniting a strong, clear voice with energetic movement, which was beginning to lift people right out of their seats. Ethel had seen it before, but now it was confirmed with the recognition by others. The review in *Variety* strengthened her conviction that Frances was no mere talent. From that time on, she was more attuned to outside interest in Frances. She didn't dwell on the written praise, but the Paramount engagement and the review had become a watershed event in her mind—a turning point which Frances wasn't aware of. Nothing, not even Frank, would thwart her now.

The momentum of the summer would give sustenance to Ethel's aims for the act, but in September she was forced to bring the girls back home for school, reluctantly canceling four more weeks of bookings, including two weeks in San Francisco. It was Janie's senior year in high school, and all three girls were eager to resume life in Lancaster. Ethel had enough impetus to keep her planning for the trio, even though most of the attention was being directed at Frances. Ethel wasn't blind to the fact that Frances was being sought as a solo, but she was loyal to the family tradition of singing together and deferred to Frances's dislike of singing alone.

She thought of success for the trio in terms of vaudeville or radio, with Frances as the focal point, her dream being no further defined at this time. A year later, when an agent asked Ethel why Frances wasn't in the movies, she told him: "I've never thought she was pretty enough." Perhaps Frances herself was still able to influence her own life, thus limiting her mother's plans for her, since, as her friend Ina Mary recalls: "Babe never liked performing except in the family act." But now audiences, bookers, and agents were paying more attention to Frances and only polite deference to the older girls. Soon they would come all the way from Los Angeles to hear Frances sing.

The autumn began with pumpkins ripening and with kids in Lancaster using the expression "nothing but the truth." All the youngsters descended on the annual Alfalfa Festival, saying "everybody's a hick and proud of it." Frank and Ethel attended Parents' Night at the high school in November—"Ma and Pa are kids again," the students joked. Frances was entering the fifth grade, while Janie and Jimmie were in high school. Frances applied herself diligently. After school she would be at Muggsie's. One day the two girls were out barefoot and encountered some fresh cement. They recorded their footprints for posterity at the corner of Newgrove and Fig.

That fall saw no abatement of Frances's professional performances. Christmas came, and Frank and Jimmie picked up Grandma and Aunt Norma in Los Angeles while Ethel and Frances drove to Santa Barbara where she was to appear at the Fox Arlington Theater. Back home for a couple of days, they headed for the Million Dollar Theater in Los Angeles where Frances had a one-week engagement.

The Christmas appearance in the city angered Frank, causing strife at home and putting stress on Frances. It interfered with the holiday, but all the family went in to see the show as usual. These conflicts were recalled vividly in later years, especially the trips away from home. "Sometimes we'd stay in Los Angeles overnight. Other times we'd drive all the way back to Lancaster . . . actually, my father didn't want us to perform, and it certainly wasn't a financial necessity. He was doing very well with the theater. But whenever we worked any place, he'd come and watch."[9]

The disagreement that Christmas did not affect the decision that Ethel had already made. Using the Kusell Studio affiliation as a wedge and an excuse, she told her friends that after New Year's, she would

Mary Jane Gumm in senior class
photo, Lancaster, California, 1933.
Courtesy of Terry Helgesen Collection

Virginia Gumm as "Queen of the
Fairies" in high school play *Iolanthe*, March 17, 1932, Lancaster,
California. *Courtesy of Adelaide
Kinnamon Ladd*

Fifth-grade class at Lancaster Grammar School with Frances in second row, third from the right, 1932–1933. *Courtesy of the Tropico Gold Camp Museum*

"spend the greater part of her time in L.A." where she would work for Mr. Kusell. This break with Lancaster was no surprise, since townspeople were now accustomed to her being away on business. They knew of her goals for the girls. Only their closest friends recognized it as a marital separation. Ethel was resolute; she would not relent. She noticed things or thought she saw things in Frank's camaraderie with customers at the theater which alarmed her. There were arguments and recriminations and the ensuing departure by Ethel and the girls.

Maurice Kusell dropped a publicity note to one of the Los Angeles papers, regarding the expansion of his staff: "An addition to the Kusell faculty is Ethel Gumm, personality and harmony jazz singing teacher. Mrs. Gumm trained the sensational juvenile singing trio, the Gumm sisters, who have won acclaim as modern rhythm harmony singers."

The Depression was deepening. It was 1933. President-elect Roosevelt was focusing his attention on the economic ills of the country while on Broadway *As Thousands Cheer* opened, in movies *King Kong* made its debut, and in Chicago "The Century of Progress Exposition" opened its gates.

Ethel lived in Los Angeles, trundling the girls back and forth between the two cities. She was so busy at her job that she enlisted Norma, who was still visiting, to accompany Frances to Long Beach for a three-day engagement at the Strand Theater. This meant a weekend at the Pike, the oceanfront amusement park, right next to the theater on the boardwalk. Her Aunt Norma gave her a freer rein, which Frances relished, and this spontaneity resulted in Frances doing some experimenting with her usual billing. Always trying to improve the sound of her name, perhaps thinking it was holding her back but never really getting at the root of the problem, she attempted a variation this weekend, since Ethel wasn't there to take care of such details. The advertisement listed her as one of the acts:

STARTS TODAY 6 BIG VODVIL ACTS 6 NEW STRAND
GRACIE GUMM "RADIO'S YOUTHFUL STAR"

Frances's prankishness continued. A few months later, when Frank accompanied her to the Garfield Theater in Alhambra for a weekend engagement, she ended up third on the bill:

ANOTHER GREAT SCORE!!
ORPHEUM BIG TIME VAUDEVILLE
—Alice Gumm—

She was the one who had to go out there and sing. A name change at least gave her some choice, although real choice for her, as she was beginning to learn, was merely the freedom she had on stage. But the stage had not, by any means, become a refuge where life and fantasy merged, as it would later when Judy Garland would tell people that even when she was physically ill and depressed, singing somehow made her feel good.

The spring of 1933 was spent half in Lancaster and half in Los Angeles. After the Garfield appearance, Frances played the Fairfax Theater on Beverly Boulevard and made a radio engagement with "Al Pierce and his Gang" on KFI. She found time to visit friends, the Wright girls, who had moved from Lancaster to Canoga Park. The whole family got together as guests of Marcus Rabwin at the Brown Derby in Hollywood for dinner, following an appearance of the Gumm sisters at a reception at the Hamburger Memorial Home, a home for Jewish working girls.

The girls continued to take lessons at the Kusell Studio, being directed by either Kusell or their mother. Kusell recalls them as an "act that didn't require being pushed—the act spoke for itself in its quality." All of the Gumms were a common sight at the studio. Ethel would leave the kids there as she went about her business, and Frank, when in town, would meet them there.

Kusell saw Frank frequently during these years, and, like everyone who knew him, thought Frank a likable, fine person. But Kusell also described Frank as being "double-gaited," that is, bi-sexual. He concluded that Frank "wasn't flagrant . . . he was discreet about his conquests . . . it didn't get out of hand. . . ." It is to his credit that, despite his inability to practice the cardinal virtues, Frank's sexuality didn't pervade his entire personality nor did he agonize over his situation. Nonetheless, there were many tribulations for him, many long-range effects on his wife and children. "Frank was gay, most people at the dance studio knew . . . but everyone loved him . . . he was a helluva guy. . . ." But, Kusell added, "I hear he got into some trouble along the way because of it."

Ethel returned to Lancaster to attend Janie's graduation with the rest of the family, but it was back to the city right away. " 'Baby' Gumm is filling an engagement with radio station KFWB this summer," it was reported. She was appearing regularly on Friday nights, and intermittently Janie and Jimmie joined her on the air. That the act was a good one was attested to by a *Los Angeles Examiner* critic who cited the excellence of the trio as a whole: "When the Gumm sisters of KFWB's Junior Revue sing, I imagine them stomping and infusing their vigor into all spectators. They have radio personality so sadly lacking in most trios, 'doubles' and 'quartets.' . . ." And on June 23 he wrote:

Those three juveniles from Lancaster are masquerading under false colors. They are not imitators. Nothing on the air at the moment is so original. Perhaps we should be abstemious in our praise of these youngsters for fear of curtailing their prospects of rising to full effulgence. Still, it is better to assist them with a mild, gentle boost than to retard their progress with a well-meant constructive criticism which might be misconstrued. The kids frolic this evening at 7:45 through KFWB. . . . Catch these sisters tonight. . . . Last week they "Shuffled off to Buffalo" with a spirit and originality that must have moved every listener. . . .

Bookings were becoming more accessible. Now items such as "Vaudeville Acts Sought" appearing in the theatrical sections of newspapers did not mobilize Ethel as they had in the past. The sisters were not headliners yet, but they did have a following among radio listeners, regular Los Angeles vaudeville-goers, and, of course, Lancaster residents. There was a lively interest in Frances that summer.

On a stifling hot Sunday afternoon in mid-July 1933, Messrs. King and Winkler from the RKO vaudeville booking office drove to Lancaster to hear Frances. After dinner the girls sang for them. "I was so impressed with the child's voice and delivery," King said years later, "that I made

Mrs. Gumm promise to bring . . . the sisters the next night to go on the Weekly Review Vaudeville Bill, a Monday night fixture at the RKO Hillstreet." King was so impressed that he arranged for them to be worked into the show which was booked weeks in advance.

Frances and Ethel quickly readied some new songs, and they went to Los Angeles the next night. The trio did a number, then Frances sang a solo on the big RKO stage. King recalls the number she sang. "I'll never forget it—'Rain, Rain, Go Away.' It impressed a man in the audience as much as it did me." Ben Piazza, from MGM casting, was there. He asked about Frances, but nothing more was heard from him.

The growing interest in the three girls, as well as Ethel's almost total absorption in Los Angeles, led to the inevitable break with Lancaster. Her move was a wise one for her, since it wasn't long before Frank's personal crisis. Although she was deserting Frank, there was really little left in their marriage. With Janie graduated from school and the girls having been gradually weaned from the little town, her intention was announced in mid-summer: "THE GUMMS WILL RESIDE IN LA. Mr. and Mrs. Frank Gumm and family moved to LA at the week end. Mr. Gumm will continue to spend part of his time in Lancaster."

The girls had told all their friends about the move a few weeks earlier. There were rounds of dinners and farewells. The Order of the Rainbow for Girls, an organization Janie and Jimmie had belonged to, gave a party, as the newspaper reported, ". . . a farewell compliment to two of their members, Misses Mary Jane and Virginia Gumm. . . . 'Baby' Frances Gumm was invited to join the festivities." The parting ended in a typically Gumm manner: "The three sisters sang together for the pleasure of the group and Frances responded with solos."

11

A SHORT REUNION

*It's hard to explain, but all the times I had to
leave him, I pretended he wasn't there; because
if I'd thought about him being there, I'd have
been too full of longing.*

At the end of her life Judy was a neurotic, desperate, baffling woman.
She was an unstable performer who, after 40 years of singing, was
losing her voice. Nonetheless, she was still charming and magnetic, traits
which even Mel Torme in his ode to Judy's awfulness as an adult, *The
Other Side of the Rainbow,* had to admit she possessed: "It was senseless
to be angry with her, unthinkable to hate her. . . . Very few sacred cows
can and did get away with some of the things Judy did throughout her
later life. She prevailed . . . she created a mystique that served her well
through some incredibly troubled times. . . ."[1] In Torme's love-hate study
of the older, declining Garland during her "last moment at the top"
television series, he hits on the most telling factor of her willingness to
be charming and give a good performance: "First and foremost, she had
to be interested . . . involvement was impossible unless she felt it was
worth the effort. . . ."

The basis for this petulance was not understood by Torme or most
of her contemporaries; nor would it have been any more palpable if it
had been understood. Judy wanted perfection. She was no mere performer; her charms and talents were a gift to those who gave her love
and attention

Everything had to be going her way, everyone had to be on her wavelength. Unconditional devotion and loyalty around her—producers, coworkers, conductors, audiences, friends, and family—was the order of the day. As Torme admitted: "the whole mishigoss revolved around Judy Garland." He concludes, almost in awe of her unique charisma, that despite her impossible temperament, "prominent, talented people from virtually every walk of life idolized her, swore by her, defended and protected her. . . ." She did, indeed, prevail.

This unswerving allegiance was already taken for granted by Frances in the early thirties, just as the rhythm of her days and her perception of the world were established by the departures and returns, the long drives to places—vaudeville houses, nightclubs, carnivals, and ballrooms —to appear before strange audiences and sing.

Down the street from the entrance to the Fox Theater in San Francisco was the Oasis Club, filled to capacity one night in March 1934, in the middle of the music-crazy swing era. The entire Gumm family went there after their last show at the Fox. The robust nature of the family and the vivaciousness of the three girls dressed in matching outfits was immediately noticeable. Someone there knew that the girls were playing at the Fox. Soon "they sat her on the bar" as everyone turned to listen to the girl with the bubbling demeanor—Frances perfectly at ease in a white dress and black patent boots ready to sing with the band. She sang for more than an hour, smiling and giggling in response to the crowd's enthusiastic reaction to each song.

This was the heady air she breathed as a child; the narcotic effect of these years would never wear off. It would have to, at the very least, make her self-centered as an older person; for if most children fantasize about being someone other than themselves, Frances was living such fantasies. With this dual life she could choose between reality and fantasy, the two gradually becoming inextricable. Because of the gradual immersion in this milieu, with the tragedy, success, and unreality eventually piling on one another in her life, it is doubtful that Judy ever realized how extraordinary the years of her youth were.

Throughout her life, Judy depended on those around her, which goes to prove what is traditionally said about the "baby" in a family, that he or she will always be taken care of by the others. Vincent Minnelli, in remarking on their marriage in the 1940s, said she had a "desire for constant approval which was pathological." Judy was aware of her dependence. Periodically she would say, as she did in 1962: "Now I'm getting a little too old to be towed around. . . . I'm not a half child anymore. . . . before, nobody ever let me do anything for myself. Everybody took care of things for me. First my mother, then my husband. . . ."[2] But she had to include her family and friends in the "business" act. There was no other alternative. It had to be as much like Grand Rapids and Lancaster as possible. Her children would eventually join her onstage, boyfriends would become press agents or musical arrangers, in-laws became conductors, and husbands became promoters or managers. She demanded it. Perhaps the most fruitful, though tempestuous, of these associations was with her fourth husband, Sid Luft. Luft, who strikingly resembled Frank Gumm, best cultivated her theatrical genius and brought to the fore some of her greatest triumphs. It was touching that this legendary entertainer needed such large amounts of support. When her mother's lawyer came to the Curran Theater in San Francisco in 1952 to discuss a legal matter with Sid Luft, Judy interrupted the conversation and forced them to "come and watch" her while she sang.

With great amounts of love and guidance from her family, Frances was carefree. The only time she wasn't dependent on anyone was when she was singing. Perfectly content offstage, she performed magic onstage. Life for her was exhilarating, intoxicating—pure pleasure. It is no wonder that she could display a quality at this time which demonstrated the cliché, "stopping the show," an ability that was rare among performers, then or now. She believed in what she was doing; she threw herself into a performance; she gave totally of herself and in turn made people forget themselves. The life of Frances Gumm verged on the sublime. She could partake of two worlds without losing either, although the scene was now set for the eventual tearing apart of those worlds.

Comparisons are often made between Judy and other self-destructive entertainers such as Marilyn Monroe and Janis Joplin. Judy had become a wayward bus careening into failure. Although she shared with Monroe and Joplin a certain helplessness and vulnerability, the analogy to the other two troubled persons fails because there were differences in talent and personality. Marilyn was a mutation, forever struggling to discover her identity as a woman and artist. She was a lamb next to the lioness Garland. Judy was always the triumphant artist; she had been a complete person once, and she had never lost the vitality of that completeness. Even her public stance of masochism in her later years was more tempestuous than pathological, more in the histrionic tradition of a Lola Montez, Sarah Bernhardt, or Aimee Semple McPherson. She had observed and undoubtedly admired Aimee McPherson, since she wanted to play the movie role of Aimee. Notwithstanding her genuine disturbed condition, she knew all too well what was expected of her; she played the flamboyant role in this tradition, to gain both publicity and sympathy.

Marilyn and, more recently, Janis Joplin were two disparate people who came from drab, ordinary backgrounds. They sought theatrics in a search for meaning and fantasy, because in their natural setting they could never feel special or privileged. They became ebullient only in their outside world. As a youngster, Judy never knew deprivation; her artistic emergence differs at the core. She was privileged and indulged in both worlds and would remain high-spirited in both settings. She differed from the other two women because of another factor—toughness. As Marjorie Rosen points out: "this adaptability created a spring board of resilience, ensuring survival. . . ."[3] In Myra Friedman's biography of Janis Joplin one reads how hurt and dismayed she was when an interviewer called her "the Judy Garland of Rock and Roll."

Aside from the problems of being a celebrity, these women shared little. Marilyn was searching for herself; Janis perhaps never knew who or what she was except perhaps when singing her gutsy blues; whereas Judy was fighting for survival because she had been disinherited.

In his biography, Torme relates a conversation with Judy in 1963 in which she returned to her past: " 'We were good, you know that? The Gumm sisters. We had fun singing together. Long time ago,' she said forlornly. '*Long* time ago. Did you know my dad was a good singer?

And writer? He wrote "I Will Come Back." Did you know that? No, you didn't. You're so wrapped up in your own damn world, you never took time to find out about mine.' "[4] Torme could not respond to her. How could anyone? No one could sympathize with her any more than she could piece the story together. There was a semblance of madness here; she could neither show nor prove how marvelous and sad this life was. She could not articulate the joy and loss of her youth.

The marquee on the Golden Gate Theater in San Francisco announced its week's vaudeville offering which included the "GUMM SISTERS Harmony Deluxe with Frances." Ethel had booked herself and the girls on a cruise leaving San Pedro Monday night and docking in San Francisco the following day. Frank drove up to join them in one of their few professional engagements together. The booking came just a few days after they had moved to Los Angeles. It was due to Frank that they were appearing together, as he moved quickly in an attempt to reunite himself with his family. Despite his and Ethel's impasse, he felt that for the girls' sake he should be with them as much as possible. He knew the move to Los Angeles had been Ethel's victory, that his influence was growing weaker. In San Francisco he would introduce his girls with a new song-and-dance routine.

The seven acts of vaudeville were, according to *Variety:*

a slap at whoever stated that "vaude is coming back". . . . it was everyone for himself, let the customers flee where they may. . . . The Gumm sisters, with Mamma Gumm at the piano, and Papa Gumm in advance, deuced. Three girls of assorted sizes who sing in mediocre voice and style, with majority of the burden falling to the youngest one, a mere tot, who lustily shouted three numbers, decidedly not of her type. And much too long.[5]

This first review of the entire family was Frances's first negative review and one of the few times she hadn't managed to "stop the show." As usual she stood out enough for her to be singled out by the reviewer who was perhaps merely puzzled by her style. On the other side of town, however, George C. Warren of the *San Francisco Chronicle* seemed

Golden Gate Theater, San Francisco, where entire Gumm family played in the summer of 1933. *Courtesy of Terry Helgesen Collection*

more in tune with the audience, which had roared its approval, as he noted: "the Gumm sisters, who harmonize, and have a strong-voiced small woman, who imitates and sings in a big way. . . ."

The next week, at the Fox West Coast Theater in Long Beach, all agreed that "the Three Gumm Sisters, featuring the Radio sensation of KHJ, Frances Gumm," were terrific. After two weeks of the five Gumms appearing together, Frank went back to Lancaster and Ethel returned to Los Angeles. The girls attended Lawlor's Professional School in the morning and rehearsed at Kusell's studio in the afternoon.

In Lancaster, the Valley Theater continued to show the best of the current crop of films, but the absence of Sunday-night vaudeville was obvious. Frank had wanted to stay on in the house there, but it became an impractical, lonely enterprise. He moved into a tiny bungalow just off Antelope Avenue, a block from the theater.

In Los Angeles, Ethel rented a small house, which did not please Frank. He thought his family deserved better. In another attempt to maintain some influence in the family, he set out to find a more suitable residence. By mid-November he had rented an impressive home in the Silverlake district of Los Angeles. The three-story white structure, which resembled a small medieval castle, seemed extravagant, but it was into this elegant setting that Frank and Ethel welcomed their Los Angeles and Lancaster friends for a housewarming.

It was an effective facade. The appearance to Frank's brother Bob and his family visiting from Alabama, and to the Goods and Gilmores and others, was that the Gumms had "gone Hollywood." It was assumed that they were prospering. By then the charade that had begun so many years before had been perfected; no one knew that they were merely going through the motions of being man and wife.

Some friends from Lancaster drove in to see the girls onstage at the Warner Brothers Downtown Theater after they finished a booking at the Warner's Hollywood moviehouse. *Variety* reviewed the show that night and the trio—especially Frances—were again panned:

. . . the Gumm Sisters, three harmony warblers, with Mother Gumm accompanying at the piano. Two of the sisters are grownup, while the third is a precocious juve whose mild attempts at comedy add nothing to the offering.

Frances, Frank, and Virginia on porch of home on Ivanhoe Drive, in Silverlake District of Los Angeles, 1933. *Courtesy of the University of the South*

Frances was getting her first dose of "hard knocks" which had heretofore gone to other performers in other acts. Even the review at the Golden Gate Theater seemed to be qualified.

Whatever went wrong with the Warner booking was perhaps inevitable and had begun on opening day when the local papers advertised the movie *Captive* and the vaudeville bill featuring, among others, the "Drumm Sisters."

Although most would have agreed that *Drumm* was a more theatrical name than *Gumm,* Ethel had spent a lot of time getting the act well known. She saw to it that the booking agent notified each newspaper immediately, and the misbilling was corrected in the next issue.

While they were touring that summer, Frances might have met a teenage performer named Kay Thompson, billed as "popular blues singer," at the Paramount. Kay later became a confidante and devotee of Frances's, as well as godmother to Liza.

As the weeks passed, Frank commuted to and from Los Angeles, often taking the girls with him to Lancaster. On these trips they stayed in the homes of their friends because the cottage Frank had rented was too small. The trips gave Frank a chance to be with the girls. Frances would stay with Muggsie, and they would do the things they had done before the Gumms left. At first Jimmie and Janie visited frequently, but they got used to Los Angeles, particularly Mary Jane who, like her mother, felt less at ease in Lancaster. Still, all three remained a part of Lancaster as long as Frank managed the theater and kept the valley folks in touch with the girls' theatrical endeavors. For Frances, though, something had begun to change as soon as the move to Los Angeles took her away from the distractions of everyday events: show business would now be allowed to prevail. Ethel's groundwork was paying off handsomely; interest in the trio was mounting. With her career fast becoming the dominant force in her life, Frances began to think of herself more and more as a singer.

By January 1934 Ethel had decided to spend less time at Kusell's studio and more on the girls. Her liberation from small-town life had given her options she had not been able to take advantage of in the past, and she found the prospect exciting. In her own mind she had reached

Warner's, Los Angeles, where Gumms were misbilled and earned third *Variety* notice in 1933. *Courtesy of Terry Helgesen Collection*

a point of self-realization, an opportunity to put to work her abilities in promoting the trio; but her emancipation would have the effect of narrowing Frances's choices for any other kind of life.

If Ethel's goal at some earlier time had merely been to get away from Lancaster and keep busy, she now made it known that she wanted the trio to get important bookings, to be successful. Her goal was inseparable from that of the girls and their theatrical success. "In L.A. my sisters began to lose interest in being performers, and I can't blame them. They never got a chance to sing a solo, like I did . . . and I was always getting too much attention on stage anyway."[6] Mary Jane added that she and Jimmie were "just charming background . . . we didn't mind because it took a lot of the responsibility away from us."[7] While Janie and Jimmie may have been aware of their professional place in Ethel's scheme of things, she was the first to realize Frances's potential. She intended to keep the girls together, if possible; if the little one carried the largest share of the act, she seemed to get the biggest kick out of it.

In 1934 Frank and Ethel bought a house on Lakeview Terrace East, just a block over from where they had been living. It was a fine, but less pretentious, house than the former one. For them, whose marriage now existed only for the girls, the purchase of an elegant new home seemed less a good choice than a compromise. Indeed, this impression of their marriage was communicated by one of the older girls to a friend in Lancaster. The friend received a letter in which Janie or Jimmie told her that the "folks" were going to get a divorce.

Almost immediately after moving into the house, Ethel arranged a month-long tour on the Paramount circuit in Washington, Oregon, and Idaho. At the same time, she and Frank got a letter from friends in Chicago who were operating one of the cabarets at the World's Fair. The Gumms were invited to spend the summer at the fair and work in the cabaret.

The tour was to be a combination of "outing and business" for the family, as Frank told his neighbors. Ethel and the girls boarded a train for Seattle, their first stop. The Paramount Theater in Seattle would be a full week's booking before the troupe hit the smaller communities for one day each. Frank would meet them on the last day of the Seattle stint.

"The pick of ENTERTAINERS from Los Angeles and the East . . . in New BIG TIME," blared the *Wenatchee World* as it advertised "The Only STAGE and SCREEN show in town." Wenatchee welcomed the troupe of minstrels on their fourth stop. Frank had been providing the transportation from town to town. They drove into Wenatchee, Washington where the Liberty Theater promised its patrons "BIG TIME" and proudly listed the acts on its billboard:

Featuring
DUCI DE KEREKJARTO
(Wizard of the Bow)
CLAUDIA COLEMAN
(Comedy Motion Picture Star)
TOLMACK AND BARLOW
(Comedy Team)
THREE GUMM SISTERS
(Trio Unusual)
HOWARD, SIDELL AND BERNICE
(Varieties of the Dance)

The Orpheum Theater in Spokane brought the troupe back to a large city where the local paper, the *Spokesman-Review,* commented:

The Three Gumm Sisters are harmony singers in a dainty bit of vocal entertainment that features the youngster of the lot in a clever imitation of Helen Morgan. The crowd gave the girls a great hand.

Whether spurred on by the two recent *Variety* reviews lambasting the act, particularly Frances, or by her own efforts to keep the act up to date, Ethel hit on a sure-fire show-stopper. Frances would sing "Bill," the plaintive song from *Showboat,* while sitting on a piano with her legs crossed and hands reaching out. As Helen Morgan, Frances's shouting became a strong and crisp lyrical line. The songs that weren't "her type" became the kind of theatrical show tune for which she would be known all over the world someday. Frances was now stopping shows because she was so good and not because people couldn't believe that the big voice and flyaway arms and legs came from so small a person.

The tour ended at the Liberty Theater in Lewiston, Idaho where the trio was billed as "Radio's Sweethearts." For the Gumms, however, the trip back to Los Angeles via the coast meant a week's engagement at the Fox Theater in San Francisco where the *Chronicle's* George Warren this time merely noted: "the Gumm Sisters, with a turn they term 'unusual.' "

They drove into Lancaster on March 16. The *Antelope Valley Ledger-Gazette* welcomed them back and in passing notified its readers that "the Gumm sisters will make a tour this summer east to Chicago. . . ."

Ethel had written her friends in Chicago that she and the girls would drive to the fair but that Frank would not be able to leave the theater. Because of commitments she had already made for the trio in Los Angeles, it would be late June or early July before they could reach Chicago.

As if singing and dancing to gawking fair visitors weren't enough, Ethel had arranged a booking that would fill the weeks before they left for Chicago. Frances would join the circus for the next three weeks, and her sisters would be in the act during the final week. The circus was the Gilmore Circus, which sent radio and vaudeville "stars," along with the traditional bigtop acts, around the circuits.

At the age of 11, Frances was the only born and bred, and by far the most precocious, vaudeville trouper among the 23 stars, most of whom were radio personalities of the day, such as "The Sheriff," "Aunt Addie," "Soda Pop," and the "Fortified Five." Frances belted and bounced for three weeks among the elephants, tigers, and trapeze artists, first in San Diego at the Spreckles Theater, the State Theater in Long Beach, and finally the huge Shrine Auditorium in Los Angeles where she was joined by Janie and Jimmie.

Even in the confusion of the circus, young Frances was singled out by the San Diego *Union-Tribune:* "Little Miss Frances Gumm, a child, sang 'Why Darkies Were Born' in such a fashion that she shared the encore honors with 'The Sheriff' who is the star performer of the show," while in Long Beach, the local paper commented: "Frances Gumm, a charming youngster who is the 'baby' of the troupe, sings 'That's What a Darkie Is' and 'Dinah' in a singularly grownup little voice."

The circus ended, but the girls continued working. Ethel had lined them up for a week at the Million Dollar Theater in Los Angeles and a three-day stint with the "Movie Star Frolics" at the Gilmore Stadium. The Screen Actors Guild staged the extravaganza which was billed as a circus, rodeo, and mardi gras and featured Eddie Cantor, plus 500 stars; the Gumm sisters were somewhere among the 500.

In Lancaster Frank tried to give his patrons something special even if his girls no longer had time to perform on the Valley Theater stage. That week they could get a glimpse of Frankie Darro, a popular teenage star of the day whose picture, *Wild Boys of the Road,* was playing at the theater. Darro had become a friend of Jimmie's in Los Angeles and would make future appearances at the Valley Theater.

The car was once again readied to roll across country. With Ethel's short, slightly plump, figure hidden behind the wheel, it seemed to be a massive, independent machine. The departure from Lancaster shortly after Frances's twelfth birthday was reminiscent of the day the family had left Minnesota, with the Milne family huddled around the car. This time, though, Frank was one of those standing around the car saying good-bye. Just before they left, Frances took a publicity photograph out of her mother's portfolio and quickly wrote: "To my old pal Muggsie" on the face of it, and signed it "Frances Gumm." She handed it to Muggsie before her mother could say anything. She hadn't spent much time with her friend lately; the gesture was a combination of anxiety and sentiment and perhaps a glimmer of recognition that her carefree days were being whittled away. She wanted her best friend to remember her. As the car headed across the Mojave Desert, Frances was scolded for giving out a professional photograph as if it were a common snapshot.

Indeed, Muggsie's friendship with Frances *was* drawing to an end. They would see each other a few more times in Lancaster and one or two times in Los Angeles. In Silverlake Muggsie remembers playing with Frances in the bedroom. "Ethel came in and told Frances she had someone outside who wanted to hear her sing . . . she made a face . . . Frances always made faces when she didn't want to perform."

How radically altered her life eventually became can be seen through the eyes of her friend Muggsie who, after 1935, would see

Frances at age twelve in solo performance in 1933. The only known picture autographed by her—"To my old pal Muggsie, Frances Gumm." *Courtesy of Ina Mary Miller*

"Babe" only twice again. Once Judy became a part of MGM, Muggsie didn't hear from her again until the late thirties. Her letters to Judy were either returned by the studio or unanswered. After the success of *The Wizard of Oz* Frances and her mother made one trip to Lancaster. Frances went to Muggsie's house. They talked and walked around the town while Ethel sat in the limousine supplied by the studio. It was a haunting visit. Muggsie was a young woman now, while Frances, who was 17, was living in a dream world. As she looked about she could scarcely grasp the life she had lived in Lancaster. They said good-bye. There was no further contact for over 25 years.

Denver was the first stop. They stayed with relatives of a Lancaster schoolteacher, Shirley Eyler. Although Frank had given Ethel a check for $200, she and the girls were determined to work their way across country and make the trip pay for itself. With a letter of introduction and her own skill in getting spots for the act, she arranged a week at the Tabor Grand Theater in Denver.

The engagement was a cliff-hanger for them, at least on opening night. Someone had evidently given the man who operated the spotlight incorrect information about which side of the stage the Gumm sisters would make their entrance from. At the piano in the pit, Ethel introduced the first few bars with the 10-piece orchestra joining in on the downbeat. The girls launched into their strut, gaily greeting the audience —in complete darkness. The operator heard them shouting out the opening lines of "Avalon Town" from somewhere in the darkness at the other side of the stage. The girls wasted no time in heading for the spotlight, only to have it swing to the other side. Finally, after they were several lines into the song, the spotlight found them desperately trying to sing above the uproar in the audience.

After that, the act went without a hitch. In fact, it proved such a success that the girls were offered and signed for another week in Denver and two weeks in Colorado Springs. They were eager to get to Chicago but glad "The Trio Unusual" seemed to be paying for itself.

The concentrated movement of people—on foot, in automobiles, streetcars, and the elevated trains encircling the center of the city—pro-

vided Chicago with seemingly continuous sound. The Chicago World's
Fair had begun its second year on May 26; the carnival atmosphere contrasted sharply with the city's well-known gangsterism. The ever-inven-
tive Frances later concocted stories of their not being paid for one
engagement because gangsters ran the club, and they ran out with the
money. She was influenced by such events as John Dillinger being
gunned down as he left Chicago's Biograph Theater on July 22 that
summer.

Chicago's "loop" was the theatrical section of town. Ethel pointed
out the important theaters to Frances, Janie, and Jimmie. Making the
rounds of the Oriental, Palace, Chicago, and newly revived State-Lake
that summer were such names as George Jessel, Jane Froman, Helen
Morgan, Rudy Vallee, Texas Guinan, Bob Hope and Company, and
Alice Faye. Ethel hoped her letter of introduction would get the girls
into one of these big theaters, but for the moment she wanted to get
herself and the girls situated at the fair.

The Old Mexico Cabaret was on the boardwalk at the "Century of
Progress" exposition. Many of the concessions at the fair were having
trouble making money because of the competition from vaudeville shows;
but the Old Mexico Cabaret was doing well with its popular bill. The
Gumms joined Sandra Medrano, "Exotic White Dancer"; Skippy Reale,
"1934 Sensational Fan Dancer"; Myron and Evelen, "Society Dance
Team"; John Poat, "Golden Voiced Baritone"; and a comedy act, Hank
the Mule. With the bill heavy on dance, the Gumm sisters, "Blue Harmony," were a welcome addition to the club.

Now that the girls were into daily work at the fair, Ethel, characteristically, felt the need to see what else could be arranged in the city.
She went to the Consumer Building on State Street where she had been
told an agency there might be able to help her. The agency explained
that the city was swamped with vaudeville acts this summer, but that if
they found that they had a spot for them, the girls would be asked to
audition. Ethel left her address and phone number.

By mid-July, though some aspects of the fair were dismal, the Gumm
sisters were clicking. Ethel wrote back to Frank that Frances had been
seen at the Old Mexico by Captain Riley, the man who was in charge

Ethel and three daughters during a 1934 tour. *Courtesy of The Garlandia Collection of Wayne Martin*

of special events and that he had chosen her to be guest of honor on "Children's Day." Mr. Riley couldn't have chosen a kid more up to the task of being the center of the ballyhoo. The "honor" included riding in an official car, leading a procession of musicians and clowns handing out balloons and candy to children lined up along Leif Ericson Drive. More like a pied piper than a guest of honor, Frances led the parade to one of the large auditoriums where she entertained the children and their parents in a special program of songs and dances.

Some of their stay in Chicago was with Frank's relatives from Murfreesboro, who were now living in Chicago. A distant cousin, Mrs. Barbara Goenne, who recalls the visit, says that Frances "was a happy girl with a fine sense of humor . . . and she was so natural and unaffected."

They were having a wonderful time at the fair, but Ethel had not been able to get the act booked at even one Chicago vaudeville house. She tried again at the agency in the Consumer Building but got the same response as before. By early August she had had enough of the pandemonium of the fair and wrote Frank that they would be leaving in a few days to visit Grand Rapids before coming home.

But before leaving, she was handed a note by her host at the Old Mexico Cabaret which read, "Call the talent agency." She was told that they had an opportunity for the trio, which, as it turned out, meant they needed a fill-in for one night only at the Belmont Theater. The agency said that this would also serve as an audition for the trio, that an agency representative would be in the audience.

Frances did her Helen Morgan imitation which the audience loved. The next day Ethel phoned the agency to get their reaction, only to find out that no one from their office had been there. They finished the week at the fair and for the second time prepared to leave for Grand Rapids.

Again Ethel was contacted by an agent who needed a fill-in act; but this time it was at the important Oriental Theater. It was for the five remaining days of the bill and featured George Jessel. The drummer in the orchestra at the Belmont had mentioned the girls' success that night to the agent, and he wanted them to replace another singing group on the bill.

The Oriental Theater, Chicago, where name change occurs along with "break" for the act, 1934. *Courtesy of Terry Helgesen Collection*

Their proud entrance was marred by, for them, their worst mis-billing so far. If ever a name lent itself to such accidents, *Gumm* seemed to have almost unlimited possibilities. At the Oriental Theater, the marquee announced: THE GLUM SISTERS.

Ethel agreed with Jessel that she should change the girls' name and accepted his suggestion of "Garland," purportedly after his friend, the theater critic, Robert Garland. Others say Jessel told the three girls that they were as pretty as "a garland of flowers," in an effort to console them about the misbilling. But the girls were never upset by their name being garbled; it had happened before. It is just as likely that the name came from a movie playing at the time, fixing the name in all their minds because of Carole Lombard's part as a rising actress named Lily Garland battling with a producer played by John Barrymore in the movie *Twentieth Century*. The girls saw the movie, and the name must have seemed appropriate.

If they thought the matter could be taken care of by changing their name the surest indication that it hadn't appeared in *Variety* and the *Chicago Daily Tribune*. Because the girls were a last-minute replacement, the *Variety* bill had not listed the Gumms as part of that week's bill. When Ethel accepted a booking at the Marbro Theater on Chicago's West Side immediately after the week at the Oriental, the trio made the *Variety* bill for the week of August 24 at the Marbro. Along with the headliner, Larry Adler, and seven other acts, the bill added "GLUM SIS." Not only the *Variety* bill, but the opening night ad in the *Tribune* announced the eight acts of vaudeville, including the "GLUMM SIS."

The error at the Oriental followed them across town. The story of the big break and the name change, which would be embellished over the years, was related to Frank when Ethel phoned the weekend of the Oriental booking, telling him of the girls' success and the other bookings. While Frances continued to knock them out with "Bill," Frank passed the story on to the *Ledger-Gazette* which appeared on August 23, 1934:

GUMM SISTERS SHOW IN THE EAST
VALLEY GIRLS MAKE HIT IN SHOW WITH GEORGE JESSEL

The Gumm sisters of Lancaster who, with Mrs. Gumm, have been presenting

Marbro Theater, Chicago, where the Gumm trio was first misbilled as "Glum Sisters" in 1934. *Courtesy of Terry Helgesen Collection*

their song and dance specialty at various points on the grounds at the Century of Progress in Chicago, got one of the proverbial "breaks" in the show business this past week according to reports from Chicago. An act at the Oriental theater, one of Chicago's best show places, proved a disappointment, and the Gumm sisters were called in to fill the vacancy. They opened last Friday with George Jessel and have proven a real sensation according to all reports. Little Frances shares headline honors with Jessel who is the star of the show. Frances makes a hit in her impersonation of Helen Morgan when she sits on a white grand piano and sings "Bill," one of the outstanding numbers done by Miss Morgan in "Show Boat." All three girls render two selections accompanied by Mrs. Gumm at the piano.

By September 7, when the girls opened at the Michigan Theater in Detroit on a bill featuring Arthur Tracy, "the Street Singer," all theatrical sources in town had reached a consensus. The name Garland appeared for the first time:

3 Garland Sisters
Grace—Beauty—Songs

The singing, dancing Garland sisters spent the next four weeks pounding out rhythm and harmony in theaters in Milwaukee, St. Joseph, Cincinnati, and Kansas City. In mid-October Ethel called a halt, and they headed home. It was early morning when they drove up the narrow street to the Silverlake house. Frank emerged from the house, with his arms outstretched. The girls ran to him. Judy later recalled the homecoming, saying: "all the time we were away from home, my sisters and I were lonesome for our father, but we didn't dare mention it to Mother. We hit Los Angeles at three o'clock in the morning, and my father was outside the house. It was the first and only time I can remember that I ran into his arms. I cried out of happiness . . . the family was back together again, and I was very happy about that."[8]

But it was a short reunion. Frank returned to Lancaster and the girls to the Lawlor School, while Ethel began to line up more work for the girls. Within a few days of their return, the girls sang at the Beverly-Wilshire Hotel with the Vincent Lopez Orchestra, and within another week Ethel had arranged bookings that would fill the remainder of the year.

Ethel, Mary Jane, Virginia, and Frances pose at piano in Chicago, 1934.
Courtesy of The Garlandia Collection of Wayne Martin

An item appeared in a Los Angeles paper, saying that Sam Goldwyn was "within the next six months" to film *The Wizard of Oz,* based on the fables which had been a favorite of children since 1900. But the movie would not appear for another four years.

The Gumm, or Garland, sisters—depending on which city paper you were reading—opened at Grauman's Chinese Theater in Hollywood in the prologue to the film *The Count of Monte Cristo.* Almost five years later to the day, Frances would return to the same theater, transformed into a star. The prologue was a stage show that carried a theme drawn from the companion film. It was the kind of vaudeville for which Grauman's was famous. Raymond Paige's orchestra backed the bill which had a "lot of punch" and entertained "in full measure." The punch was a knockout performance by 12-year-old Frances who drew from a previously cool *Variety* critic the first public pronouncement of the mature and accomplished professional she was rapidly becoming. "Gumm Sisters next and stopped the show," he said as he continued his review in the "New Acts" section of *Variety.* This review later led to the belief that the booking at Grauman's was the Gumm sisters' first *Variety* review, when, in fact, it was their fourth.

Hardly a new act, this trio of youngsters has been kicking around the coast for two years, but has just found itself. As a trio, it means nothing, but with the youngest, Frances 13 [sic] years old, featured, it hops into class entertainment, for, if such a thing is possible, the girl is a combination of Helen Morgan and Fuzzy Knight. Possessing a voice that, without a p.a. system, is audible throughout a house as large as the Chinese, she handled ballads like a veteran, and gets every note and word over with a personality that hits audiences. For comedy she effects a pan like Knight and delivers her stuff in the same manner as the comic. Nothing slow about her on hot stuff and to top it, she hoofs. Other two sisters merely form a background.

Kid, with or without her sisters, is ready for the east. Caught on several previous shows, including the 5,000 seat Shrine Auditorium here, she has never failed to stop the show, her current engagement being no exception.[9]

Now the "precocious juve" whose attempts at comedy added "nothing to the act" the previous year, was a noteworthy comedienne; the tot

Frances in performance with sisters on cross-country tour 1934. *Courtesy of The Garlandia Collection of Wayne Martin*

who "lustily shouted" her songs that year was now an accomplished balladeer and rhythm singer. But if Frank and Ethel expected offers from studios or agents, they did not appear. In March of the next year Frances would be singled out by the trade paper as "a bet for pictures." Two months later she was tagged "talented beyond doubt," but with all the notice of her extraordinary natural talent and her improvised moments of comedy, panning and vocal surprises, stretching as far back as the Loew's State debut, she was not picked up by a studio or agent. Few vaudeville acts could have hoped for more exposure yet this one kept plodding along.

One of the problems, not only for the Gumm sisters but for all vaudeville at this time, was that talent was being developed by the movie studios and sold to the public on film and not in vaudeville. Producers no longer sought to discover talent among the declining quality and number of acts in the moribund vaudeville. Nevertheless, as late as the middle thirties some important theatrical people were predicting continued life and better times for the stage show. This provided a small ray of hope, which was all a vaudevillian needed. Few families had been in the business as long as the Gumms, so Ethel grabbed any booking she could get for the girls, and they continued their assault on a goal which many were already abandoning.

The girls made their last appearance as a trio under their Gumm family name at the small Strand Theater where Frances had appeared the year before as "Gracie Gumm." Evidently the management felt the girls were fairly well known in town and would do better as the Gumms than as the Garlands. After the prestigious Grauman's engagement, however, the girls had to wince, being squeezed in between Donna Day, "America's Premier Fan Dancer," and "Olga's Trained Seal."

They returned to the Orpheum Theater which they had played the previous February. The manager was familiar with the act and was impressed with Ethel's promotion of it. He remembered her as a "very sweet woman," who had "the appearance of a school marm." The Orpheum, which had been Los Angeles' only straight vaudeville house, now had the same vaudeville movie policy as the other downtown theaters. The Garland sisters and the other four acts of "Vodvil" were appearing

Frank Gumm in front of Lakeview Terrace home in Silverlake District of Los Angeles, 1934. *Courtesy of the University of the South*

between showings of the two feature pictures, *Lemon Drop Kid* and *Desirable.* The girls enjoyed their bookings there because of the still flourishing grandeur of the ornate auditorium, the large lobby, the "green room," and the dozens of dressing rooms which occupied several floors above the stage.

The trio had been drawing good comment and were called "excellent harmonists," although the trio was now clearly no more than a showcase for the little one. This was obvious to people in Lancaster who had not seen the girls perform there for a long time, as they returned to the Valley Theater in December. Frank had published his usual theater ad, saying that on Friday "the Garland Sisters, formerly known as the Gumm Sisters, will appear at the Valley Theater in song and dance numbers." This was to be their last appearance there.

A few days before Christmas they all drove up to San Francisco where Irving Strauss's Frolics had been booked at the Curran Theater for a holiday extravaganza.

They had been appearing at the Wilshire-Ebell Theater in Los Angeles in a series of concerts, where the Frolics had been given a preliminary run on Sunday nights. The Wilshire-Ebell attracted the movie crowd and other professionals, as well as the regular theatergoers, which gave the theater a more sophisticated audience who paid prices as high as $1.50 a ticket. "With the success of the Sunday Nite Frolics at the Wilshire-Ebell, town has gone Sunday vaude concert screwy" commented the *Los Angeles Times.*

That Christmas season in San Francisco would always be a fond memory for the Gumms. They were together again, involved in a show that was being highly touted in town, with newspapers promising that Irving Strauss's Frolics would bring back echoes of the two-a-day regime to the Curran Theater.

The large company of 60 comedians, singers, dancers, and acrobats scored a hit during its seven-day engagement. Frances, of course, got a lot of attention, including some doubts from George C. Warren of the *Chronicle* that she was the juvenile the program indicated. He decided that she was great, "whether she is young or old."

One wonders how vivid this memory of the week with the Frolics and the family reunion was when Judy returned to the Curren 18 years later with the vaudeville road company of her Palace comeback show. Did she recall this poignant time when she, her sisters, and mother and father spent their last Christmas together in San Francisco?

The new year began for the family as it always did—Frank, Ethel, and the girls working the family specialty, vaudeville. The very thing so often responsible for taking Ethel and the girls away from Frank and home was that which brought them back together and gave them their happiest times. The girls knew that their father and mother were happiest when involved in the act. It was almost as if the old family spirit and laughter had depended on it.

In an open letter on January 3 in the *Ledger-Gazette,* Frank ostensibly took the opportunity to state his theater policy, but it was an obvious display of bitterness which substantiated the rumors that problems had emerged in his theater operation. He thanked those who had expressed themselves as pleased that he had remained in town and continued to manage the theater. He then announced a change in theater policy, noting his displeasure with those who made it a practice to remain in the theater for a second showing or those who expected free admission or credit or complained that the admission price should be less. He was also limiting charity benefits to one a month. Then with his old aplomb, he closed with "Rest assured our policy is 'the pick of pictures' clean and wholesome entertainment for the whole family in pleasing surrounds and with RCA Victor equipment, 'the perfect sound' hence, our slogan, 'The Valley Theater, the Home of BETTER pictures.'"

Whit Carter, who owned the theater building, told Frank that his lease would not be renewed when it expired at the end of March. Carter had been generous in allowing Frank to make only partial payment on the theater during the past year. Now, more than $2,000 owed in back payments, he was unwilling to let Frank continue his deficit payments. Frank was never ambitious in his theater operation. His benevolent attitude, along with the family's extravagance, the expenses of living in the city, the girls' careers, and the seeming loss of momentum and direction for himself when the family moved to Los Angeles—all contributed to his financial troubles. In an effort to keep his lease, he hired a lawyer to negotiate the contract.

Frank contacted Marcus Rabwin's brother, Harry, who was also an old friend of the Gumms, dating from their Minnesota days. He was now practicing law in Los Angeles. Harry drove to Lancaster, unaware of the pressures that had led to Frank's business crisis. He did manage to get a delay in a decision about the lease. Harry Rabwin says that he "never suspected" Frank's homosexuality; he never had the slightest hint of it.

Rumors about Frank's financial and personal problems were being circulated in Lancaster. It wasn't like Frank who had for almost eight years greeted his neighbors with a warm, reassuring smile. Perhaps, though, he thought he would have their support and understanding after all he had given them. But his problems were deeper than his financial problems or the break-up of the family or Frances's career.

Judy Garland might have had more peace of mind in later life, and more sympathy for her mother, if she had known that the demons that drove her mother were real and not fanciful and if she had known that her father was a much more troubled person than she knew.

Beyond the apparent problems of his theater operation, there were at this time "unsavory" stories about Frank. Once again established in another small town, Frank and Ethel were confronted with the same stress that had shattered their lives in Grand Rapids. Four decades later, people spoke sympathetically of the struggle that divided him and forced his wife to devote herself to her daughters' careers. Many who were fond of Frank said it was "too bad." One Lancaster resident said that "they just about ran him out of town" because of one incident.

One who was a close friend of the Gumms' in the thirties remembers his first awareness of Frank's vices. In gym classes at the high school where conversations inevitably ranged over the subject of sex, Frank was mentioned in a ribald way. Several boys boasted of how they let Mr. Gumm "use them." When they went to the show at the Valley Theater, the family friend recollects, everyone had to pay their way except those who consistently got in free when they asked Frank. "Several of the boys took liberties with Mr. Gumm." This became a dilemma which, added to others, prompted Frank's open letter. During those years, "Frank made a pass at several other boys in town," which were sufficient to bring about a mildly vigilante atmosphere in Lancaster.

Townspeople, of course, did not know that accounts of Frank's sexual proclivities went as far back as Grand Rapids and that this had caused their departure from Minnesota. Whit Carter says that he, too, heard the gossip but that the change in the lease was strictly business. Nevertheless, Frank, in effect, was once again being run out of town.

Most valley residents liked the Gumms and patronized the Valley Theater. They were at a loss to know why Judy hated them. Judy, who was usually sensitive to undercurrents in her life, swore a lifelong fealty to her father's memory, buried her happy memories, and turned on the town with a vengeance because they turned her father out. She never knew about her mother's desperation, her gallant and protective instincts, or her anguish when, toward the end, Ethel knew she had failed to protect her child. She never knew that it was Frank's nature that had determined for his family the vagabond motif of their lives and imposed on each of them the unhappy ending syndrome of his own life, particularly for Frances, who would reap the full havoc of her parents' dilemma.

The burden of all this fell on his wife, and Ethel chose alternatives. Her daughter, later judging her mother's actions, portrayed her as a symbol of her disenchanted life, and this opinion replaced the knowledge that her father's hope for stability and a home for his family was always an illusion. It was he as much as her mother who was the cause of her unhappiness.

Judy was preoccupied with her father and inquired of his friends in later years about him. Marcus Rabwin was close to Judy. After her death, when he was asked about the sad, melancholy side of Frank, he said: "Yes, Frank was a homosexual . . . but I never knew it while he was alive." He said that it was only in retrospect, by putting various things together, that he knew this about Frank. "I believe there was an arrest in Los Angeles."

It was widely noted in Judy's last years that a conspicuous part of her audience and coterie were homosexual. Rabwin recalled how surprised he was to see how she was "drawn" to them. Although psychologists said that it was natural for the gay crowd to be sympathetic to a celebrity who was a public school symbol of a martyr and long-suffering woman, Judy was equally fascinated with these men. She didn't reject attention from anyone, and in her insomnia would spend many of her sleepless nights at New York clubs or private parties with homosexual crowds.

Marcus Rabwin watched Judy's life and career. He became a second father to her. He watched her rise and decline at MGM and then her comebacks in the 1950s and 60s. His most poignant memory was of a meeting with her about a year before her death, during which she "asked me if her father had been a homosexual." Rabwin replied with a resolute no. He didn't tell her the truth. "I didn't see what sense it would make to tell her."

By the usual standards, Frank Gumm was a failure. Forced to move from town to town, hedonistic, thinking he could do anything he wanted and get away with it, ultimately self-destructive, he was a success only to himself. He was charming, enigmatic, mysterious. "He had a way about him, a charm, a jolly quality." He was all this to Frances. If she, too, became self-destructive and failed "to become a great person," it was because she repeated her father's tragedy. It was enough for her that he, above all others, like a true Sewaneean, had paid "delightful attention" to her; this would carry her through.

The picture of Frank that is best remembered, which probably was the truest image of what he was really like, was seen through the eyes of his daughter:

I loved my father. . . . He was a wonderful man with a fierce temper . . . and an untrained but beautiful tenor voice . . . he was the only thing in my life! . . . handsome and so friendly . . . he had a funny sense of humor, and he laughed all the time—good and loud, like I do. . . . I adored him. We sang together. . . . And he wanted to be close to me, too, but we never had much time together.[10]

Frank's streak of indominability helped him fight against odds to save everything he had worked for. He believed that his lawyer, Harry Rabwin, would be able to arrange a last-minute agreement to save the lease. In the March 28 issue of the *Ledger-Gazette* he announced his screen attraction for March 31 and April 1, adding an "if possible" after the April date. In a note to his patrons he said: "I regret that my lease ex-

Valley Theater, Lancaster, California, at night two years after the departure of the Gumms. *Courtesy of John Reber*

pires April 1 and the building has been leased to an outside party. Unless I can obtain this lease I will be forced out of business temporarily but expect to open a new show as soon as possible." But on the front page of the same issue, the hopelessness of the matter was apparent:

THEATER LEASE CHANGES HANDS

W. B. Carter leases building to Mentor and Shearer, April 1. . . . Negotiations for the leasing of the Valley Theater in Lancaster have been concluded. . . . Frank Gumm, present manager of the theater, has not yet announced his future plans.

Frank kept his promise; he returned with a new show. He and Ethel rented the Lancaster Grammar School auditorium and presented "The Lawlor Professional Revue of 1935, with 50 talented young people of screen, radio, and stage." He promised the patrons "two hours of clean wholesome entertainment." As a farewell offering to the people of Lancaster, or perhaps out of bitter disappointment and an attempt to show the town what they would be missing, the Gumms gave their last performance in town.

Later in the month they made the familiar Lancaster-to-Los Angeles trip for the last time, Frank saying good-bye to the town he had once hoped would be a lasting home for his family.

They took some friends to see the wildflowers in bloom in the Antelope Valley. They had dinner with their best friends, the Goods, then left, driving past the Valley Theater. Frank took one more look at his desert showplace, the Valley Theater, now under new management. A sign in front read: REOPENING OF THEATER TODAY. Ethel, of course, didn't share Frank's nostalgia for the town; her disdain was now fixed.

Although Frank was disheartened, he outwardly exhibited confidence and optimism; Ethel was used to this. The family, though sometimes with different goals, had the ability to persevere, the ability to pick up and start over again. With this spirit, and 20 years of moviehouse experience, Frank quickly made another theater deal and assumed the management of the Lomita Theater.

12

L. A. APOTHEOSIS

*Daddy decided to take me to the audition
just as I was.*

As a teenager in Hollywood in the late 1930s, Judy was world famous. But she was also aloof, pensive, and introspective. She did not like being a movie star and was reluctant even to go out to dinner because of fans and autograph-seekers. Whereas later in life she played the role of Judy Garland to the hilt, in the early years of fame she could see it only as false compared to the true celebrity she was as a child. At this time, a couple of years before her first marriage, she wrote some poems of an imitative, romantic nature, but still, poems that show she knew, at some level, what had happened to her life. In one titled "An Illusion" she tells of the death of an illusion, which is like a child lost who had been protected from the hurts of the world—her ideal is lost too, a candle is lighted in her heart in "remembrance" of something which will not ever be recaptured.

Soon the door closed on these days. Fantasy became her best way of expressing her real self. The growth of film musicals was only being postponed until she made her appearance, her primary lessons in music and life now nearing an end. More couldn't be asked for: a girl whose voice, whether speaking or singing, was full of rhythm and melody and whose heart was about to be so wrenched that she would be able to better understand and express human feeling.

In the movies of the thirties and forties, whether they were frothy or sad, brassy or bittersweet, Judy enacted her own tale of woe, singing of hope and nostalgia, pain and happiness. Reality and fantasy become one to her, whether it was her sincerity in singing to Mr. Gable, her high spirits and determination in the endless vaudeville rags-to-riches chronicles, her gaiety and pathos in *Meet Me in St. Louis,* or her bravery and earnest cries for help in *The Wizard of Oz.* She was 16 when the film was made, and many scenes are symbolic and prophetic about the end of her own childhood; so it is no wonder that she was so convincing, that viewers thought she *was* Dorothy and not merely playing a role as they watched the little girl trapped in Oz crying for home and her family. She hears voices from home. Desperate and sobbing, she says: "I'm frightened . . . frightened. . . ." She hears her Aunt Em saying, "Dorothy, where are you?" "I'm here . . . I'm here . . . and I'm trying to get home."

Frances never stopped trying to get home. She lost this wonderful life which she was perfectly satisfied with and which was the source of her greatness. By the time she made *The Wizard,* her life as Frances was fully repressed; she communicates the sense of loss, nonetheless. In one of her best movies, the reason she can empathize is clear. As one critic put it: "'Meet Me in St. Louis' is the first Hollywood movie to confront the fact, and in a nostalgic family mileau, that childhood can be 'a dark time, a time of troubles.' "[1]

That Frances could attest to this tragic theme is evident as one watches her childhood come to an end and sees the life she leaves behind as she becomes the fabulous Judy Garland.

Frank once described Lomita as a "funny little old place," but it wasn't very different from the town he had spent the last eight years in. It was merely closer to Los Angeles. Lomita was a little settlement about 20 miles from Hollywood. Frank leased the Lomita Theater, which was on the main street of the town. By the end of May he was routinely running it. It was all second nature now. The only difference was that he had to commute to Lomita. The family did not move there. Again the theater became a family enterprise. The girls pitched in to help the new theater get off to a good start. Jimmie drew Frankie Darro, by now her boyfriend, into the operation by having him make a personal appearance after one of his movies. The girls' professionalism on stage came in very handy now. They were at their peak.

The girls had just completed their longest and most successful engagement so far, playing for three weeks at the Paramount, the theater which two years earlier had been their greatest goal and dream. It was the "Palace" of the circuits of vaudeville they had played since 1926. This was a return engagement—their third—and would turn out to be the final appearance of the Gumm sisters in a vaudeville theater.

Just two months earlier they had played the Paramount for a week. In part of his house review, the *Variety* critic said the Garland sisters had "panicked." In vaudeville parlance, a panic was even better than a riot. There is no doubt that they were well known by now. They earned up to $110 a week at a theater such as the Paramount. To record their billing during this engagement, one member of the family went outside and photographed their name—Garland Sisters—on the marquee, for the family scrapbook.

They were featured in the Fanchon and Marco stage show which was coupled with the latest Mae West movie, *Goin' to Town*. Again *Variety* reviewed the act.

Frank and Ethel were there for the opening night, May 16. Business was good in general for that performance, as well as the entire run. Mae West was the big screen attraction in 1935. The big stage show opened with three dozen chorus boys and girls wrapped in red, white, and blue, doing a patriotic drill routine. *Variety*'s reviewer cited the generally "mediocre" talent of the show's opening but then said that it warmed up with Rube Wolf, band leader and trumpet player, perennial favorite at this house and the brother of Fanchon and Marco. Wolf did a solo, Franklyn and Warner did a burlesque ballroom dance routine, and Max Ong, a Chinese singer, did an Italian aria and an American folk song.

But the reviewer's enthusiasm was reserved for the Garland sisters,

The sisters doing a song on the stage during 1934–1935. *Courtesy of The Garlandia Collection of Wayne Martin*

who were sensational; the impact of Frances's stage presence and musical vitality was evident. They got a good review. Even the manager of the Orpheum came down to his cross-town rival to catch the show.

Four decades later, it is evident that something stunning and phenomenal was happening in Judy's performances in late 1934 and early 1935. She was putting all her experience into action. She was electrifying audiences, and it was inevitable that she was going to be observed by those who would know what to do with her talents, and how to exploit them. The decade of singing with her family had led to the peak of her early form. In part, she may have thought that by becoming so good, she'd satisfy both her mother and father and somehow quell the discord between them, keep them together. But now her performing was an entity in itself, and her giving her all would become her undoing. More than a trouper, she was now the "little Mozart" of her milieu. In the last days of vaudeville, when critics and experts lamented that no great talent was being produced, there emerged perhaps the greatest of all vaudevillians—almost the ideal performer—Frances Ethel Gumm. That something astounding was taking place within the young Gumm child is documented in five reviews from the time, viewed both in light of her later triumphs and her early years. From Grauman's to the Paramount, the impact is the same:

Voice . . . audible throughout a house as large as the Chinese, she handles ballads like a veteran, and gets every note and word over with a personality that hits audiences. . . . Nothing slow about her on hot stuff, and to top it, she hoofs. . . . Kid is ready for the east . . . She has never failed to stop the show. . . .
    Variety review of Grauman's Chinese, November 1934

. . . The Garland Sisters scored a hit, with the youngest member of the trio practically stopping the show with her singing.
    Los Angeles Times review of Wilshire-Ebell "Frolics," December 1934

The Garland Trio made a great hit last night, especially the small member of the three, called "little Francis" [sic] on the program, but whose singing and action seem much more mature than the short frock and the bare legs indicate. She is very clever whether she is young or old, and deserved the applause.

San Francisco Chronicle—George C. Warren, review of "Frolics" at Curran Theater, January 1935

Garland Sisters, three femmes, one of whom, Frances, is still a child and about 80% of the combination, are excellent harmonists, but it remained for the youngster to tie things up in a knot. Girl looks like a bet for pictures and should make rapid headway. However, she should be coached more proficiently in her foreign tongue songs, particularly the German, as her pronunciation is none too accurate. Otherwise, the kid is tops and deserved everything she drew today.

Variety—Edwa, review of Paramount, L.A., March 1935

Class act on bill is the Three Garland Sisters, which, for the Paramount booking seems to have concentrated heavily on Francis, the youthful member of the family. Girls do only a couple of harmony numbers, leaving rest of performance to kid sister, who is talented beyond doubt, and who scores heavily with her rendition of 'Eili, Eili' plus a couple of songs in foreign tongue.

Variety—Edwa, review of Paramount, L.A., May 1935

For several months Ethel had been introducing herself as Mrs. Garland. Possibly she and Frank, in their zeal, legally changed their surname at this time. In subsequent newspaper advertisements, Frank billed the moviehouse as GARLAND'S LOMITA THEATER.

The girls' performance in Lomita was greeted enthusiastically, and Frank and his "family" theater were quickly accepted in town. The paper reported:

The three Garland Sisters, daughters of Frank Garland, owner of the Lomita Theater, made a very favorable impression with their stage entertainment. The three young ladies are talented and Lomita people gave their first appearance here a fine reception at both performances.

To keep up the momentum, Frankie Darro appeared in person the following Saturday, with Chapter 1 of his *Burn Em Up Barnes* serial. "All theater goers have seen and heard Frankie Darro in his several screen exploits. Now you will see this 17-year-old young movie actor in person. Frankie, a close friend of the Garland family, has graciously consented to appear. . . ."

So, in a new location, the cycle began all over again for Frank Gumm, smalltime vaudevillian and moviehouse manager.

In the summer of 1935 they went up to Lake Tahoe for a six-week working vacation at the Cal-Neva Lodge. It was a routine engagement, with the trio doing their act for the resort vacationers in the evening and swimming and having fun during the day. However, while they were at the lake two incidents occurred that they would always remember. First, Frances met a young musician who played in the orchestra there and introduced him to Mary Jane; before leaving for the city, Frances caught the attention of Lew Brown, a songwriter, and Al Rosen, an agent from Los Angeles. Brown had seen the trio perform and knew that Frances was something special; but Rosen had not seen the act. The Gumms were heading home. Frances recalled it:

We were ready to return to Los Angeles; my sister Jimmie had left all her hats in a hatbox in her room, and I went back to the bungalow to get them while my mother and sisters waited in the car. And "Bones" Remer, one of the owners of the place, asked me to come into the casino and sing for some friends of his. . . . I sang "Dinah." . . . When I was through, Al Rosen gave me a slip of paper with his phone number on it and told me to have mother call him when we got back to Los Angeles. . . .[2]

Back in Los Angeles, Ethel made some inquiries about Rosen. Learning that he was reliable, she agreed to let him search for opportunities for Frances. Rosen took Frances on a round of auditions which, with the exception of one, were like all the rest she had been to over the years.

Although the family was now going by the name of Garland, they had done nothing about their first names except for Janie who was nicknamed "Suzanne." Starting that summer, Frances adopted a stage name for professional purposes, but it was never used in the billing of the act. But then she was insisting on its use, even though she must have known her family, especially her father, preferred to call her

Babe. It was a name she liked, from a song of the same name. She told Rosen that he could call her Judy—Judy Garland.

Janie went back to Lake Tahoe. Frances's introduction of her to the young musician had sparked a romance, and Janie soon announced an elopement of sorts, a wedding at Tahoe, because the groom couldn't get any time off from the band. The couple would come to spend a week or so with the family in September. Frank told their friends, and the *Lomita Progress* announced the romance and marriage:

The Garland Sisters, daughters of Frank Garland of Lomita Theater who recently fulfilled a six week's vaudeville engagement at Cal-Neva Lodge, Lake Tahoe, were this week broken up as a trio when Dan Cupid waltzed in claiming Suzanne Garland for the bride of Lee Kahn, orchestra leader at Tahoe.

The paper went on to say that Jimmie had informally announced her engagement to Frankie Darro but that Frances "is only 12 so Cupid must wait a while." Being left out of romance didn't prevent Frances from being impressed with Janie's new-found happiness. When the family took Janie to the airport to catch a plane to Reno for the wedding, the three sisters tearfully parted.

The days of the Gumm sisters trio were over. They had had much fun together. A trend had started. Jimmie could be next, and then Frances would be all alone.

Jimmie liked the trend, since she hoped to marry Frankie soon. Frank accepted Janie's marrying philosophically and nostalgically. Ethel, too, would miss Janie, but she was undeterred as ever. Still teaching music, she now made Frances the focal point of her activities.

For the third time, Frank was well known in a small town, and family entertainment was succeeding. He made some improvements in lighting, sound, and projection. Everything was running smoothly; life was, or at least he said it was, "congenial." But Frances was aware of the slightest changes—the moving again, saying good-bye to friends, and now Janie's leaving. She was sensitive to everything and everyone. Her real self, according to Jimmie, was and always would be, "earnest, tender, and lyrical." The other side of her personality was fun-loving and high-spirited, and nothing could change that.

It was a crisp, beautiful fall. Their daily lives brought only ordinary changes until the autumn of 1935 when the golden fruit called "success" came to Frances.

Her initial success didn't alter her life. After all, even with a new name, she was still Frances Gumm. Most of all, she had her family, especially her father who, to a young girl, was practically her whole world. In the Gumm house they now talked about Lake Tahoe as being her "discovery."

On Friday, November 15, 1935, Frank went down as usual to oversee the evening show. He was proud of Babe's success. Their youngest was now on the threshold of movie-making. As he drove into Lomita that Friday he was thinking about the events of the past few weeks, of Frances's good fortune, and of their life in Grand Rapids and Lancaster. Only last month he had written some friends in Lancaster to bring them up to date about the family. In this letter, saved by John Perkins of Lancaster, Frank's love for his family, as well as his failures, achievements, hopes, and dreams, can be seen. It was written in response to a birth announcement from his friends in Lancaster:

Dear Friends Johnny and Billie:

Just a line to congratulate you upon the arrival of your new daughter. What a nice family you have now. Suppose Ronnie is some tickled over having a little sister. It sure is swell and I just hope the little girl gets along fine and dandy and that her mother will "recuperate" in good shape; to say nothing of her FATHER. If you are anything like me, Johnny (and God help you if you are), you feel a great relief after another one arrives safe and sound; at the best those little "parties" are no "pink tea" affairs I can tell you. History seems to be repeating itself in the Perkins family; first a boy and then a girl, like your mother and dad, eh? Now my candid advice is to "call it a day" and believe me kids you have your hands full if you raise the two of them up right and give them advantages.

I have been on the point of dropping a few lines to you, . . . but, I didn't know if you would care to hear from me or not; that is, if you would be at all interested; but when you DID think of us and send us the attractive little arrival card, it makes me happy to feel that someone in that old burg does think of me once in awhile.

How are things up there anyway? I hope you are doing O.K. Lomita is a funny little old place, but you know, I have done really very well down there and its so nice to be able to come home at night and have my meals etc. at home all the time. Another thing I look forward to is missing out on that damn cold weather in Lancaster when I would have to go to bed in Martha's shack with my bathrobe and sheep-line shoes to keep from freezing at nights. Boy those were miserable days and nights for me up there after the folks moved down here. I feel pretty much like an "old man" now that Janie got married and Jimmie is engaged and baby beginning to give the boys the "once over." I was just saying to Ethel today that in a little while I guess we will be left at home with nothing but the Pekingnese pup for company. Ethel's mother is with Norma, who is singing in a night club at Reno and doing very well. She has been there since last February. She stood up with Jane at her marriage; you see her husband, Lee Kahn, was playing in the orchestra at Cal-Neva and couldn't very well get away to come down here because the season is so short up there anyway and he plays the lead violin, saxaphone and clarinet in the band and it would have meant quite a loss to the band and to him too if he had taken a whole week off. They were married August 14 and stayed up at the lake until about the middle of September and then they came home for about ten days and are now living in Frisco where Lee is playing with Jimmie Davis at the Cairo Club and Jane sings with the band; a very nice arrangement and between the two they pull down about $120 per week. Babe got her seven year contract with M.G.M. and it started October 1 at $150 per week and the last year she gets $1,000 a week as the salary advances every six months; a very attractive deal. Of course, its all on six months' options and she has to make good or they have the privilege of letting her go at the end of each six months' period. . . .

It was September 13, a Friday, about midday. Frances, dressed in gray slacks, rode her bicycle up the street toward Melrose Avenue and then back to the house. Not having made any friends on the block yet, she was content to play by herself in the front yard. Inside, the phone rang, and after a few minutes Frank called Babe. An agent had phoned and arranged an audition at MGM studios. They were to meet him there. Frances was surprised that they had to go right away, since Ethel usually arranged those things, and she was now in Pasadena playing the piano at the Community Playhouse. But Frances was delighted that Frank was going to take her, since her mother always got her all gussied up. "Daddy decided to take me to the audition just as I was"—in slacks, white blouse, and grass-stained sneakers.

As they drove to Culver City, Frank talked rather brusquely, assuring Frances that they would either like her as she was or not at all. He didn't mind going over to MGM; he knew that his going with her would help avoid the distress of her having to perform alone. Everything turned out fine when he was around.

They entered the fabled gates of the fortresslike studio. Frank looked about as much as Frances, both equally awed by Hollywood's greatest studio. Al Rosen, the agent, took them into the rehearsal hall where she was to sing for Jack Robbins, the talent chief. "I'm looking for a woman singer. Why are you bringing me a child?" Robbins said. But Rosen talked him into listening to one number. Frank played the piano; Frances sang "Zing! Went the Strings of My Heart," a hit song of the year that she had been doing, based on an arrangement by Ethel. When she was through, Robbins called in Louis B. Mayer's executive secretary, Ida Koverman, an influential power at the studio, who was known for her musical taste. This time they brought in their own pianist, Roger Edens, who would become a lifelong mentor and disciple of the musical prodigy he was to play for now. Frances sang "Zing" again, and the "professional" listeners around her heard for the first time the sincerity and effervescence that would become her trademark. To Edens and the other MGM personnel, Frances had "unbelievable control, full power in the high register and shimmering warmth in the low." Ida Koverman picked up the phone and said a few words, then put it down and said: "He's coming." In a few minutes a burly little man entered the room, followed by a corps of secretaries, and sat right down to listen to Frances. The former nickelodeon owner, known to be both sentimental and ruthless, vulgar and shrewd, was "L.B." Mayer, the archetypal movie mogul. Here was the first encounter between the infamous movie czar and the movie exhibitor from Lomita and his youngest daughter. Mayer, who had a good eye for talent and who believed that all talent eventually reached its own level, surveyed the little girl whose face was at once impish, with a wide smile, and mourn-

ful. She sang "Zing" for Mayer, and, according to her, "the expression
on his face didn't change one bit." When she finished, he got up "without saying a word" and left the room. Frank said, "Let's go home" to
Frances. That was the end of the audition.

They drove back home, thinking that this had been just another
performance before a group of people who liked her singing. When
Ethel returned from Pasadena, Frances said: "Do you know where I
was today?" and before Ethel could respond, she said "Metro." "Who
took you?" Ethel asked. "Daddy!" "And what did you wear?" "Just what
I've got on."

Ethel had missed out on the big moment, for at MGM that day
Louis Mayer did something he had never done before. Without any
specific plans for her in mind, and without a screen test, he ordered a
seven-year contract. Frances Ethel Gumm had reaped the ultimate re-
ward of vaudeville. It was of the stuff of the American Dream. Whether
Frances realized the significance of this isn't known.

Within a few days of the audition they were told the good news.
Frances was thrilled with the prospect of being part of the world's
greatest movie studio. She had long internalized the ambitions, for her,
so she was now exhilarated. For all the Gumms there was an airy feeling, a suspension of reality as they told their friends. Frank tried to
temper the occasion by reminding Baby that she would still have to
prove herself.

For the first few months there were no immediate plans for her.
She would study at the studio a couple of hours each day after attending
school there, working with Mr. Edens on new songs. It didn't sound
very difficult for a starting salary of $150 a week with the eventual boost
to $1,000. Two weeks after the audition, she went with Frank and Ethel
to sign the contract: Frances Gumm, professionally known as Judy
Garland.

By the time Frank had written John Perkins, the Superior Court in
Los Angeles had approved the contract, and Frances was going to MGM
daily. Within a few days of the court's approval the Gumms told their
old friends, as well as their new associates, of Frances's good fortune. In
Lomita the first headline ever to use the new name by which Frances

would always be known appeared in the *Lomita Progress:* "JUDY GARLAND GETS MGM CONTRACT . . . Daughter of Manager Garland of Lomita Theater."

In Lancaster, where friends still considered the Gumms as part of their lives, people were curious but not stunned by the news of Frances's discovery, since they assumed this is what the family had been working toward all those years. Still, they had to feel a personal involvement in her life as they read the *Ledger-Gazette* item: BABY GUMM GIVEN SEVEN YEAR CONTRACT BY FILM CO. To the people of Lancaster, who 38 years later would still refer to Judy Garland as "Baby Gumm," the headline must have seemed to mark the end of an era, during the decade in which the remarkable family had captured and held their attention.

John Perkins and his wife got the news directly from Frank a few days before the item in the local paper. The letter to the Perkinses continued, discussing Frances's contract and the rest of the family:

. . . She is set for the first six months though and her first picture will probably be "This Time It's Love" in which Robert Montgomery and Jessie Matthews will be the stars and baby plays opposite Buddie Ebson a 6 foot 2 comedian that made a big hit with his sister in the new Broadway Melody of 1936. The picture goes into production in January next to be released about next April. Babe, or "Judy" as she is now called, will broadcast Saturday night, October 19th with Wallace Beery on the Shell Chateau hour from 6:30 to 7:30 P.M.

Frances appeared on the broadcast Frank mentioned, although it was postponed until October 26. The show was indirectly under the auspices of MGM, since Beery was one of their leading contract stars, and Frances was introduced on this show as a new find, with no mention of the contract that had been signed. They also said she was 12, instead of 13, in an effort to make her sound more precocious than she already was. Those who heard her that night could have been led to believe that she was 20, since she sounded like a mature woman.

The Los Angeles newspapers previewed the show in their radio sections. The *Herald and Express* said that "the tip we have is that little Judy Garland, child singer, is the surprise package," while the *Los*

Angeles Times informed its readers that in addition to Fannie Brice, Jack La Rue, and others, "an added attraction will be the appearance of Judy Garland, a youngster, who has just been signed to a motion picture contract by MGM."

A reviewer listening to a recording of the performance 35 years later said:

Her performance of "Broadway Rhythm" on that broadcast virtually defies belief; for Judy's poised assurance, effortless vocal control, sense of dramatic dynamics, pathos, and skill at syncopation were as fully developed as they ever would be. At the age of thirteen, she was a consummate performer. . . .[3]

Late on a Saturday afternoon Ethel, Frank, and Frances drove to the KFI studios for the show. Beery introduced her:

Now for the surprise of the evening, this is the opportunity spot of the show, one portion of the show that we donate each week to someone whom we feel has exceptional ability and we want to help along. We have a girl here who I think is going to be the sensation of pictures. She's only twelve years old and I take great pleasure in presenting to you, Judy Garland—wait until you hear her—twelve years old [applause]. Come on, Judy [more applause]; there you are, here Judy, if you're scared, you hang right on to me, honey. I'm right with you [Judy giggles]. Now come on, we'll talk a minute. Now where did you learn to sing?
Judy: My mother taught me [she responds without hesitation].
Beery: Your ma, huh? Never had any regular music lessons at all, huh?
Judy: Well I did take some piano lessons.
Beery: Can you play pretty good?
Judy: Oh, I don't know, mom says I play pretty well.
Beery: Hmmm, well, of course, mom would! All right Judy, now tell me this, now what do you want to do when you grow up to be a great big girl, huh?
Judy: I want to be a singer, Mr. Beery, and I'd like to act too.
Beery: Well you will, Judy, don't you worry. Now I'll tell ya, you just stand here and sing that piece you sang for me the other day and show these folks what a singer you are. Now go right to it. If you need me I'll be standing right there [Judy laughs]. Step right on it; go ahead, Judy.
[She sings "Broadway Rhythm"]

This dialogue was intended to coincide with MGM's gradual introduction of "Judy" and publicity connected with her "discovery." But

Frances's guileless, sincere demeanor transcended the dialogue and captured one's attention. After the conversation with Beery she sang, leaving her sweet and innocent speaking voice and becoming a dynamo of rhythm and feeling. Her performance was greeted at the end by applause and cheers.

Frank, Ethel, and Jimmie were in the front row, also applauding and cheering. Frank had listened to his "Baby" earnestly tell Wallace Beery that she wanted to become a singer and an actress; he, too, shared this dream for her. Knowing that her dreams and the family's dreams for her always came true, he embraced her after the show, confident that she would make good.

Frank concluded his letter to Perkins, reminding them to listen to the show:

Jimmie's fine and still going around with Frankie, claiming they are engaged: maybe it will all blow over as they fight like cats and dogs at times, he is so ungodly jealous. So much for the kids. Ethel is O.K. and just finished rehearsing a musical show for the Pasadena Community playhouse and has several private pupils she is coaching in personality singing, so with the Lomita theater, etc. we are all kept pretty much busy, but it's all congenial work and we are getting by nicely enough. Mr. and Mrs. Gilmore were here yesterday: you know, I suppose she had a stroke and her left arm and left leg, in fact, her whole left side is practically dead: awfully pitiful: I feel sorry for them. Bernice and Vesta Wright spent the night here last night and Jimmie went back with them to Canoga Park this morning for a few days' visit. Bernice is such a pretty girl now: think she is not well though as she is terribly thin. She goes with Dorothy Wilson's cousin; you know Dorothy Wilson of the pictures, I can't recall the guy's name but he brought her here several times and seems a fine chap and lots of dough; I hope she lands him as she is a nice girl. The two little girls were here with baby last week for several days and are such cute kids now; Mary Mae and Marjorie Ruth, you remember them. Just picked up the paper from Grand Rapids and in the "twenty years ago" column it announced Mary Jane's birth; gosh just think of it; she was 20 Sept. 24th.

Must close this up now before you get too tired of my line. Would like to send the baby a nice little gift but you know it's so hard to go down town or even to Hollywood to shop; takes hours to make one little purchase so I am taking the liberty of enclosing you a buck with which to buy her some little something she would like if she knew what it's all about. Lots of good wishes to you all and I would love to hear from you anytime; or if you are down, drop by and see us.

He signed the letter, "Sincerely, Frank" and added a P.S.: "Ethel and the girls send their regards and best wishes to you all."

In this letter to his friends is an undeniable statement of Frank's paternal feeling toward his family and an expression of his love and hopes for Frances.

Mixed feelings overwhelmed Frank, in his reverie about his family, past and future, as he arrived in Lomita that Friday ahead of showtime. It was dark when he entered the theater. He picked up the local newspaper and glanced at the advertisement for his new show that was starting Sunday:

Nov 17–18–19
Dante's Inferno and *We're in the Money*

He remained until the staff arrived—everything was in order—but left before the show, complaining of a headache. He was tired as he started the long drive back to Hollywood. He would go home and rest, tomorrow being another exciting day for the family.

Saturday night was another triumph for Frances, the only difference now being that her every performance would be chronicled and evaluated by the professionals of the entertainment industry. The transition from a "property" of her family to one of corporations and money men was taking place. But none of this mattered; Frances was doing what she liked. She was happy pleasing everyone, especially her mother and father. The appreciation of her and her talents would undergo a qualitative change, but the talents of the Gumms' youngest child, which could be exploited, could never be duplicated.

Ethel and Frances drove alone to the KFI studio for the broadcast Saturday afternoon. For the second time in a month, she made an electrifying impact on the show, her style now established. If on the previous broadcast she was the consummate performer, it was now clear that she was an artist and would always be one. At air time Ethel sat alone in the audience as Wallace Beery again introduced her daughter:

. . . her name is Judy Garland. And I'm sure that you remember her singing here about four weeks ago. Well since her last appearance here she's signed a seven year contract with the MGM studios. Isn't that great, gosh, and the minute she was signed, Sam Katz brought her into his new picture, *Yours and Mine*. I knew that, uh, Judy would make good. The last time she was here she was so good that everybody said, Wally, why you've got to have that little Judy Garland back again, so here she is and I'll tell you right now, we are very proud of her. Wait until you hear her sing. All right Judy, whip along . . .

She sang "Zing! Went the Strings of My Heart," the same song she had sung for Mayer. But this performance was different. Dad wasn't with her, and this night she sang with a purity, a depth of feeling, pathos, and intensity that she was capable of but had never quite reached before. This was the night before the world of Frances Gumm came to an end.

Early that Saturday morning Frank woke up in severe pain and by afternoon had been taken to the hospital. All of his life, Frank had had a draining ear, a common problem; but now, without much warning, it had ruptured into the inner ear. He was in a stupor when he arrived at the hospital and was soon diagnosed as having spinal meningitis.

Marcus Rabwin, who had, years earlier counseled the young couple to have their third child, was one of Frank's doctors. When he saw Frank he knew it didn't look hopeful for him. This was before the time of antibiotics, and brain surgery was not readily ventured. Every effort was being made to save his life. Ethel returned home in the late afternoon to get Frances ready for the broadcast; there was a show business tradition that wouldn't be broken by the Gumms. Rabwin called Frances before the show that night because he wanted to encourage her to do the show because she might have known her father was very sick. Frank did come out of the coma to some degree that night his "Baby" sang, and a radio was put in his room.

Whether or not he heard her singing to him that night in November 1935, he was never to hear her again. The one person she wanted to impress the most, the man who made her whole childhood worthwhile, would never again sit in the audience, cheering her from the front row, praising or embracing her as she came off the stage.

To Frank and Ethel Gumm must go the eternal credit for the qualities Frances possessed as a person and as a performer. At 13 she was a veteran trouper, a true artist. Frank gave her the depth of feeling; Ethel singlehandedly brought about her success. She had it all by 1935. Neither Louis B. Mayer nor any of his talent scouts, nor any of those who claimed to, discovered Judy Garland. She was there all along— Frances Ethel Gumm of Grand Rapids and Lancaster. When they found her she complied, since she had never refused to sing for anyone. She did not do it for fame or money, but as she had always done, to please. This is crucial in understanding her later notorious temperament and her unreliability as a performer. As a friend later stated, "Judy can only sing for nothing." Her art came out of the joy of singing with her sisters and parents; singing would always remain a matter of her heart.

Judy was not a product of Hollywood but of the commonplace, of good and gentle influences, of a tender background. Frank and Ethel were true innocents. Ethel thought that her actions were a solution to her and Frank's dilemma. Frank thought he could insure happiness for his family despite himself. Because of their actions, and chance, Judy would come to know tragedy.

They cultivated a quality in Frances which is a rare goal: to make a child believe in his or her own value and to always live up to this feeling of self-esteem. The Gumms were adventurers. Their like will never be seen again, any more than there'll ever be a minstrel remotely like young Judy. She would come to feel betrayed, although her mother and father could never have dreamed of such a betrayal.

But until the end of childhood she had never known suffering. Those first 13 years had been a joyous period in her life. Frances had always come first; her parents gave her everything but a sane and secure future. They provided for her greatness while unwittingly insuring her eternal disenchantment.

Judy inherited it all—the burden of her parents' actions—but it is a testament to the innocence of the Gumms that neither Frank nor Ethel ever comprehended the consequences of their actions. And Judy only slowly perceived the broken promise of her youth.

This life remained Judy's private vision of perfection, and an energy source for her, notwithstanding the myths which arose to bury the true incandescence of these years. If she had been unhappy, introverted, and cruelly treated, as the traditional accounts would have us believe—if she had not known joy and delight as a child—she could not have become the magnetic and vital woman she became.

Judy forever feigned the story of her mother's culpability while all the time recognizing that she had, in fact, been a dauntless individual. Curiously, Judy never damned her mother while Ethel was alive, her worst anger being saved for times when she felt betrayed and isolated, usually as her career deteriorated. She was in agony at having gradually lost everything after having begun life with incredible and unlimited promises of love, attention, and indulgence. When these eluded her as her illusions were destroyed, she could always seek refuge in her talent which she thought was eternal. When this became finite, there was no meaning at all. It was her unfortunate destiny to have been given too much and then to have it all stripped away. Maybe she became most angry at her mother for never telling her about loneliness and loss.

What Frank gave Frances ran deeper than any awareness on her part of his personal suffering, for Frank's discontent and melancholy was more existential; his romantic bent was thoroughgoing, and there is no question but that Frances inherited these. His memory always remained uncorrupted to her. It maintained her universe, and the ideal was justified. Despite his vulnerability, he did dominate his family and the affections of his three daughters. He held his wife, and kept the family together to the very end. And what of the love story between Frank and Ethel that Judy never spoke of? How much pain did their love for one another cause them in the midst of their torment? Judy, the victim, missed the touching aspects of their love. But she did carry the trauma of this love for the rest of her life.

The most poignant aspects of Frank's and Frances' love for one another is that Frank never got to see, and she never got to show him, her accomplishments on the stage and screen. She later said: "at the preview of my first picture I remember I cried when I realized he was not in the audience to watch my performance." He had had such great hopes for her to reach the pinnacle, with the strutting and tap dancing, syncopation and rhythm, and the vocal dynamics she had first tried out and then perfected on his stage. This was the saddest part of her success.

It is the paradox of her life that the childhood she reveled in, in which she was always contented despite its disjointedness, should leave her with intense needs. What perception of the world did this childhood give her? What direction did it set for her? She believed in the preeminence of herself and her cherished place in the scheme of things. Judy's need for mass love and devotion from audiences would be frequently remarked on; certainly her confidence and security as a child came from this total indulgence, on and off stage. This collective love and concern from everyone would make individual love intricate and difficult for her as an adult. The foundation for terrible emotional dependencies was here, and later indulgences, such as her use of drugs in response to stress, unhappiness, and exploitation at MGM, inevitably stemmed from the expectation molded in these early years.

Mainly, these years left her addicted to the stage and singing. The vaudeville life, with its tinsel and glamor and excitement, accelerated her senses. With the ultimate loss now, singing would save her from madness as she tried to convey her experience. This unconditional love she expected from all—she had long before taken for granted the advice of the Wizard to the Tin Man: "A heart is not judged by how much you love, but by how much you are loved by others"—made any other life impossible.

Fantastic things were ahead for her in the years to come. Triumphs, artistic brilliance, love, fortune, and acclaim. Could Frances imagine any of these? A cult forming around her, of being idolized and defended by unknown masses, of knowing the greatest artists and stars, and even presidents, of millions of words, in newspapers, magazines, and dozens of books, discussing and analyzing her, of a life with pitfalls, that a child could never imagine, bringing suffering and loss, or of a death which millions mourned, and a funeral like a general's or a president's, or lying in state, while over 20,000 persons file past her coffin. Could a little girl conceive of becoming one of the few authentic legends of her time? The life of Judy Garland was ahead. But what "adult life could have satisfied" Frances Gumm?

The rest of her life would be an attempt to recapture what was lost, to pick up the thread of her serene life as Frances Gumm. On stage in later years she would match the emotional richness and perfection of her childhood. In her private life, she would search for the equivalent of her extraordinary early life. With the exception of fleeting moments of romantic love and the mutual love between her and her three children, she would never find anyone who loved and accepted her for herself as her father had. She had known a great friendship with him, which would always be her basis for comparison. Her loss blurred and fragmented her being, never to be whole again. She had been indoctrinated to believe that all turned out well, never knowing that somehow her success was tied to family failures. Many would say that insecurity was the base of all her problems. But it was this childhood which was at the root of her heartache, or rather the catastrophe which brought these years to an end. Insecurity? At least. But more than that, it was the cataclysm of a soul, of innocence. She had been shielded from the unhappiness and sorrow of the world, and had never even been to a funeral, and now suddenly, the golden years were over, the gallant years were ahead.

On November 21, 1935, the *Lomita Progress* reported Frank's death: "Sad news reached Lomita Sunday evening telling of the sudden death of Frank A. Gumm (Garland) proprietor of the Lomita Theater. . . . Everything possible was done to spare his life but at 3 o'clock Sunday afternoon death closed the showman's career. . . ."

Judy later spoke of her father's death as "the most terrible thing that ever happened to me in my life . . . but the terrible thing about it was that I couldn't cry at my father's funeral. I'd never been to a funeral. I was ashamed because I couldn't cry, so I feigned it. But I just couldn't cry for eight days, and then I locked myself in a bathroom and cried for fourteen hours."

In the MGM period Judy refused to let his memory be extinguished. Neither her mother nor the studio ever referred to her father in publicity releases other than as the vaudevillian who died before her entry into movies. No photograph was ever released of the young star's father. And 40 years later, with the exception of one local article in the South, there was still no published photo of the father whom Judy idolized, despite her recollections of him.

For the rest of her life she would remark about him: "My father? Why, he was the only thing in my life." For a while she silently blamed her mother for his death, and in her grief and anger she later said that she had acted selfishly in thinking that only she felt the loss. Yet in light of all the overheard arguments, the separations, and vaudeville tours, what was she to think? And what of the special significance of the day of his death to her mother? In the child's mind it had to make an impact of more than a coincidence. Was her father being punished, her mother vindicated and rewarded? Was there a sense of release or relief on her mother's part? Or was Frances being punished for some unknown reason? She had done her best to hold it all together, and now the person she wanted to be closest to was gone. "And he wanted to be close to me, too," she would repeat, "but we never had time together."

If he had lived a few years longer, he would have seen Frances in a screen classic about an average American girl, not unlike herself, who, having a normal amount of yearning and desire, dreamed of an existence other than the drab and ordinary. The girl's life was interrupted by a tornado, never to be the same again. In this dream, or nightmare, or reality, she encounters incredible adventures—wonderful and terrifying, good and bad—while all the time wanting to go home. In the end Dorothy returns to her Kansas farm, to her family and home, to a normal existence. In real life, Frances Gumm could never return. In November 1935 she must say good-bye to Frances Gumm. The plaintive cries of Dorothy are of no avail. In the story she awakens from the dream, and in her touching and unforgettable voice, repeats over and over the moral, "There's no place like home . . . there's no place like home . . . there's no place like home."

By the Sunday morning after the radio show, Frank had gone into a deep coma. It was November 17, 1935, Ethel's birthday. He died at 3:00 P.M. at the age of 49. The Gumm family saga was over.

The night before, Frances got a thundering ovation. She always remembered that night; she knew that her father was very ill. She knew that the doctor had put a radio in the room so that he might hear her. "I sang my heart out for him, but by morning he was gone."

Frances would always do her best. For the rest of her days she would be a heroic trouper. That Saturday night, as she had so many times, she put on her trouper face for the world to see. She sang the love song, and then Wallace Beery talked with her:

Beery: That was marvelous Judy, oh how you can sing. Ladies and gentlemen, that was Judy Garland. That wasn't me singing [Judy giggles]. Oh I want to thank you for that Judy; it was marvelous.
Judy: Wait a minute, Mr. Beery, I want to thank you.
Beery: Oh no.
Judy: Yes, really I do, I want to thank you for giving me two chances to come here and sing at Shell Chateau and for all the other things you've done for me.
Beery: Oh, I'm so proud of you Judy. I bet your mother is proud of you too; isn't that your ma, sitting down there in the front row?
Judy: That's her.
Beery: Um, hmm.
Judy: Well, do you think, do you think my mother would care if I gave you a great big hug?
Beery: Oh I don't know what she'd think, but maybe that little Carol Ann of mine might object [Judy laughs]. Go ahead [laughing, Judy gives him a hug]. That's awfully sweet of you. Now come on, just a little, little bitty, teeny weeny encore.
Judy: All right.
[Orchestra reprises, and she sings again]

> Dear, when you smiled at me,
> I heard a melody,
> It haunted me from the start.
> Something inside of me
> Started a symphony,
> Zing! went the strings of my heart. . . .[4]

EPILOGUE FROM LANCASTER

FRANK

"Frank Gumm Dies in LA. . . . Mr. Gumm came to Lancaster with his family from Minnesota nine years ago and moved to Lomita about a year ago where he has operated a theater. He and his family contributed generously of their musical talents to many community gatherings while in Antelope Valley and are kindly remembered for their public spirit."

Ledger-Gazette, November 21, 1935

ETHEL

"Death of Star's Mother Noted by Antelope Valley Friends. . . . Many of her old friends in Lancaster mourn the recent passing of Mrs. Ethel Gilmore, mother of world famous stage and screen star Judy Garland . . . the wife of the owner of the first theater in Lancaster. Mrs. Gilmore was a very active person. . . . The Gumms were known as a very talented family. . . . The Gumm family lived on Cedar Avenue."

Ledger-Gazette, January 8, 1953

MARY JANE

" . . . Miss Garland's sister, Sue Gumm Cathcart, 48, died in Las Vegas, Nevada, Tuesday night. . . . "

Ledger-Gazette, May 29, 1965

FRANCES

"Judy Garland Dead at 47. . . . Although she expressed little fondness for the area in later years, Judy Garland was a former resident of Lancaster. . . . During the late 1920's her father operated the theater on Sierra Highway, Judy and her sisters appeared on stage there. . . ."

Ledger-Gazette, June 23, 1969

The old Valley Theater was destroyed by fire on February 27, 1953. The newspaper published a photograph of the burnt-out building, stating, "This is all that was left of the old Valley theater when the embers cooled last Friday morning. . . . This is where the film star, Judy Garland got her early training when her parents, Mr. and Mrs. Frank Gumm, owned the theater and lived in Lancaster."

Ledger-Gazette

VIRGINIA

The last of the Gumms is married and lives somewhere in Texas.

APPENDIX

This is a heretofore undocumented chronology of Judy Garland's early years, as we have reconstructed it. For every two or so documented appearances, there was possibly an anonymous one, either an impromptu or a professional occasion. Where there are gaps, especially on the family stage, the girls undoubtedly continued to perform as theater ads indicated vaudeville at regular intervals. While Ethel Gumm is not cited as a performer, she almost always played the piano accompaniment to the family act, as well as to the silent movies. Frank Gumm occasionally substituted as pianist. When they were booked on the professional vaudeville circuit, there were two to four shows daily.

PERFORMANCES, 1923–1935

1923   Central School, Grand Rapids, November 16; Ethel; she accompanies school operetta, *Snow White and the Seven Dwarfs.*

Episcopal Guild, Grand Rapids, December 12–13; Frank, Ethel, Mary Jane, Virginia; play, *Mary,* staged by Ethel; sisters sing "Hello" song; Frank plays "Gaston Marceau, the funny Frenchman."

1924   Legion Hall, Grand Rapids, January 14; Frank.

Grand Rapids Commercial Club meeting; Frank sings town song.

Hibbing, Minnesota, May 7; Frank, Ethel, Mary Jane, and Virginia; Encore of *Mary* musical.

Itasca Dry Goods Store, Grand Rapids, May or June; Frances; sings at annual style show, her public debut.

New Grand Theater, Grand Rapids, Christmas week; Frances, Mary Jane, Virginia; spontaneous theatrical debut, when Frances interrupts her sisters to sing "Jingle Bells."

New Grand Theater, Grand Rapids, December 26; Frances, Mary Jane, and Virginia; formal theatrical debut of young Judy.

1925 Central School, Grand Rapids, March 6; Mary Jane and Virginia; in operetta, *Cinderella in Flowerland;* Mary Jane stars, Virginia as a page.

New Grand Theater, Grand Rapids, March 21–22; Mary Jane and Virginia.

New Grand Theater, Grand Rapids, March 29; Frank and Frances; Frances between shows, and vocal solo by Frank.

New Grand Theater, Grand Rapids, May 23; Gumm Sisters.

1926 Garrick Theater, Virginia, Minnesota, April 30–May 1; Frank and Ethel.

Cross-country tour, June–July; Gumm family; six-weeks tour on way to California; theaters unknown—Minnesota, North Dakota, Montana, Idaho, Washington; Liberty Theater, Shelby, Montana where girls sing "In a Little Spanish Town."

1927 Valley Theater, Lancaster, May 22–23; Gumm family; theatrical debut of family on their new family stage.

Valley Theater, Lancaster, June 5–6; Frank and Ethel.

Valley Theater, Lancaster, July 3–4; Gumm family.

Valley Theater, Lancaster, July 17; Frances.

Valley Theater, Lancaster, July 24; Frank and Ethel.

Valley Theater, Lancaster, July 31–August 1; Mary Jane and Virginia.

Valley Theater, Lancaster, August 7–8; Frank and Ethel.

Valley Theater, Lancaster, September 4–5; Frank and Ethel; they sing between shows.

Valley Theater, Lancaster, September 18–19; Frank and Ethel.

Antelope Valley Fair, Lancaster, October 14; Gumm family.

Valley Theater, Lancaster, November 22–23; Gumm Sisters.

Valley Theater, Lancaster, December 2; Gumm Sisters; Frances solos.

Valley Theater, Lancaster, December 9; Frank and Ethel.

1928 Valley Theater, Lancaster, March 23; Gumm family.

Valley Theater, Lancaster, May 3–4; Gumm family.

Valley Theater, Lancaster, August 26–27; Gumm Sisters.

KFI Radio, Los Angeles, August–October; Gumm Sisters; radio debut of Frances, with sisters, "The Children's Hour."

Valley Theater, Lancaster, September 14; Gumm Sisters.

Shrine Auditorium, Los Angeles, December 13; Frances; *Los Angeles Examiner* Christmas All-Star Benefit, including Meglin Kiddies.

Loew's State Theater, Los Angeles, December 20–26; Frances; solos with Meglin Kiddies in Christmas show, with Jess Stafford and Brunswick Orchestra.

1929 Grammar School, Lancaster, February 28; Gumm Sisters; Virginia has lead as Cinderella, Mary Jane plays the prince, and Frances, Bonnie Bee.

Better Babies Contest, Los Angeles, March; Frances; she wins Honorable Mention.

Egyptian Theater, Los Angeles, March; Gumm Sisters; Meglin recital at Hollywood theater.

Figueroa Playhouse, Los Angeles, April 7; Gumm Sisters; Frances a soloist with Meglin Kiddies.

Valley Theater, Lancaster, May 16; Gumm family; Ethel at piano, Frank soloist; Gumm Sisters close with song-and-dance specialties in Antelope Valley Band "Minstrel Show."

Shrine Auditorium, Los Angeles, June; Gumm Sisters.

Valley Theater, Lancaster, June 10; Gumm Sisters.

Grammar School, Lancaster, June 13; Mary Jane; she sings solo at her graduation commencement.

Unknown theater, Lone Pine, July 15; Gumm Sisters.

Bishop Theater, Bishop, July 16–17; Gumm Sisters.

Valley Theater, Lancaster, July 28; Frances; she and Eugene Taylor in novelty song-and-dance specialty.

Loew's State Theater, Los Angeles, August 14–20; Gumm Sisters; they perform with 56 Meglin Kiddies and Stepin Fetchit in Fanchon and Marco show.

Valley Theater, Lancaster, August 25; Gumm Sisters.

Kiwanis, Lancaster, September 19; Frank.

Kiwanis, Lancaster, October 2; Ethel; plays in local orchestra.

Jazz Cafe, Lancaster, October 19; Frances; sings a song at reopening of candy shop.

Haubrich's Department Store, Lancaster, October 19; Virginia and Frances; Virginia and Frances in three solos.

KNX Radio, Los Angeles, Monday afternoons, November–December; Gumm Sisters; in special Christmas shows with Hollywood Starlets group on Big Brother Ken radio show.

Walker's Department Store, Los Angeles, November 16; Gumm Sisters.

Valley Theater, Lancaster, November 24; Gumm Sisters; girls appear under new name, "Hollywood Starlets Trio"; Frances sings "Wear a Hat with a Silver Lining."

Warner's Film, Los Angeles, December; Gumm Sisters; showing of vitaphone short; Frances in movies at age 7, with sisters singing "The Sunny South" in *The Meglin Kiddie Revue.*

Kiwanis, Lancaster, December 4; Gumm Sisters.

High School, Lancaster, December 6; Gumm Sisters; entertainment featuring songs and dances by the girls.

High School, Lancaster, December; Ethel; she performs her own composition, "Deep Deep in My Heart," at school "Hi Jinx."

American Legion, Fillmore, December 13; Gumm Sisters.

Los Angeles Country Club, Los Angeles, December 23; Gumm Sisters; they appear with Hollywood Starlets group in Christmas entertainment.

Munz Country Club, Antelope Valley, December 22; Gumm family.

Kiwanis, Palmdale, December 26; Frank; he sings "Swanee River."

1930   Valley Theater, Lancaster, January 12; Gumm Sisters; the Hollywood Starlets Trio sing songs from their second vitaphone film short.

KNX Radio, Los Angeles, January 13 and following Mondays; Gumm Sisters.

St. Paul's Church, Lancaster, February 16; Frank.

High School, Lancaster, February 28; Mary Jane and Frances; Mary Jane as Meg in *The Gypsy Rover* and Frances as one of the little children.

Grammar School, Lancaster, March; Virginia and Frances; Frances stars as Goldilocks and Virginia plays the Wood god in school operetta.

Better Babies Contest, Los Angeles, March; Frances.

Warner's film, May 9–10; Gumm Sisters; Valley Theater features second Meglin-Warner's technicolor film short; the girls are billed as "three kute kiddies," with Frances singing the featured song, "Blue Butterfly."

High School, Lancaster, May 22; Frances; as mistress of ceremonies at a piano recital, she does song specialties.

Shrine Auditorium, Los Angeles, May 24; Gumm Sisters; benefit performance with Hollywood Starlets for Milk Bottle Fund.

Hotel Del Coronado, San Diego, July 4; Gumm Sisters; professional appearance with Hollywood Starlets group.

Million Dollar Theater, Los Angeles, July 17–23; Gumm Sisters.

Warner's film, August 1–2; Gumm Sisters; Valley Theater shows third Meglin-Warner's technicolor film short, *The Wedding of Jack and Jill,* in which Frances sings "Hang on to the Rainbow."

Million Dollar Theater, Los Angeles, August 14–20; Gumm Sisters.

Loew's State Theater, Los Angeles, August 21–27; Gumm Sisters; with the Hollywood Starlets in a Fanchon and Marco show, featuring Rube Wolf in *Southern Idea.*

Kiwanis, Victorville, October; Gumm family; Gumm children and Kiwanis Quartet, with Frank, sing with band.

Kiwanis, Barstow, October; Ethel; she plays piano accordion at Kiwanis affair.

Grammar School, Lancaster, November; Gumm Sisters; school playlet, *The Old Sleuth,* with the sisters singing "My Baby Comes for Me."

1931   Funeral, Lancaster, January; Frank.

Valley Theater, Lancaster, January 11; Gumm Sisters; theater ad cites "harmony songs and dance numbers."

Pantages Theater, Los Angeles, January 31; Gumm Sisters; Saturday matinee with the Meglin Kiddies.

KFVD Radio, Hollywood, January 31; Gumm Sisters; afternoon broadcast at Hal Roach studio.

Savoy Theater, San Diego, February 21; Gumm Sisters; benefit midnight matinee for the Red Cross Drought Relief Fund.

Kiwanis, Lancaster, March 13; Frank.

Agricultural conference, Lancaster, April 1–2; Gumm family.

Funeral, Lancaster, April 24; Frank and Ethel.

Grammar School, Lancaster, June 12; Virginia.

Wilshire–Ebell Theater, Los Angeles, July 10–16; Gumm Sisters; in Kusell's *Stars of Tomorrow;* sisters featured in three song-and-dance numbers; Frances featured in two other solo acts; orchestra under Ethel's direction.

Valley Theater, Lancaster, August 30; Frances.

Valley Theater, Lancaster, September 6; Frances; first name change: "On the stage, Frances Gayne in a group of song specialties."

High School, Lancaster, September 15; Frances in PTA show.

Valley Theater, Lancaster, September 21; Frances.

Order of the Rainbow, Los Angeles, September 26; Mary Jane; sings duet with Lancaster friend, Jean Weaver.

High School, Lancaster, October; Frank.

Eastern Star Lodge, Bakersfield, October 5; Frank and Frances.

Eastern Star Lodge, Tehachapi, October 6; Frank and Frances.

Kiwanis, Lancaster, October 28; Virginia.

Eastern Star Lodge, Lancaster, December 12; Ethel and Frances.

Kiwanis, Lancaster, December 16; Frances.

Warner Brothers Theater, Hollywood, December 24–30; Frances; "Little singer at Hollywood Theater," with Jess Stafford's orchestra, in Christmas show.

1932 Cocoanut Grove, Los Angeles, January 25; Frances featured at Ambassador Hotel club.

High School, Lancaster, March 17; Virginia "Queen of the Fairies" in *Iolanthe*.

Cocoanut Grove, Los Angeles, March 21; Frances.

High School, Lancaster, April 10; Frances; school talent show.

Valley Theater, Lancaster, April 17–18; Frances.

Valley Theater, Lancaster, April 24–25; Frances.

Philharmonic Auditorium, Los Angeles, April 30; Gumm Sisters; girls perform in revue staged by Maurice Kusell.

Valley Theater, Lancaster, May 1–2; Frances.

High School, Lancaster, May 21; Frances; May musicale of the PTA, with "Only God Can Make a Tree" and "Cherie" sung by Frances.

Valley Theater, Lancaster, May 22–23; Gumm Sisters.

Vaudeville tour, July–August; Gumm Sisters; summer tour of 12 theaters, under management of Fanchon and Marco.
?, Los Angeles, July 7–13
?, Los Angeles, July 14–28, three engagements
Fox West Coast Theater, Long Beach, July 29–31
?, August 1–10, two engagements
Manchester Theater, Los Angeles, August 11–13
?, August 14–23, three engagements
Paramount Theater, Los Angeles, August 25–31

At the Paramount, the sisters are billed as "Blue Harmony," in a show headlining Fuzzy Knight, with the George Stoll orchestra; the girls get their first *Variety* review.

KFI and KECA Radio, Los Angeles, October 29; Gumm Sisters; broadcast with Uncle Tom Murray and the Hollywood Hillbillies.

Valley Theater, Lancaster, October 30; Gumm Sisters.

Theater unknown, Los Angeles, October 31–November 6; Gumm Sisters.

Lancaster, week of November 20; Gumm Sisters; three sisters in a musical program for the Southern California Gas Company.

Fox Arlington Theater, Santa Barbara, December 16–17; Frances.

Million Dollar Theater, Los Angeles, December 29–January 4; Frances.

1933   Valley Theater, Lancaster, January 29; Frances; she and a Kusell student, Clark Williams, in a stage specialty.

Strand Theater, Long Beach, February 3–5; Frances; among "6 Big Vaudeville Acts," she appears as Gracie Gumm, "Radio's youthful star."

Unknown radio station, Beverly Hills, April 1; Frances.

KFI Radio, Los Angeles, April 20; Frances; sings with "Al Pierce and his gang."

Hamburger Memorial Home, Los Angeles, May 6; Gumm Sisters.

High School, Lancaster, May 10; Gumm Sisters; song-and-dance numbers by Mary Jane, Virginia, Frances, and Clark Williams, for junior class promenade.

Valley Theater, Lancaster, May 12; Frances; special musical numbers by Frances for spring fashion show.

Garfield Theater, Alhambra, May 13–14; Frances; billed as Alice Gumm, she sings in "Orpheum Big Time Vaudeville."

Fairfax Theater, Los Angeles; May 25–26; Frances.

KFWB Radio, Los Angeles, June; Frances; performs in "Junior Hi Jinx" every Friday.

KFWB Radio, Los Angeles, June 16–July; Gumm Sisters; Mary Jane and Virginia join Frances on the "Junior Hi Jinx" show.

Audition, Lancaster; July 16; Gumm Sisters; RKO vaudeville bookers audition sisters at Cedar Street home.

RKO Hillstreet Theater, Los Angeles, July 17; Gumm Sisters; the three girls appear on Monday program of vaudeville; Frances solos with "Rain, Rain, Go Away."

Lancaster, July; Gumm Sisters; Order of Rainbow farewell party for Gumm Sisters, at which they entertain.

Golden Gate Theater, San Francisco, August 2–8; Gumm family. Earn second *Variety* review.

Fox West Coast Theater, Long Beach, August 9–15; Gumm Sisters.

Warner Brothers Theater, Hollywood, August 24–30; Gumm Sisters as "Harmony at its best," in show featuring Teddy Joyce.

Warner Brothers Theater, Los Angeles, August 31–September 6;

Gumm Sisters; second on bill, as "Harmony Supreme." Earn third *Variety* review.

Acacia Club, Los Angeles, September 21; Gumm family.

1934   Paramount Theater, Los Angeles, February 2; Frances; KHJ "Friday Nite Frolics" radio program, originating at the Paramount.

Orpheum Theater, Los Angeles, February 8–13; Gumm Sisters; one of seven acts on vaudeville bill.

Vaudeville tour, February–March; Gumm Sisters.
Paramount Theater, Seattle, Wash., Feb. 16–22
?, Bellingham, Wash., Feb. 24
Empire Theater, Yakima, Wash., Feb. 25
Liberty Theater, Wenachee, Wash., Feb. 27
Orpheum Theater, Spokane, Wash., Mar. 1
Liberty Theater, Lewiston, Idaho, Mar. 6
Fox Theater, San Francisco, Mar. 9–15

Spreckels Theater, San Diego, April 12–18; Frances; billed as "Baby Gumm," among 23 stars of the Gilmore Circus.

Agua Caliente Hotel, Mexico, April 15; Frances; midnight "Frolic" broadcast by Gilmore troupe.

State Theater, Long Beach, April 19–25; Frances; she sings "Why Darkies Were Born" and "Dinah" with the Gilmore Circus.

Shrine Auditorium, Los Angeles, April 26–May 2; Gumm Sisters; Mary Jane and Virginia join Frances and Gilmore Circus for Shrine booking.

Million Dollar Theater, Los Angeles, May 3–9; Gumm Sisters; girls are part of *Big Stage Show.*

Gilmore Stadium, Los Angeles, May 18–20; Gumm Sisters; billed as "Trio Musicale" for *Movie Star Frolics.*

St. Catherine Hotel, Catalina Island, June 2–3; Gumm Sisters; weekend professional engagement.

Cross-country tour, June–October; Gumm Sisters.
Tabor Grand Theater, Denver, Col., June 8–14
?, Denver, June 15–21
?, Colorado Springs, Col., June 22–July 5
World's Fair, Chicago, mid-July (the girls appear regularly at the

"Old Mexico Cabaret" on the fairgrounds, billed as "Blue Harmony")

World's Fair, Chicago, July 19; Frances selected as guest of honor and star performer for "Children's Day"

Belmont Theater, Chicago, mid-August

Oriental Theater, Chicago, Aug. 17–23; misbilled as "Glum Sisters"; headliner George Jessel suggests they change their name

Marbro Theater, Chicago, Aug. 24–30

Michigan Theater, Detroit, Sept. 7–13; first billing using Garland name

?, Milwaukee, Wis., September

?, Kansas City, Mo., September

?, St. Joseph, Mo., October

Beverly–Wilshire Hotel, Los Angeles, October 24; Gumm Sisters; trio sings with Vincent Lopez orchestra.

Grauman's Chinese Theater, Hollywood, November 1–7; Gumm Sisters; receive fourth *Variety* review and are cited as promising new act.

Strand Theater, Long Beach, November 9–11; Gumm Sisters; billed as "the Gumm Sisters direct from Grauman's Chinese."

Orpheum Theater, Los Angeles, November 14–20; Gumm Sisters; from this engagement on, the sisters appear under the Garland name.

Valley Theater, Lancaster, December 7; Gumm Sisters.

Wilshire–Ebell Theater, Los Angeles, December 8; Gumm Sisters; Garland trio on bill headed by Fuzzy Knight, in Irving Strauss's "Frolics."

Hollywood Playhouse, Hollywood, December 23; Gumm Sisters; billed as "Garland 3" and "Frances Garland" at Sunday night vaudeville, headlining Gilda Gray.

Curran Theater, San Francisco, December 25–January 1; Gumm Sisters; Los Angeles "Frolics" show, with 60 members, including "Frances Garland and Sisters."

1935 Paramount Theater, Los Angeles, March 7–13; Gumm Sisters; receive fifth *Variety* review in Fanchon and Marco show, with Rube Wolf.

Paramount Theater, Los Angeles, May 16–June 5; Gumm Sisters;

three-week engagement during which Frances sings "Eili, Eili"; sixth *Variety* review.

Lomita Theater, Lomita, June 8; Gumm Sisters; trio performs on family's new theater stage.

Cal–Neva Lodge, Lake Tahoe, July 1–August 14; Gumm Sisters.

KFI Radio, Los Angeles, October 26; Frances; she sings "Broadway Rhythm" on Wallace Beery's radio show, "Shell Chateau."

KFI Radio, Los Angeles, November 16; Judy Garland; MGM contract is announced by Beery; Frances, now called Judy, sings "Zing! Went the Strings of My Heart."

NOTES

EPIGRAPH

"Little Girl Blue" by Richard Rodgers and Lorenz Hart. Copyright © 1935 T. B. Harms Company. Copyright renewed. Reprinted by permission of the publisher.

PREFACE

1. Budd Schulberg, "A Farewell to Judy," *Life*, July 11, 1969.

PROLOGUE

1. *Variety*, July 2, 1969.

CHAPTER 1

Epigram: *McCalls*, April 1957.
1. Schulberg, "Farewell to Judy."

241

CHAPTER 2

Epigram: *McCalls*, April 1957.
1. *Ibid.*
2. Percy, *Lanterns on the Levee*, Knopf, 1941. Copyright © 1941 by Alfred A. Knopf, Inc. Copyright renewed 1969 by Leroy Pratt Percy.

CHAPTER 3

Epigram: *McCalls*, April 1957.

CHAPTER 4

Epigram: *McCalls*, April 1957.
1. Marjorie Rosen, *Popcorn Venus: Women, Movies and the American Dream*, Coward, McCann and Geoghegan, 1973.
2. *Grand Rapids Herald Review*, February 24, 1915.
3. *Ibid.*, April 19, 1915.
4. *McCalls*, April 1957.
5. *Ibid.*
6. *Ibid.*
7. *Grand Rapids Independent*, December 26, 1924.
8. Henry Pleasants, *The Great American Popular Singers*, Simon and Schuster, 1974.
9. *McCalls*, January 1964.

CHAPTER 5

Epigram: *McCalls*, January 1964.
1. *Ibid.*, April 1957.
2. *Ibid.*,
3. *Ibid.*, January 1964.
4. *Newsweek*, July 7, 1969. Copyright Newsweek, Inc. 1969. Reprinted by permission.
5. Torgersen, *Los Angeles Times*, June 23, 1969.
6. From Notes and Comment in *The New Yorker*, July 5, 1969.
7. *Time*, July 4, 1969. Reprinted by permission from TIME, The Weekly Newsmagazine; Copyright Time Inc.
8. Warga, *Los Angeles Times*, June 1969.

9. *CBS Sunday News with Harry Reasoner,* June 22, 1969. Reprinted by permission.
10. *Ibid.*
11. *Ibid.*

CHAPTER 6

Epigram: *McCalls,* January 1964.
1. *Ibid.*
2. Antelope Valley *Ledger-Gazette,* May 20, 1927.

CHAPTER 7

Epigram: *McCalls,* January 1964.
1. Hedda Hopper, "No More Tears for Judy," *Woman's Day Companion,* September 1954.
2. *My Mammy* by Sam Lewis, Joe Young, Walter Donaldson. © Copyright 1920 Bourne Co. Copyright renewed. Used by permission.
3. Ralph J. Gleason, "The Enigma of Judy Garland," *San Francisco Chronicle,* September 2, 1965.
4. *Variety,* February 17, 1965.
5. Mickey Deans and Ann Pinchot, *Weep No More My Lady,* Hawthorn, 1972. Reprinted by permission of Hawthorn Books, Inc. Copyright © 1972 by Mickey Deans and Ann Pinchot.
6. *Time,* August 18, 1967. Reprinted by permission from TIME, the Weekly Newsmagazine; Copyright Time Inc.
7. Korall, "The Garland Phenomenon," *Saturday Review,* September 30, 1967. Copyright © by Saturday Review 1967. Reprinted by permission of Saturday Review.
8. Canby, *The New York Times,* June 29, 1969. © 1969 by The New New York Times Company. Reprinted by permission.
9. *Los Angeles Times,* December 24, 1928.
10. *Los Angeles Evening Express,* December 24, 1924.

CHAPTER 8

Epigram: *McCalls,* January 1964.
1. Alexander, "Judy's New Rainbow," *Life,* June 2, 1961. Shana Alexander, LIFE Magazine, Copyright © 1961 Time Inc. Reprinted with permission.
2. *Ibid.*

3. De Toledano, "The Cult of Judy," *National Review,* August 28, 1962.

4. *Variety,* August 21, 1929.

CHAPTER 9

Epigram: *McCalls,* January 1964.

1. *Ibid.,* April 1957.

2. *Ladies' Home Journal,* August 1967. © 1967, Downe Publishing, Inc. Reprinted with the permission of Ladies' Home Journal.

3. Shana Alexander, "Judy's New Rainbow," *Life,* June 2, 1961.

4. *McCalls,* January 1964.

5. David Shipman, *The Great Movie Stars: The Golden Years,* Crown, 1970.

6. Harold Clurman, "Punch and Judy," *New Republic,* November 26, 1951. Reprinted by permission of THE NEW REPUBLIC, © 1951, The New Republic, Inc.

7. Fadiman, "Party of One," *Holiday,* March 1952.

CHAPTER 10

Epigram: *McCalls,* January 1964.

1. Korall, "The Garland Phenomenon," *Saturday Review,* September 30, 1967.

2. Clurman, *Lies Like Truth.* Reprinted by permission of Macmillan Publishing Co., Inc. Copyright © 1946, 1947, 1958 by Harold Clurman.

3. Rosen, *Popcorn Venus.*

4. Shipman, *Great Movie Stars.*

5. *McCalls,* January 1964.

6. *Ladies' Home Journal,* August 1967.

7. Antelope Valley *Ledger-Gazette,* May 26, 1932.

8. *Variety,* August 30, 1932.

9. *McCalls,* January 1964.

CHAPTER 11

Epigram: *McCalls,* January 1964.

1. Torme, *Other Side of the Rainbow,* William Morrow, 1970.

2. *Time,* November 16, 1962.

3. Rosen, *Popcorn Venus.*

4. Torme, *Other Side of the Rainbow.*

5. *Variety,* August 8, 1933.

6. George Benjamin, "Setting You Straight on Judy," *Modern Screen,* June 1939.

7. *Ibid.*

8. *McCalls,* January 1964.

9. *Variety,* November 6, 1934.

10. Hyams, "The Real Me," *McCall's,* April 1957. Reprinted by permission.

CHAPTER 12

Epigram: *McCalls,* January 1964.

1. Richard Schickel, "Men Who Made the Movies," WNET, New York, 1974.

2. *McCalls,* January 1964.

3. Miles Krueger, *Judy Garland, Collector's Items,* Decca Records, 1970.

4. "Zing! Went the Strings of my Heart" by James F. Hanley, © 1935 Harms, Inc. Copyright renewed. All rights reserved. Used by permission of Warner Bros. Music.

BIBLIOGRAPHY

BOOKS

Clurman, Harold. *Lies Like Truth*. Grove Press, 1958.

Crowther, Bosley. *Hollywood Rajah; The Life and Times of Louis B. Mayer.* Holt, 1960.

Deans, Mickey, and Pinchot, Ann. *Weep No More My Lady*. Hawthorn, 1972.

DiOrio, Al. *Little Girl Lost*. Arlington House, 1973.

Gruen, John. *Close-Up*. Viking, 1968.

Guiles, Fred Laurence. *Marion Davies*. McGraw-Hill, 1972.

Hall, Ben M. *The Best Remaining Seats*. Clarkson N. Potter, 1961.

Hill, Norman. *The Lonely Beauties*. Popular Library, 1971.

Lahr, John. *Notes on a Cowardly Lion*. Knopf, 1969.

Lloyd, Herbert. *Vaudeville Trails Thru the West*. 1919.

Mailer, Norman. *Marilyn*. Grosset and Dunlap, 1973.

Mattfeld, Julius, *Variety Cavalcade of Music*. Prentice-Hall, 1962.

Melton, David. *Judy: A Remembrance*. Stanyan Books/Random House, 1972.

Morella, Joe, and Epstein, Edward. *The Films and Career of Judy Garland,* Citadel, 1970.

Minnelli, Vincent, with Hector Arce. *I Remember It Well*. Doubleday, 1974.

McLean, Albert F., Jr. *American Vaudeville as Ritual*. Univ. of Kentucky Press, 1965.

Parish, James, and Bowers, Ronald L. *The MGM Stock Company*. Arlington House, 1973.

Percy, William Alexander. *Lanterns on the Levee*. Knopf, 1941.

Pleasants, Henry. *The Great American Popular Singers*. Simon and Schuster, 1974.

Rosen, Marjorie. *Popcorn Venus: Women, Movies and the American Dream*. Coward, McCann and Geoghegan, 1973.

Shipman, David. *The Great Movie Stars: The Golden Years*. Crown, 1970.

Spitzer, Marion. *The Palace*. Atheneum, 1969.

Steiger, Brad. *Judy Garland*. Ace, 1969.

Sobel, Bernard. *A Pictorial History of Vaudeville*. Citadel Press, 1961.

Torme, Mel. *The Other Side of the Rainbow*. William Morrow, 1970.

Zierold, Norman J. *The Child Stars*. Coward, McCann, 1965.

——————. The Moguls. Coward, McCann, 1969.

ARTICLES

Alexander, Shana. "Judy's New Rainbow." *Life*, 2 June 1961.

Anon. "End of the Rainbow." *Time*, 4 July 1969.

Anon. "Judy Garland at the Met." *Newsweek*, 11 May 1959.

Anon. "Judy Garland, 47, Star of Stage and Screen, Dies." *New York Times*, 23 June 1969.

Anon. "Notes and Comment." *New Yorker*, 5 July 1969.

Anon. "Only a Touch of Judy Left in Singer's Pathetic Concert at Toronto Date." *Variety*, 17 February 1965.

Anon. "Over the Rainbow." *Newsweek*, 7 July 1969.

Anon. "Seance at the Palace." *Time*, 18 August 1967.

Barber, Rowland. "The Eternal Magic of Judy Garland." *Good Housekeeping*, January 1962.

Benjamin, George. "Setting You Straight on Judy." *Modern Screen*, June 1939.

Burke, Tom. "The Private Lives of Liza Minnelli." *Rolling Stone*, 10 May 1973.

Canby, Vincent. "Judy Garland: Loneliness and Loss." *New York Times*, 29 June 1969.

Chitty, Arthur Ben. "Visions of Greatness." University of the South, Tennessee.

Clurman, Harold. "Punch and Judy." *New Republic*, 26 November 1951.

Coates, Paul. Article in *Los Angeles Times–Mirror*, 1952.

Crissey, Forrest. "Chicago's Encore." *Saturday Evening Post*, 14 July 1934.

Davidson, Bill. "Judy—Another Look at the Rainbow." *McCalls*, January 1962.

De Toledano, Ralph. "The Cult of Judy." *National Review*, 28 August 1962.

Douglas, W. A. S. "The Passing of Vaudeville." *American Mercury,* October 1927.

Edwards, Anne. "Under the Rainbow: The Lost Childhood of Judy Garland." Excerpted by *McCalls,* June 1964, from *Judy Garland: A Mortgaged Life,* Simon and Schuster, 1975.

Fadiman, Clifton. "Party of One." *Holiday,* March 1952.

Garland, Judy. "The Plot Against Judy Garland." *Ladies Home Journal,* August 1967.

——————. "There'll Always Be an Encore." Parts I and II, *McCalls,* January 1964.

Gleason, Ralph J. "The Enigma of Judy Garland." *San Francisco Chronicle,* 2 September 1965.

Goode, James. "Judy." Parts I, II, and III, *Show Business Illustrated,* 31 October 1961.

Hopper, Hedda. "No More Tears for Judy." *Woman's Home Companion,* September 1954.

Hyams, Joe. "The Real Me." *McCalls,* April 1957.

Korall, Burt. "The Garland Phenomenon." *Saturday Review,* 30 September 1967.

Ray De O Fan. *Los Angeles Examiner,* 23 June 1933.

Reed, Rex. "A Break for Judy's Little Girl." *Los Angeles Times Calendar,* 1972.

Reilly, Peter. "Judy Garland: At Home at the Palace." *Hi Fi Stereo Review,* November 1967.

Ripley, John W. "All Join in the Chorus." *American Heritage,* June 1959.

Schulberg, Budd. "A Farewell to Judy." *Life,* 11 July 1969.

Shipp, Cameron. "The Star Who Thinks Nobody Loves Her." *Saturday Evening Post,* 2 April 1955.

Spitzer, Marian. "The People of Vaudeville." *Saturday Evening Post,* 12 July 1924.

Torgersen, Dial. "Judy Garland Dies in London at 47/Tragedy Haunted Star." *Los Angeles Times,* 23 June 1969.

United Press International. "Judy Captures the Palladium." *Washington Post,* 25 July 1964.

Variety, 21 August 1929; 30 August 1932; 8 August 1933; 5 September 1933; 6 November 1934; 13 March 1935; 22 May 1935; 2 July 1969; 17 February 1965.

Warga, Wayne. "Judy Garland—She Walked a Cruel Path." *Los Angeles Times,* June 1969.

MEDIA

Reasoner, Harry. "CBS Sunday News with Harry Reasoner." CBS Television Network, 22 June 1969.

"Shell Chateau." KFI Radio, Los Angeles, 26 October and 16 November 1935.

Schickel, Richard. "The Men Who Made the Movies." WNET, New York, 1974.

Wizard of Oz, The. Metro-Goldwyn-Mayer, Mervyn LeRoy, producer, 1939.